CRIME SCENE INVESTIGATION

SECOND EDITION

Thomas F. Adams

Professor Emeritus, Criminal Justice
Santa Ana College, Santa Ana, CA
Former Lieutenant, Santa Ana Police Department

Alan G. Caddell

Detective Sergeant
Santa Ana Police Department
Adjunct Professor, Santa Ana College

Jeffrey L. Krutsinger

Forensic Specialist II
Santa Ana Police Department

Prentice
Hall

Upper Saddle River, New Jersey 07458

Library of Congress Cataloging-in-Publication Data

Adams, Thomas Francis

   Crime scene investigation / Thomas F. Adams, Alan G. Caddell, Jeffrey L.
Krutsinger.—2nd ed.

     p. cm.

   Includes bibliographical references and index.

   ISBN 0-13-139797-4

   1. Crime scene searches. 2. Criminal investigation. 3. Evidence, Criminal. I. Caddell,
Alan G. II. Krutsinger, Jeffrey Lee. III. Title.

HV8073 .A528 2004

362.25'2—dc21

                                               2002034590

Editor-in-Chief: Stephen Helba
Executive Editor: Frank Mortimer, Jr.
Assistant Editor: Sarah Holle
Production Editor: Janet Kiefer, Carlisle Publishers Services
Production Liaison: Barbara Marttine Cappuccio
Director of Production and Manufacturing: Bruce Johnson
Managing Editor: Mary Carnis
Manufacturing Buyer: Cathleen Petersen
Creative Director: Cheryl Asherman
Cover Design Coordinator: Miguel Ortiz
Cover Designer: Scott Garrison
Cover Image: Bill Fritsch, brandXpictures
Editorial Assistant: Barbara Rosenberg
Marketing Manager: Tim Peyton
Formatting and Interior Design: Carlisle Communications, Ltd.
Printing and Binding: Phoenix Book Tech Park

Pearson Education LTD, *London*
Pearson Education Australia PTY, Limited, *Sydney*
Pearson Education Singapore, Pte. Ltd.
Pearson Education North Asia Ltd., *Hong Kong*
Pearson Education Canada, Ltd., *Toronto*
Pearson Educación de Mexico, S.A. de C.V.
Pearson Education—Japan, *Tokyo*
Pearson Education Malaysia, Pte. Ltd

10 9 8 7 6 5 4 3
ISBN 0-13-139797-4

This edition is dedicated to Maria Elizete Adams, minha bela esposa.

TFA

To Frank Stastny and Joe Boyd
Fallen but not forgotten.

AGC

This is for all my coworkers who make me feel like I can do anything I set my mind to doing and for all the support they have given me over the years.

JLK

Contents

Preface

The headlines blare: "DEFENSE ATTORNEY CHALLENGES THE PO-LICE EVIDENCE IN MURDER TRIAL, charge the police with planting and sloppy handling of evidence." Stop! Back up! How did that happen? The officers did everything according to the book, they explained, although the book was beginning to miss a few pages and the officers got sloppy in carrying out their work in the fashion they believed the book had (or should have been) written. The problem is, we have to write an updated version of the book, and then require our personnel to read it and adhere to its precepts.

For many years, as crime scene investigators, we collected the evidence, took the photos, prepared the reports, and eventually presented the evidence in court. Hardly ever did anyone, especially defense attorneys, challenge our motives and our methods. We did our job as professionals do. It was a debatable presumption that a job done by professionals was believed to have been done completely and correctly.

Then something happened. Attorneys found that by challenging the evidence and the way it was collected and handled, and by suggesting that perhaps the evidence collectors had some ulterior motive, the case could be won by raising sufficient reasonable doubt about how the entire case was handled. This was not a new tactic, but with the mega-publicity blitz given the so-called "trial of the century" and the media-hyped "dream team" of high-priced attorneys, other attorneys have taken the baton and run with it.

The purpose of this book is to focus on the basics of crime scene investigation as it should be done by professionals. Not only must the crime scene investigators perform a perfect job, but the crime scene investigators' work must appear to others as having been done perfectly by unbiased investigators searching for the truth in every case. The crime scene investigator is not an advocate for one side or the other—that is the role of the opposing attorneys. As a CSI officer, your advocacy is for the evidence and whatever it proves.

As authors of this text, we face the challenge of writing to at least three distinctive audiences: the student, the sworn crime scene investigator, and the non-sworn crime scene investigator. To be sure, there are others we hope to reach, such as officers assigned to patrol, investigators, educators, prosecutors, defense attorneys, journalists, and others, but the primary focus is on those three groups.

We, too, have varied backgrounds: one is a college professor who is a former police lieutenant, one is a forensic specialist assigned to crime analysis duties, and the third is a detective sergeant assigned to crimes against persons. We all have one thing in common, having all been involved in police training. It is this collection of talents that allows us, we believe, to deliver a text that can meet the needs of our varied audience. Here is what we hope to accomplish:

TO THE STUDENTS

You are likely studying criminal justice or forensic science. Perhaps you have decided that crime scene investigation is your calling. Or maybe you are not sure yet and are looking for information to help you make up your mind. Maybe you are just taking a class to learn more about what is certainly an interesting topic. In any case, this text has been designed to provide you with current, realistic information that presents an accurate overview of the role of a crime scene investigator. We provide both basic and advanced information. While you may not yet actually be responding to crime scenes or processing evidence, this text will provide you with a good idea of how and why it is done. We deliberately included a great deal of background information about how CSI personnel do their job. This ranges from getting to the scene to conducting various aspects of investigating the crime scene to testifying in court.

TO THE NON-SWORN CRIME SCENE INVESTIGATOR

You are perhaps new to the field or are interested in reviewing basic crime scene concepts, or adding some new concepts to your repertoire. As a non-sworn investigator, you represent the typical CSI officer for most larger departments. Because of longer, more stabilized assignment to CSI, it is not unlikely that your work will be superior to that performed by an officer who is not particularly happy in his or her current assignment. We applaud your dedication and your efforts to seek out additional information to enhance your skills and expand your knowledge. In this text, we provide you with solid advice on how to go about your investigation of crime scenes. In addition, we have devoted many paragraphs to enhace your well-being, both fiscal and physical, and your career development. There is little in this book that will not apply to you, either as a head start in your chosen profession or as a valuable refresher, or to keep your career moving "fast-forward."

TO THE SWORN PEACE OFFICER CRIME SCENE INVESTIGATOR

As a peace officer, you might be assigned full time as a crime scene investigator, or you might be on an auxiliary assignment, or on an assignment you plan to pass through after a few months. In many jurisdictions, the entire crime scene responsibility rests with the patrol officer assigned to respond to the call. Perhaps you are assigned to patrol and want to expand your knowledge and improve your skills in this area. If so, we strongly support your efforts to better serve your department and community. All officers who respond to crime scenes have some responsibility, and the more knowledgeable you are about your role as well as everyone around you, the better the job you will perform.

This text will provide you with the high level of relevant and realistic information you need to process crime scenes in today's environment. As a sworn officer, your needs will differ from those of the non-sworn investigator. For example, we have included information about safely responding to the crime scene. This entails a different set of issues for you than it does for the unarmed investigator. We recognize the differences between the players and have included basic safety information pertaining to all who read the book, whatever your assignment.

To all our readers, thank you for sharing your time with us. We believe you will consider it time well spent. Crime scene investigation is a critically-important component of our criminal justice system. We wish you the best of success as professionals.

ACKNOWLEDGMENTS

Special thanks to Santa Ana, CA Police Chief Paul M. Walters, who authorized Jeff Krutsinger's participation in this project as co-author (who produced most of the photographs in this book), and Sergeant Alan Caddell, who joined the team and helped bring us up to the 21st century.

I would like to thank my editor, Kim Davies. I would also like to acknowledge the following who were instrumental in helping us get through the second edition: Sarah Holle, Barbara Cappuccio, Korrine Dorsey and any others whose names we have missed. Thanks for your faith and encouragement. Thanks also to Janet Kiefer at Carlisle Publishers Services.

Special thanks to our mentors, instructors, and colleagues who inspired us and, through example and other media, have been instrumental in our development in the fine art and science of crime scene investigation. Thanks also to our colleagues who do their jobs in a professional manner and make us look as though we know what we are writing about.

The authors would also like to thank the following reviewers:

Alex del Carmen, University of Texas at Arlington, Arlington, Texas; Warren Clark, California State University-Long Beach, Long Beach California; Mike Chamberlin, North Carolina Central University, Durham, N.C.; Pedro Crescente, Brevard Community College, Melbourne, Fla.; and Bill Calalathes, New Jersey City University, Jersey City, N.J.

From T. Adams: Special recognition of my wonderful sons, Tom and Brian, who make a father proud, and in memory of my daughter Norina, who was killed by cigarette smoke.

From Alan Caddell: My involvement in this book would not have been possible without the help of others. Foremost, I thank my wife, Suzette, for her support and willingness to provide me the time needed to research and write. I thank my children, Jacqueline, Valerie, Stephanie, and Lauren for serving as my inspiration and for understanding why this project took time away from family. I thank my co-authors for allowing me the opportunity to join them in this important endeavor. Lastly, I thank Maria Sugranes, my high school librarian and life-long friend, who long ago provided me with the encouragement and direction that has shaped my personal and professional life.

From Jeffrey Krutsinger: I would like to thank Kathy Saviers, who gave me the foundation and motivation to pursue a career as a forensic specialist. The excitement of being able to solve a case as a result of forensic evidence is a feeling I hope every reader will one day experience. And to my daughter, Ariel, who I strive to make proud of her daddy, I love and thank God for you every day. You constantly make me strive to work harder and do the best I can in everything I do.

Chapter One
Overview

INTRODUCTION

Serious crimes are being committed every minute of every day, but most go unnoticed in a society besieged with crime and violence. Some particularly heinous crimes, or those involving famous or notorious participants, receive an inordinate amount of national, and sometimes international attention. While sensational cases may get more attention than the mundane ones, they are similar in one important aspect. Each crime is committed by an offender and each involves one or more victims. From each victim's perspective, the crime they suffer is just as important as the ones that get all the notoriety.

Despite billions of dollars and hundreds of thousands of hours spent on law enforcement, the vast majority of crimes go unsolved. Additionally, many people have no confidence in the system, and therefore do not report their crimes because they see no advantage in doing so. This "dark figure" of crime is not only an indicator that many people in our society lack faith in the system, but it is also an acknowledgement by victims and law enforcement personnel alike that we have a lot more to do to address the challenges confronting our communities, and a resolve to do more to improve the odds and to build the public's confidence.

When we solve a crime, the resulting arrest does not automatically guarantee that the prosecutor will file criminal charges or that the trial will end in a conviction. The myriad of court-imposed rules can limit police procedures concerning the collection and analysis of evidence and lead to exclusion of crucial evidence from the trial. Other limiting factors are a lack of sufficient reliable evidence to sustain a conviction, the reluctance of victims and witnesses to come forth and testify in court, limited court resources, and even a lack of "jury appeal."

All the while the victims wait for justice, and for some victims, justice never comes. Why? Perhaps because of lack of interest by prosecutors and restrictive rulings by the courts, but also because far too many investigating officers and prosecutors do not pay enough attention to business, or because so many defense attorneys are successful in punching holes in what appear to be "iron-clad," open-and-shut cases.

So what does this have to do with crime scene investigation? Simply this: Cases are solved with evidence, offenders are prosecuted on the basis of evidence, and victims receive justice because of evidence. It is not enough just to have evidence; it must have been collected and processed properly, lawfully, and in a manner that is above reproach and proves guilt of the accused "beyond all reasonable doubt." Not an easy task, but it is one which you as an investigator must perform with diligence and attention to detail.

The crime scene investigator is, therefore, much more than a mere collector of items, photographs, or fingerprints. He or she is a collector of TRUTH. It is often the initial work of the crime scene investigator that is the deciding factor in whether that truth will assure the victims of the justice they deserve. In some police departments, original reports of crimes are taken over the telephone by a Telephone Reporting Unit (TRU). Later, at an arranged time at the convenience of the victim, a crime scene investigator will visit the scene and collect evidence. A follow-up investigator specializing in the type crime under investigation will also contact the victim and witnesses and conduct more thorough interviews, but the CSI officer must be alert to statements victims and witnesses make in his or her presence and pass the information to the follow-up investigator. Sometimes victims and witnesses choose to share considerable information with the crime scene investigator. When that happens, you must be attentive and empathic and translate all the information you collect into a follow-up report.

Never minimize the task of conducting a crime scene investigation. It is a serious undertaking. Errors reflect not only the case at hand; they reflect on the entire investigative process. There was a time when the work product of crime scene technicians was routinely presumed to have been done correctly and thoroughly. A lab result was rarely questioned, and the testimony of an expert taken at face value. This is no longer the case: many defense attorneys now critically challenge every act by all participants in the process.

Today's crop of ingenious defense attorneys are perceptive enough to see through the facade of rebuttable presumptions that professional duties performed by well-trained and educated professionals have been done with impartial care and efficiency. Defense attorneys are often successful in raising reasonable doubt about the "perfect" performance by police officers and crime scene investigators.

When you respond to a crime scene, you are confronted by an exhibition of confusion and chaos. There may be property damage, wounded or deceased persons, angry or devastated victims and their families, and bewildered and confused witnesses and bystanders. Even at the most routine scene you are likely to be confronted by a crowd of spectators, many of whom will not be happy with your presence for a variety of reasons. But what is also present at the scene—and what poses your greatest challenge—is the one opportunity to determine the success of the investigation.

One opportunity is usually all you will get. Once the tape is down, the barriers are removed, and the scene is released, there is little chance for you to return to redo work or to correct errors and omissions. It will be impossible to recreate an identical crime scene. It is, therefore, imperative that you hone your skills as a crime scene investigator to be as sharp as possible. Few professionals face the challenges of a crime scene, but few professionals are able to reap the rewards associated with assuring justice for the victim and accountability for the offender. Without your efforts, the crime might go unsolved.

In this book we will provide you with the information you need to successfully process a crime scene in a manner that will withstand scrutiny and instill confidence in those who rely on your work. A criminal investigation is like a chain, and each link is critical to the overall strength of the case. For most cases, the first link is the crime itself. Let's get started.

When you enter the crime scene, you are generally trying to answer several important questions: What happened here? Is what happened a crime? Who is the suspect? Who is the victim? The answers to these questions form the basis for a criminal investigation. The answers might fix blame on the guilty or exonerate the innocent. The answers might turn out to be insignificant, or they may send someone to prison or death row. Whatever the case, these questions need to be answered quickly and correctly.

THEORY OF TRANSFER

The reason we investigate the crime scene is because we expect to find evidence that can help us answer the questions we asked in the previous paragraph. Although we are not likely to find all the answers at the scene, the crime scene is the best place to start if for no other reason than it will not remain a crime scene for long. The basic premise to the transfer theory is that whenever a person enters or exits a crime scene, he or she alters it in some way, however significant or insignificant it may be. We may or may not discover whatever may have been transferred, but we should operate on the assumption that we will find something.

Although you may tend to believe that there is no truth to this theory after so many investigations and finding nothing, you should always consider the possibility that the perpetrator left something behind at the scene and took something away from the crime scene. You don't have to be a psychic to sense someone's presence at a crime scene (although psychics are sometimes used). Sometimes the odor of a person's cologne or after-shave lotion lingers at the scene, or the distinct pungent aroma of a particular mixture of pipe or cigar tobacco permeates the immediate vicinity, especially if the space is enclosed and there is poor ventilation. It is even possible that you might later smell this same odor when encountering a suspect away from the scene. While it may not stand up in court, the use of scent evidence—using sophisticated technology—is now part of the crime scene investigator's toolbox.

Generally, when we speak of transfer evidence, we are talking more along the lines of blood, fibers, hair, fingerprints, and other items that are left at, or removed from, the scene of the crime or the body of the victim. Many sensational cases have been solved by the discovery of such items as carpet fibers from the suspect's home found on the clothing of the victim found miles away floating in a river, or the victim's clothing fibers found at the suspect's home. Other cases have been solved by less subtle methods. Suspects have been known to discard cigarette butts at the scene (leaving their DNA in the saliva on the cigarette), or chewed gum (leaving bite impressions and DNA), or washing or relieving themselves in the victim's bathroom (leaving blood, urine or hair, all containing DNA).

Some perpetrators have even left behind their wallets containing photo identification, such as driver's licenses and student ID. Some suspects steal items from the scene and keep them as mementos of their visit. Also, thanks very much to the popularity of the video camcorder, some criminals record their crimes to show their friends at the next party they attend. These tapes sometimes serve as authentic enactments (not reenactments) of their crimes.

Evidence Types

There are two primary types of evidence that you might find at the crime scene: direct and indirect, or circumstantial. Your understanding of these types of evidence and some examples of how they are found will be helpful when you are processing the scene. Although experts will disagree about which type of evidence is more valuable than the other, both are of equal value, depending on the unique circumstances under which they are collected and later presented in court.

Success Story: DNA Database

On a dark night in November of 2000, a woman was attacked and raped in a stairway of her apartment complex. The woman was unable to provide much of a description of her attacker, but the forensic medical examination revealed traces of the suspect's semen. A DNA sample was forwarded to California's database, but the case remained unsolved.

In May of 2001 a woman was sexually assaulted outside a fast food business in the same city where the previous rape occurred. The suspect was apprehended and convicted. Prior to his release from jail in January of 2002, a DNA sample was obtained in accordance with California law. The sample was forwarded to the sexual offender database where a match was made with the sample obtained in the earlier rape. Investigators located the suspect, who was arrested on charges of rape, failing to register as a sex offender, and probation violations.

The innovative use of a DNA database allows suspects to be identified by their DNA in a manner similar to that used to identify suspects by their fingerprints. This application of science and technology is removing sexual predators from our communities.

Direct Evidence. Direct evidence is generally eyewitness testimony by the victim or witness who were at the scene at the time of the event and can relate the details from their personal experience. On its face, or your *prima facie* evaluation of this information, this is about as good as you are going to get. Let's say there has been a robbery. If an officer picks up a suspect near the scene and the victim and/or witness make a positive identification, what more do you need to convict the suspect? The same would be true if the victim and/or witness picks the suspect out of a collection of photographs. That is also direct evidence. Unfortunately, direct evidence is often flawed; victims and witnesses make honest mistakes. The amount and type of available lighting during the crime and subsequent identification may distort the view, the use of disguises as simple as baseball caps and eyeglasses, and the fact that many people look the same to an emotionally traumatized witness, can easily lead to a misidentification.

Even when eyewitness testimony is correct, the prosecution may have a problem, such as a witness with a felony record or poor eyesight. He or she may have been under the influence of alcohol or a drug while making the identification, or the eyewitness turns out to be just a poor communicator who falls apart during cross-examination by a defense attorney. Some people have "court fright" the same as others have "stage fright" when appearing before an audience. The prosecutor may find direct evidence to be a boon or burden, depending on varying circumstances. Sometimes jurors find it hard to believe the credibility of people who have a stake in the outcome of the case.

Indirect or Circumstantial Evidence.   Information or facts that are used to imply a reasonable conclusion are considered circumstantial. Let's return to the example of the robbery. If the suspect rested his or her hands on the glass countertop during the crime, and if fingerprints were immediately removed from the countertop and used to make the identification, it is implied that the person who left the fingerprints is the one and same person who held up the establishment. Of course, you may ask, "What about the innocent customer who left a set of fingerprints at the same location on the glass counter top immediately before or after the robbery?" However, if the clerk testified that he had wiped the counter clean immediately prior to the robbery and that no one touched the counter after the robbery, your fingerprint evidence might hold up. So you see, no evidence is perfect.

In reality, criminal investigations often include a variety of evidentiary items that, when put together, make a case provable beyond a reasonable doubt. Our robbery case would have been handled by patrol officers who would have asked the clerk for a description of the suspect. Later, the crime scene investigator would have located the fingerprints on the counter. A fingerprint technician would have later compared the prints against those of suspects. Detectives would have taken photographs of the suspect, and would note that his description was consistent with that provided by the victim and witnesses. They would then show the suspect's photo to the victim and witnesses in separate sessions. The combination of a "hit," or a match of prints and photo identification of the suspect all pointing to the same suspect, would give us a strong case made up of direct and circumstantial evidence combined.

Probability

When we speak of evidence, we often speak of the probability of something occurring. For example, what if during the robbery the perpetrator fatally shot the clerk? Who would testify to the identity of the suspect if there were no living witnesses? Without the testimony of the victim or a credible witness, we would have to rely on circumstantial evidence and probabilities to make our case. Let's say that the suspect and victim struggled during the robbery. The class counter was shattered and CSI found blood on the glass. While making an area search immediately following the robbery, an officer stops a man three blocks away who has a cut on his hand and blood on his pants. What can we imply from these circumstances? Would we have enough evidence to send the man to prison based on what we have so far? Probably not.

Without more facts, the circumstances confronting us so far might be nothing more than an unfortunate coincidence. But what if that man's blood type and DNA matched some of that found on the glass? To take it further, what if some of the blood on his pants matched that of the robbery victim? Blood type (O-Negative, for example) is not unique in itself. Many people have similar blood types, but what is the probability of the victim's and suspect's blood being found where it was in our robbery case? Also, if DNA analysis is used and results in a similar match, what are the odds now?

Because nothing is absolute in the field of evidence, the experts always speak of reliability of evidence in terms of probabilities. As a result of comparing latent prints from the crime scene with a rolled set of comparison prints taken in the office or taken from the files of the FBI or another agency, a fingerprint expert will never state that the latent prints from the crime scene are positively those of a suspect. What the expert will say is that the probability that the prints were left by someone other than the defendant is about one in 100 million. In other words, of the 100 million sets of prints scanned, only one set of prints, those of the defendant, matched the latents found at the crime scene. So far, in all the years that fingerprint files have been maintained worldwide, no two people have come up with identical sets of prints. Even twins identical in all other ways have different fingerprint patterns.

Take DNA (DeoxyriboNucleic Acid) for example. Of the current world population of about five billion people, some experts have proclaimed that no two people—except for identical twins—have the same DNA, or genetic code. The mathematical probability of duplicate genetic codes, with the exception of identical (not fraternal) twins would be five billion to one. Some experts have even stated that no two people who have ever lived, live now, or ever will live on earth have the same genetic code (except for the identical twins, that is). Of course, scientists and law enforcement have not yet catalogued the DNA of all inhabitants on earth, but they use projected mathematical probabilities not unlike opinion polls. An oversimplified example of such law of probability is that 100 randomly-selected Democrats and 100 randomly-selected Republicans (in this case allegedly representing the total population of both parties in a given region) are asked it they favor the "three strikes and you're out" law. Eighty five Republicans and 85 Democrats state that they favor the law. The pollsters would then state that 85% of all people of both parties favor the law. If they were to question ten more representatives from each side, their numbers might change, but they will go with what they have. This random sampling technique is an accepted practice throughout our society. Of course, once a second person shows up with an identical set of prints, then the odds would be one in 50 million, or if another person surfaces with an identical genetic code, then the odds would change to one in 2.5 billion. Scientifically speaking, that's good enough to get a person convicted.

CRITERIA FOR DETERMINING EVIDENTIARY VALUES

1. *Mathematical probability.*   As long as every attempt to replicate an examination to produce identical results comes up negative, the criminalist can say that of 3,000 attempts to produce an identical result, it did not happen a single time. Therefore, the probability of matching two pieces of broken glass as in a jigsaw puzzle, and being able to duplicate a match of one of those pieces of broken glass with another is 1:3,000 because of the 3,000 unsuccessful attempts by the criminalist. So it can be said with some scientific certainly (but not absolutely) that two pieces of broken glass that fit together in all likelihood came from the same pane of glass and that they were previously both part of one piece, and now there are two that fit together at the place they were separated.

   Here are a few more examples. When you toss a coin, the probability that it will come up "heads" is one in two, 1:2 (because there are two sides to the coin). If 40 percent of all humans have type O blood, you can say that two of every five people have type O blood. Even if you come up with five people in a row who have type O blood, the probability will not change because so many people have had their blood typed, and of all of those individuals, 40 percent of humans have type O blood. If you have type A blood, what is the probability that the next time your blood is typed it will be anything other than A? Zero, of course, because blood type does not change.

2. *Uniqueness.*   A shoe print that appears to have been made by a size 12 shoe is found impressed in the soil in a flower bed outside the murder victim's bedroom window. The design of the print on the sole, including a logo and some type of lettering, is characteristic of only one type of shoe custom made by a shoemaker in Milan, Italy, according to the shoe print expert of the Federal Bureau of Investigation. No other shoe maker can be found who manufactures a shoe with a similar design. The victim's son wears a size 12 shoe, and you find in a search of his apartment a sales slip showing that the son bought a pair of size 12 shoes from that same shoemaker in Milan. How many people wear size 12 shoes? How many people purchased size 12 shoes from that particular shoemaker in Milan? Further examination of the shoe print shows a distinctive wear pattern and a cut across the heel impression that appears to have been made by a knife. You find the son's size 12 shoes, and one of the shoes appears to have similar wear pattern, logo, and lettering design, and one of the shoes has a knife cut across the heel. The shoe expert will point out the similarities between the shoe and the impression that it probably made, and the improbability of any two shoes making an identical impression, but he or she will never say that a specific shoe made that specific impression. Yet the situation is so unique that it can hardly be attributed to coincidence.

3. *Inconsistency.*   A middle-aged rape victim who has lived alone for the past 20 years, who does not smoke and has never allowed anyone to smoke in her house, finds a half-smoked cigar in her bathroom sink. Because of its inconsistency with the victim's lifestyle, it is reasonable to assume that the intruder was the one who brought the cigar to the scene and left it behind. In an embezzlement case, the office manager started working late every night without asking for overtime pay and at the same time volunteered to take care of the bank deposits. One of the clerks at the bank became suspicious when the office manager opened a second account with himself as the signator, which was inconsistent with the company's previous banking practices. After the office manager started making withdrawals from the second account, the bank employee became suspicious and phoned the owner of the company, who subsequently went to the

police department and filed a complaint against the office manager for embezzlement of several thousand dollars. The manager had coincidentally taken an unscheduled vacation (which was also inconsistent with his behavior of never wanting to take time off for vacation or illness).

Physical Match.   The perpetrator of a "smash and grab" burglary broke a window. Fragments of glass taken out of a suspect's clothing were compared with the glass still remaining in the window, both as to physical characteristics and mechanical match, and the criminalist's expert opinion was that the glass fragments found on the suspect were probably—with little chance for doubt—part of the broken plate of glass. The mechanical match was made by photographing the larger fragments that have a shape to them and photographing the remnants of the window at the scene, and moving the photographs around as one would put together a jigsaw puzzle, coming up with a match. It is virtually impossible for any two sheets of glass to be broken in exactly the same way. Virtually, but not absolutely. We are dealing with the law of probabilities again.

AT THE CRIME SCENE

As a crime scene investigator, you probably deal with circumstantial physical evidence more than with direct testimonial evidence. It is important to remember, though, that your role might involve obtaining statements from victims and witnesses at any time or on a regular basis, depending on your department's requirements. Officers assigned to supervise the investigation are usually the ones who do the interviewing, but because your job puts you directly on the scene and in close proximity to victims and witnesses, you might inadvertently overhear conversations, or individuals might speak directly to you. Everything you see and hear at the crime scene might be evidence, and you are responsible for accurately documenting all of it in your reports.

So when you enter the crime scene, you are looking for evidence of a direct or circumstantial nature to answer the questions previously posed. The question as to whether a crime actually occurred is a valid one, because it is not unusual for you to come upon the scene of a situation that appears on its face to be a crime scene. For example, your initial response to a medical aid or dead body call is as though it were a homicide or personal assault. Once you determine that there has been no foul play, your job is usually finished and the scene is turned over to medical response people or family members.

Elements of Crime

For an act or omission, or passive participation to be classified as a crime, it must be written into law, or codified. There are no common law crimes that you make up as you go. The majority of crimes are found in your state's criminal codes, and thousands more are found in municipal and county codes, other state law compilations, and in Federal codes. Each crime defines the details of the offense and prescribes the punishment for a violation. For example, consider California Penal Code Section 459, Burglary:

> Every person who enters any house, room, apartment, tenement, shop, warehouse, store, mill, barn, stable, outhouse, or other building, tent {inhabited} vessel, ... {which is designed for habitation} railroad car, locked or sealed cargo container, whether or not mounted on a vehicle, trailer coach ... {etc.}. ... vehicle {when doors are locked}, aircraft ... with intent to commit grand or petty larceny or any felony is guilty of burglary. {An inhabited dwelling is one that is designed and used for "dwelling purposes", whether occupied at the time or not}. {omissions by the authors}

The law looks confusing, doesn't it? Essentially, it means that a person who enters one of those described structures with the intent to commit any felony or any theft is guilty of a burglary. This is true even if the culprit only gets inside and doesn't have a chance to commit any felony or theft once he or she has gained entry. "Of what importance is that to the crime scene investigator?" you may ask. The answer is that it is your job to locate evidence to support or disprove that a burglary was actually committed, or perhaps it was a different crime, such as trespassing or vandalism.

Consider the following scenario: Officers respond to a silent alarm at a computer store. They find the front door ajar, and they arrest a man they find hiding under a table. When you arrive, the officers ask you to process the scene for evidence of a burglary. What evidence would you look for? Before you answer, consider the statement of the man the police arrested: "I was cold and tired when I saw that the door was open. I came inside to sleep. The next thing I know I am being arrested."

Do you believe the man? Is this a plausible explanation for his being inside the store? Would one juror out of twelve believe his story? If so, you don't have much of a case so far. What evidence would you need to prove or disprove the man's story? If you found that the door was pried open and the man had a screwdriver or crowbar in his pocket, would it make a difference? What if the shelves showed signs of being ransacked and several boxes of merchandise were stacked near the back door? What if you found the man's car, which he had denied owning, parked outside the back door? When you check out the car, you find more contraband from another burglary, and when you check the man's record you find that he has a history of burglary convictions. Although prior convictions do not make him a burglar this time, it certainly helps focus attention on the investigation at hand. What you have done is disprove the man's story. You are on the way to proving the crime of burglary.

You should know the elements that constitute each of the crimes that you are going to be working. Knowledge of criminal law and the elements that make up the *corpus delicti*, or body of the crime, will put you in good stead so that you can do your work effectively. Another factor to consider when working crime scene investigations is to know when and under what conditions you can lawfully enter the premises. This requires a knowledge of the Fourth Amendment to the Constitution regarding search and seizure, and an understanding of criminal procedure. Actually, as a first responder to a crime scene, you are there by invitation, either express or implied, and you have no need to worry about getting a search warrant. Once you have completed your investigation, however, if you wish to go back and complete work that you should have done in the first place, you may need a warrant. Also, there will be times when you must search a place that is a possible or probable crime scene, or someone's residence for additional evidence. In those cases, a warrant may also be in order. Whenever you are in doubt as to whether or not you need a warrant, check with your supervisor, a senior officer, or perhaps the department's legal advisor. Search warrants are not required in emergency, or exigent, circumstances, and a crime scene almost always fits that category.

The possible loss or destruction of evidence or the personal safety of officers or other individuals also qualify as exigent circumstances. You also have to be careful not to extend your search beyond the scope of the exigency. One way to avoid a claim of making an unconstitutional entry and search is to get permission from the person in charge of the premises. Even when it is not necessary, it is a good practice to always ask for permission to enter so that you may take photographs or to search for additional evidence. It is more difficult for the defense to claim unreasonable search when permission has been granted to enter the premises.

THE FOURTH AMENDMENT

The Fourth Amendment of Bill of Rights forbids unreasonable searches of a person, his home or personal papers but it falls within the "reasonable cause" category when you are at the scene of a crime, because the goal of your search is to determine the nature of the crime and to identify the person or persons responsible for the crime. It is also reasonable to identify the victim and all of the circumstances about the person and/or place that is the object of the attack. In other words, it is only a very rare circumstance when you will need a warrant to conduct a crime scene search.

If and when the occasion arises for you to seek a search warrant from the local magistrate, the affidavit must state where you wish to search, including the exact address, an accurate description of the place, exactly what you expect to find, and what reliable information you have that leads you to believe that the search will yield the evidence that you expect to find. Once you have the warrant in hand, then you may proceed with the search, which should be consistent with what you expect to find. For example, if you are searching the residence of a burglary suspect or small tools used to gain entry and several handguns, it would not be logical to search places where one would not be likely to find those objects, such as in the pages of a paperback book or a diary. But let us get back to the crime scene. Search warrant procedures are covered in other texts in much greater detail. If in doubt about any aspect of any search that you conduct, seek the counsel and advice of your department's legal counsel or the prosecuting attorney.

CHAIN OF CONTINUITY OR CUSTODY

It will be your responsibility to guarantee the integrity of the unbroken chain of custody from the very moment an item of evidence is found until it reaches its final destination at the evidence locker or the laboratory—and then again when the item goes from one of those places to the courtroom. While the evidence is in the custody of the evidence custodians or the laboratory technicians, those individuals will share the responsibility for its continuity. Then, when it comes time for court presentation, it will be up to you to take the evidence to the court and present it at the trial with a complete explanation of its itinerary. No evidence can be introduced without a human's testimony to make it part of the trial. Anyone who has no official business with an item of evidence should never handle it, or else the chain is broken. Once the chain has been broken, the integrity of the evidence is in jeopardy.

Here is what a typical chain of evidence looks like: You locate a drop of blood on a kitchen floor. You swab the blood and place it into a container to transport to the laboratory. You seal the container and place your signature on the seal. You also attach an evidence tag or card to the container (some departments use tags with bar codes). On the card you have written the case number, date and location of crime, time of discovery, location where you found the blood drop, and that you found it. Later at the station, you put the container in an evidence locker and you again sign the card and list the date and time that you placed it in the locker. You lock the locker and drop the key through a slot into the locker so that you cannot retrieve it once you have completed your "link" in the chain. Later, the evidence technician retrieves the container from the locker from inside the laboratory and signs the card, indicating the date and time he or she took custody of it. The technician then handles the analysis or hands it to the criminalist or another specialist, who will handle the analysis, who also makes the appropriate entries on the card. After performing the necessary tests, the specialist returns the evidence to the locker or other storage unit with limited access, again making proper notation on the card. So far the chain has been unbroken, and it is imperative that everyone keep the links connected.

Three months later, you or an investigator receives a *subpoena duces tecum*, which orders the recipient to come to court to testify and to bring along certain specified articles for presentation in court. The person who checks the evidence out of the locker or other storage space, such as the compartment of a refrigerator, fills out another portion of the card, assuring the unbroken continuity of links in the custody chain. Although there may be a lapse of several months between the time of discovery and the time of presentation in court, there is a complete history of the item's itinerary. This greatly reduces the opportunity for tampering with the evidence and reduces the opportunity for anyone to challenge its unbroken chain of continuity.

So what you have here are several tests along the way before an item of evidence may be allowed to serve its purpose to prove an element of the crime. The bottom line is that every item of evidence must be carefully collected, meticulously packaged and transported to the evidence repository or the laboratory, carefully analyzed by the laboratory technicians and criminalists, transported to the courtroom for the trial, and legally presented in court. All of this has to be within the strict confines of the rules for maintaining a continuous and unbroken chain of custody. If it sounds confusing, think of the chain of custody like the tracking that the Postal Service, or Federal Express or United Parcel Service provide when you send a package. The clerk or driver affixes a tag with a bar code to the package, and then the tag is updated at every step along the way by everyone who handles the package. At any time, you can check on the current location of the package from point of origin to destination.

One very important difference between your chain of custody and that used by shipping carriers is that while no one gets too upset to learn that a package sat in a truck unsupervised for a few hours as long as it gets to its destination on time, if your evidence sits unsupervised for any length of time at any step along the way, the custody chain may not have been broken, but it leaves an opening for an attack upon its credibility. For example, instead of testifying that the gun you present in court is exactly the same one that you collected at the crime scene, you may have to acknowledge that a link in the chain has been compromised, and that all you can say is that the gun certainly looks the same, considering it is in the same sealed package and that the serial number is the same. It gives the defense attorney an opening to comment on the shoddy work of the police, which may lead a jury to find the accused not guilty.

DISCOVERY

As a crime scene investigator, you are probably working for a law enforcement agency, but as an objective investigator you are also working for the defense. It is just as important that your evidence clear the innocent as it is that it convict the guilty. Your objective is to reveal the truth, whatever that may be. All information and evidence that you discover during the investigation must be revealed to the defense. The defense must also reveal to the prosecution what evidence and information it has, with the exception of those items that may be withheld to assure the defendant's Fifth Amendment rights not to be a witness against oneself. Although not a game, the discovery process is similar to playing a hand of poker where all players must show the other players their cards. Under such conditions it would be rather hard to bluff the others with the impression that one player is holding a royal flush when they can see only a pair of eights. When the defense attorneys see that evidence is weak—which they believe does not prove an element of the *corpus delicti*, or which they believe was collected in violation of the search and seizure rules (or Miranda, in the case of statements or admissions obtained)—they are going to petition the court for a pretrial hearing to suppress that evidence. If the court suppresses the evidence because of officer impropriety, the evidence cannot be presented later at the trial.

Depending on your department's human and financial resources, consider adding to the team of crime scene investigators a videographer historian whose sole purpose is to memorialize the entire investigation from beginning to end. If the date and time feature on the camcorder is available, be sure of the accuracy of the date and time the tape is being made. In one so-called "crime of the century," the O.J. Simpson case, a videographer recorded scenes of the suspect's house for liability protection purposes yet caused some serious credibility problems when the date and time showing on the tape were different than when he and other officers testified he made the tapes. That seemingly inconsequential matter, which the videographer overlooked when checking out the camcorder, gave the defense team some good ammunition with which to attack the prosecution's case.

MEDIA RELATIONS

The public has a right to know that you are doing your job by investigating crimes for the purpose of locating the perpetrators and bringing them to justice. The public does not have a right to know the details of a case under investigation that would jeopardize the successful conclusion of your investigation, no matter what the media representatives will try to argue. "Scoops," "exclusives," and ratings are not your responsibility. Do not fall into the trap of feeling that you must pander to the media to get their cooperation. It is your duty to be polite and respectful, and to refer the media to your supervisors or to the department's media liaison person. Certain unscrupulous news reporters will create their own story completely or will give it their own slant, depending on that agency's editorial policies. Just because they print or broadcast misinformation, perhaps to bait you into giving them the "correct information," don't fall into their trap. Your job is to investigate the crime scene, not to act as a news reporter.

In a very high-profile case, such as spectacular murder or a crime involving celebrities, be careful to shield the crime scene from the cameras in the helicopters above or in the trees or on top of buildings down the street. There are some media people who set out to conduct their own investigation and to question suspects and witnesses so that they may make their own news rather than report it. How many times have you seen good cases compromised or literally destroyed because of premature release of information, or because of misinformation?

Sometimes it is necessary for your media relations people to ask the print and broadcast people to withhold certain information that they may have in the interest of common decency so that the follow-up investigators may go after the perpetrator(s) and interrogate them for their knowledge of the crime. Consider the case where only the victim (who is dead), the coroner's people, the investigators, and the murderer know what weapon was used and where it was disposed of after the crime. Later, when the suspect confesses to the crime and describes the weapon and what he did with it, you will know with some reliability that you have the right suspect. But consider how the case would be compromised if all that information were publicized and if you could not know for sure if you had the true confessor or a false confessor. Yes, there are many people who confess to crimes they never committed for a variety of reasons. Just ask the "old-timers" on your department.

SUMMARY

In this overview chapter, we have covered many topics, some of which we will discuss in more detail later in the book. It is absolutely essential that your crime scene investigation be thorough and complete. Although some people generally presume that a well-trained police officer or specialist in crime scene investigations does good work as a matter of routine, we know that all officers are not equally efficient. Many professionals make serious errors in spite of their training. For that reason, you should expect critical review of your work from many directions. Although the Fourth Amendment rules concerning search and seizure do not generally apply to crime scene investigations, there are many ancillary searches when you may have to adhere to the rules closely.

All elements of the crime, or the *corpus delicti*, must be proven in order for you to establish that a crime has, in fact, been committed and that these elements are proven by either direct or by circumstantial evidence. Evidentiary values of certain objects or information vary with each situation, but in this chapter we have discussed some of the criteria for determining those values. Keep in mind that the rules of discovery require that both prosecution and defense share information so that there are few secrets prior to and during the trial.

We rounded out the chapter with discussions of the theory of transfer and the chain of evidence custody precautions to take to avoid accusations of theft or damage to the property of victims or other persons involved in your investigations. What we will cover in Chapter Four is your relationship with the news media, the ubiquitous journalist with camera or camcorder, which is extremely important to the success of any police venture.

SUGGESTED OUTSIDE PROJECTS

1. Prepare a list of examples of criteria for determining evidentiary values in each of the categories of mathematical probability, uniqueness, inconsistency, and evidentiary match.

2. In the law library, research the principles of the discovery rules and explain what types of evidence and information the defense can withhold from the prosecution. Explain how an attorney goes about getting the court to enforce the discovery rules.

3. List and describe at least five different types of evidence you might find during your investigation that would tend to bear out the theory of transfer.

DISCUSSION QUESTIONS

1. How do you see the difference between direct and circumstantial evidence? Can you come up with a convincing argument that one is better than the other?

2. What do you know about DNA and the state of the art at the present time?

3. Can you give an example of any type of evidence that may be regarded as positive proof of a fact?

4. What is your agency's policy regarding the wearing of protective glasses or goggles and gloves while investigating a crime scene?

5. Describe the chain of custody process in an average crime scene investigation.

6. Describe the theory of transfer, and give an example of how this might work in a convenience store robbery case.

7. Explain the process known as "discovery." Which side benefits most from the discovery rules, prosecution or defense?

8. What do you think about the crime scene investigator using a checklist to assure a thorough investigation?

9. If the Fourth Amendment protects people from intrusive practices of government officials, what protection is there against intrusive private persons who force entries and conduct searches on their own?

10. Describe the process for getting a search warrant.

Chapter Two
Protecting Yourself

INTRODUCTION

A career in crime scene investigating is a rewarding one in many respects. In other respects, it is also one that involves exposures to many hazards that the average person would never encounter during their lifetime. Your work schedule is going to change frequently, and you may be required to roll out to a crime scene at any hour of the day or night, which will certainly play havoc with your eating and sleeping routines. Your senses will be shocked by the scenes of death and destruction and other human tragedies that most people don't even want to think about. Strangely, though, you will eventually come to accept those things as just part of the job.

Some of you may find that the hazards that you face on a daily basis are what set the job apart from the humdrum alternatives of another calling you might have chosen, and you look forward to the adventure, if you will, of the unexpected. In this chapter we are covering some of the hazards that you must expect in the daily routine of your job and that you must prepare yourself to deal with appropriately when you encounter them. You need make only one mistake and your life will be changed forever.

BIOLOGICAL HAZARDS

It should come as no surprise that dealing with blood and other biological materials can expose you to illness, disease, and possibly death. It should also come as no surprise that CSI personnel confront such substances on a frequent basis. The good news is that by taking reasonable precautions, you can protect yourself from these hazards and still get the job done while maintaining good health.

Biological substances can enter your body in only so many ways. The main threats are by inhalation, ingestion, through the eyes, or through an opening in the skin, such as through a cut or open wound. As a CSI officer, there are a number of situations where you will be exposed to these biological hazards. Common examples include (1) injury or fatal traffic collisions, (2) violent assaults, (3) sexual assaults, (4) death scenes, (5) homicides, (6) suicides, (7) child abuse, and (8) sexual molestation.

The simplest way to protect yourself from a host of hazards is to wear disposable gloves. It should be a department or at least your personal policy that you always wear protective gloves when performing crime scene work, and make it a practice to change gloves frequently. Even "macho" patrol officers don plastic gloves at the first sign of physical contact with another person. Greater muscular development does not decrease the risk of infection. When dealing with blood or other body fluids, it is a good idea to wear two pairs of gloves. The cost is negligible, and it is inconsequential when considering your health and longevity on the job. Gloves will protect your hands from most hazardous substances, but not against certain acids and chemicals. Also, gloves will not help at all if you rub your eyes or nose, or if you put a gloved hand to your mouth while conducting the investigation.

Eye protection, usually special protective glasses or goggles, or transparent masks that cover the entire face, are a must anytime there is a potential situation for a substance to be splashed into your eyes. The full face shield is best when the substance is likely to be splashed or sprayed onto the face including the eyes, mouth, and nose.

You should also protect your mouth and nose with a mask. Masks come in a variety of styles and levels of protection. The most basic paper mask may filter out fingerprint powder and dust, but it may be useless against other substances transmitted through the air. For example, the paper mask might block out a blood spatter only until the blood soaks through the paper. The transparent face shield might be the better choice after all, and well worth the extra cost.

Masks can only minimize your exposure to hazardous vapors. From a biological standpoint, most odors are probably just an annoyance, such as the smell of a dead body, but sometimes you will encounter odoriferous materials that are also hazardous to your health. When investigating death scenes where putrefaction has set in, you should wear gas masks with special filters to block out harmful bacteria. If you attend an autopsy, you will usually see the technicians and pathologists suited up as though they were going to go out on a space walk, with protective gear from head to toe. A few years ago, you could watch them doing their work in shirtsleeves and jeans. This practice has changed principally since the AIDS epidemic began.

Some older, experienced homicide investigators used to carry ammonia inhalants or a jar of Vick's VapoRub™ to block out the odors associated with death.

When dealing with scenes that are particularly messy, it is advisable that you wear a disposable jumpsuit over your street clothes, then dispose of the jumpsuit when you have completed the job. Also wear plastic "booties" over your shoes. These disposable "booties" perform two functions. First, they prevent you from introducing contaminants into the crime scene, such as dirt or fibers; and second, they prevent your shoes from being exposed to blood or other substances in the scene. You want to avoid picking up biologically-hazardous materials on your shoes and taking the materials back to the station or your home. Keep a solution of bleach and water in your crime scene kit so that you can decontaminate your shoes as an extra precaution.

HAZARDOUS MATERIALS

When we think of hazardous materials, we tend to visualize spilled tanker trucks or mysterious drums of leaking fluids. The reality is, however, that every home and business structure contains hazardous materials that, under the right circumstances, might cause us serious injury. When a disaster of some sort occurs in the community, police and fire units are the first to respond, and CSI is usually right behind them. It is not likely that you will be called into a scene that is known to be hazardous. Chances are that the qualified personnel will determine when it is safe for you to arrive and to begin your work processing the scene.

There is a real risk, however, of responding to a scene where the hazards are not immediately apparent. Hazards can take on as many forms as there are types of hazardous materials. Estimates place the numbers of potentially-hazardous materials existing today at 700,000, but following are some situations when you are more likely to be exposed to toxic or hazardous materials:

1. A train derails and a ruptured tank car releases toxic liquids and/or fumes.

2. A big-rig (16 wheeler) overturns in a traffic collision, spilling its load of hazardous or toxic liquids.

3. A metal plating firm in your city allows hazardous solvents to leak into the sewer.

4. A fire at a chemical plant threatens to explode several tanks of deadly chemicals.

5. A house fire pours thick, black smoke into the surrounding community.

6. An unidentified container is found in the street.

7. Patrol officers stop a car carrying a variety of unmarked bottles in the trunk.

All of the above are examples of situations where you could be exposed to hazardous materials. Sometimes the hazard is not easily recognized. An overturned truck might be leaking nothing more than water, or the leaking contents could be a substance that might kill first responders within minutes. The fire at a neighbor's house actually may have been the result of an explosion in a drug lab in the garage. Your cautious response to scenes such as these can greatly minimize your chances of being injured.

It should be a firm policy that crime scene investigators not enter hazardous materials scenes until competent experts declare the scene safe to enter. Even then, CSI personnel should wear appropriate protective gear when processing the scene. There is always the possibility that the scene has not been recognized as one containing hazardous materials. In those cases, protect yourself by taking protective gear along with you in your CSI response vehicle at all times so that you will be prepared for the unforeseen event.

Recognizing that any crime scene holds the potential for exposure to hazardous materials, it is imperative that you understand the potential ways that a toxic substance can enter your body. Perhaps the simplest point of entry is through the respiratory system by mere inhalation. Always try to enter potentially-dangerous scenes from the upwind, or leeward, side. Although your department may have provided you with paper masks, be aware that these masks will not protect you against poisonous vapors or toxic substances composed of very small particles. If you are in an area that smells dangerous, it probably is. Avoid dangerous odors when you can until you can determine from the experts your risk of exposure. Of course, there are many deadly substances that have no odor.

Ingestion is another method of exposure to a dangerous substance. While you would probably not try to eat or drink something you did not trust implicitly, be careful not to rub your eyes or lick your lips or touch anything to your mouth while at the scene of a hazardous spill, as you could unknowingly bring those substances into your body. Never eat or drink at a scene where there is a chance of exposure. Even fingerprint powder or talcum powder can be hazardous to your health if ingested.

Substances that enter your body through your skin are another area of concern. Always wear gloves, goggles or a mask, and some sort of covering over your street clothes when around materials that can be splashed or sprayed.

Another common method of exposure is having a substance or object break your skin, introducing biohazardous materials into your system. Hypodermic needles and any other sharp object are common threats. Not too long ago, a coroner's technician who was also an embalmer was embalming a body when he accidentally injected his arm and "embalmed" his entire arm. It took several weeks of treatment to get his arm functioning normally, but the incident could have been much worse had he not immediately sought medical aid. Broken glass, wrecked vehicles, and splintered doorframes are all examples of objects that could cause problems. If your eyes, lungs, skin, or throat burns while you are at any scene, leave immediately and seek medical aid.

When responding to the scene of wrecked or damaged trucks, trains, and buildings, look for warning placards that announce the type of hazardous materials they contain. The Department of Transportation (DOT), the North American Emergency Response Guidebook (NAERG), and the National Fire Protection Association (NFPA) all use standardized systems to label materials. Look for the triangular-shaped placard that is usually blue, red, and yellow (you will even see them on college and university buildings where chemicals and electronic materials are stored and used in class). The degree of hazard is designated with a numerical value, with the number 1 being "no unusual hazard" to 4 being an "extreme hazard." It is beyond the scope of this book to go into further detail concerning these placards and what they mean, but whenever you encounter any of these placards, you should proceed with caution and notify the agency in your jurisdiction that deals with hazardous materials.

Illegal drug labs are a growing hazard and are certainly crime scenes. Processing these scenes requires careful preparation and special equipment. When you come across one of these labs, which are found in hotel and motel rooms, private kitchens, garages, basements, outhouses, or even motor homes and campers, notify the special units that are designated to handle the initial investigation and eventual cleanup, such as the State or Federal Narcotics agencies, in addition to notifying your own agency's narcotics enforcement unit and usually the HAZMAT unit of the fire department. Cooking drugs, such as methamphetamine, involves use of basic cooking utensils plus beakers, tubing, glass bottles, computer circuit boards, large pots, plus a few other items that do not at first look unusually out of place, except when you find them all together along with the ingredients for preparing the drugs and sometimes distinctive odors that you will recognize with experience.

Never turn any switches on or off or disconnect any portion of the lab. It is not unusual for the operators of these places to "booby-trap" them so that the whole place, and anyone who enters without their permission are destroyed and killed in the explosion. Larger jurisdictions usually have specially-trained teams of specialists to work on illegal drug labs. They are also equipped with sophisticated Saranex™ suits with self-contained breathing apparatus and decontamination equipment. The best advice we can give you is leave the drug labs to the experts.

TERRORISM

The United States and our allies are deeply involved in our war against terrorists and those who harbor terrorists. The terrible events of September 11, 2001, involving four commercial airliners containing hundreds of innocent passengers and crew deliberately crashed by hijackers in Pennsylvania, the Pentagon near Washington D.C., and at the World Trade Center twin towers in New York killed thousands of innocent people and made it abundantly clear that the threat of future attacks in our own back yard is a real one. These events were preceded by bombings of the World Trade Center in 1993 and the Murrah Federal Building in Oklahoma City on April 19, 1995, the latter having been carried out by American citizens of Anglo-Saxon descent.

At the time of this book's writing, it appears inevitable that the situation will worsen before it gets better. We should anticipate that terrorist attacks could happen again on our own soil, and that we are no longer protected by large oceans on opposite sides of our country. Not only should we anticipate such overt attacks as bombings and attacks from the air, but a more covert, and equally-insidious type of terrorism is also strongly possible, such as the anthrax-filled letters sent in October, 2001 to news agencies and to our halls of Congress, killing several innocent people. Whether those letters were sent by a foreign or domestic terrorist is still unknown, but they were sent from a city in New Jersey. Whether the terrorist attacks originate from within or from outside the United States, they could take the form of biological or chemical violence as well as an explosive form.

Whenever you are involved in any situation which may possibly—or positively—involve chemical or biological agents as weapons of terror, you should wear protective gear, including self-contained breathing apparatus and facilities for decontamination. If the toxic substance is released covertly—that is, without advance notice by the responsible parties—there may be no recognition of the problem for several days until a pattern of illness and/or death begins to manifest itself. In cases such as these, the investigation works backwards toward the source of the release of such toxic materials.

Because the release of many biological or chemical agents as acts of terrorism, such as anthrax or smallpox (and a whole host of other materials) might not be immediately recognized, it is critical that you assume the worst and protect yourself when responding to potential incidents or threats. The Centers for Disease Control (CDC) may have already supplied your local health authorities with antibiotics to treat affected victims. The Federal Bureau of Investigation and the Office of Homeland Defense serve as clearinghouses for information concerning threats and investigation of their validity. Once they determine that the threat is credible, Homeland issues a color-coded alert, then local law enforcement and all other concerned government agencies respond to the threat or attack. When it is confirmed that there has been an actual release of a biological weapon, the FBI and the CDC will coordinate the collection of evidence and administration of counteractive procedures. You will not be called upon to perform CSI until an affected area has been completely decontaminated and declared safe.

CIVIL LIABILITY

Now that you have looked at the physical hazards, you must consider another one that seems almost inevitable in what appears to be a litigious society. There are some people in our society, including attorneys, who appear to specialize in filing claims, both criminal and civil, against law enforcement professionals for doing their job in what the claimants charge as deliberate or reckless with no regard for the safety or well-being of the people they serve.

People in our society demand perfection in a non-perfect world. They are particularly demanding of those in law enforcement who must perform under a wide variety, and frequently adverse, circumstances. Society gives tremendous power, authority, and trust to those of us in law enforcement, and with that power, authority, and trust comes commensurate accountability. But one would be naive to think that only rogue officers are targeted and "broad-brushed" with allegations of corruption and malfeasance. The reality is that some people make a good living suing the police, many of them filing false claims to forward their own agendas or to line their pockets, taking from the "deep pockets" of government. It is not unusual for some attorneys to file complaints on behalf of their clients even when the officer has done no wrong. Some insurance companies would rather pay out what they consider a "nuisance fee" of several thousand dollars to make the case go away because going to court and defending the case— even winning it—would cost more than making a cash settlement with a stipulation from the claimant that the matter be dropped.

You, like the vast majority of police personnel, are probably honest, ethical, dedicated, and above reproach. Yet you, like many of your colleagues, might well be subject to allegations of dishonesty or incompetence. How do you protect yourself against false allegations? First and foremost, ensure that you are competent and professional in all your actions, and that it is obvious to others. Always perform your tasks "by the book." Do not take shortcuts or deviate from established policies or procedures. If you are unsure about something you are doing, stop and ask someone in authority for the answer. Perhaps you remember, or perhaps you have studied excerpts from the O.J. Simpson murder trial. There were many allegations of misconduct on the part of CSI and investigating officers, such as taking critical evidence home overnight before taking them to the laboratory, or carrying blood samples around from scene to scene instead of taking them directly to the laboratory.

You must remember that as a CSI officer you will be admitted to areas usually closed to outsiders. You will be inside people's homes and offices. You will be in their vehicles and searching through their personal belongings. You will often be working alone and unsupervised. In short, you will be trusted to perform your job without worry of misbehavior. This trust to work autonomously also brings the risk of having to defend yourself against accusations of misconduct. You may be accused of theft or of damaging something of value in the house, or even of planting or manipulating evidence.

One of the best ways to protect yourself from allegations of misconduct is to have other personnel accompany you to document the findings and conditions located at the scene. This can be shared by initial responding officers, investigators, supervisors, and other CSI personnel. Every individual involved in the investigation should prepare separate reports of their specific functions and findings. The reports will differ in regards to each individual's role at the scene, but they will reinforce each other as to non-destruction or theft of property. For example, the responding officer might note in the report that a wallet was lying near the body and he or she stood by until the arrival of the investigator (name included), who took possession of the wallet. The investigator's report would show that he or she had picked up the wallet, checked the identification of the victim, and turned the wallet over to the coroner's investigator (name included).

The officer in charge of the scene should be alerted to all matters of potential liability and will similarly document the event, as will the coroner's investigator. The inventory of the victim's belongings will include the wallet and its contents. If someone is videotaping the investigation as an antiliability precaution, the wallet will also be fully documented. It will be easy to refute any allegation of theft of the wallet or any of its contents.

Speaking of videography, if you have adequate personnel and if the investigation is of major public interest, perhaps because of the celebrity of the victims, suspects, or other participants, it is a good idea to tape the entire investigation. This is, of course, in addition to the usual CSI photography and videotaping. The purpose of this tape is not so much to serve for evidentiary purposes as it is to protect those on the scene from false allegations of impropriety or even criminal conduct. Anything at the scene that is of significant value, such as jewelry or money (with the descriptions and amounts counted and documented in the presence of a witness) should be taped. Never, *ever* deviate from established policy regarding how such items are to be collected and documented. Innocently placing valuable items in your pocket or some other non-conventional means of safeguarding them for later booking into evidence is opening yourself up to big trouble.

It hopefully goes without saying that ultimately your best defense against unwarranted allegations is your own credibility. No videotaping or reporting system will provide foolproof evidence for every situation. It is imperative that you act professionally and honestly at all times. You will make mistakes, but loss of your reputation for honesty or integrity is no mistake, and your career will be ruined. Never allow yourself to be compromised. There is no room in our business for a dishonest CSI officer.

RESOURCES

The good news about facing the potential hazards discussed in this chapter is that you do not have to face them alone. Most agencies have programs and resources in place to help you. Police chaplains are at your beck and call for spiritual and moral comfort and guidance. They are usually selected because of their unique education and experience in dealing with death, posttraumatic stress, and counseling. Department psychologists and psychiatrists are available for counseling and treatment, with long-term follow-up in serious situations. Your visits with spiritual or psychological counselors are strictly confidential and designed for your emotional well-being and continued value to the department as an effective participant in the investigation process.

Attorneys are also available when you are in need of legal counseling, and under many cases there is the protection of attorney-client privilege that shields you from any interference by supervisors or staff. Many departments have full-time legal advisors who provide legal advice to the Chief or Sheriff and operational staff about legal matters involving department management and law enforcement. Other attorneys are strictly available for exclusive consultation with officers about legal matters that involve their personal liability problems and those that also involve their supervisors in the same case. There is a difference—check to see whom the attorney is representing in the matter about which you seek his or her advice.

PHYSICAL HEALTH AND STRESS

It is most important that you maintain excellent physical and mental health. To avoid stress, learn as much as possible about your job and those of the people around you so that you avoid friction with others on the job. Many times stress is caused by lack of self-confidence, or by overcompensation for incompetency. You can avoid that type of stress through study and competent experience. As for your physical health, check with your nutritionist and physical education advisor.

SUMMARY

The focus of this chapter has been devoted to protecting yourself from physical hazards and from liability claims. As a crime scene investigator, you are going to be exposed to many hazards and dangerous situations, many of which we have not even begun to cover in this text. Be aware of what is happening in the world around you to keep up with ongoing threats, and take special care on the job to protect yourself against all of the hazards of which you are aware.

No matter how well you do your job, no matter the reputation you have earned for your high integrity and honesty, you are always open to allegations of civil or criminal liability. Be extremely cautious in your contacts with the people you contact on the job, and be sure that everything you do is strictly according to policy, procedure, and the law. There is no absolute protection against false allegations of misconduct, but if you are careful to not only do everything in an honest and straightforward manner, but to avoid doing anything that even gives the impression that you are not going by the book, your life will be less complicated.

SUGGESTED OUTSIDE PROJECTS

1. Research the various types of masks and face shields available to the CSI and laboratory personnel at your local department. Compare them and recommend which is best for your use against biohazardous materials, such as anthrax. Include prices and manufacturers, as well as availability of these devices.

2. Check with your local department officers who are responsible for anti-terrorism and outline the procedures they have put into place to handle (1) anthrax or smallpox alert, (2) suicide-bomber attack, (3) defense of such vulnerable venues as reservoirs, power plants, sewage disposal plants, and other essential facilities to keep the infrastructure viable.

DISCUSSION QUESTIONS

1. What is a "biological hazard" and is it a threat in your community?

2. What type of gloves should you always wear at a crime scene?

3. Is a face mask, goggles, or protective glasses best for CSI work?

4. What is the purpose for wearing plastic shoe covers, or "booties" at a crime scene?

5. Do all hazardous materials have an identifiable odor?

6. What is the purpose for a multi-colored triangular placard with the number 4 on the wall or door outside a warehouse?

7. In your jurisdiction, who is responsible for closing down a home drug lab?

8. What planning has your department done to respond to acts of terrorism?

9. Regarding civil liability, can a police officer sue someone for making a false accusation?

10. What is the purpose for videotaping a crime scene if it is not to document the evidence?

Chapter Three
The Crime Scene Kit

INTRODUCTION

Your crime scene investigation (CSI) kit should contain all of the equipment and supplies listed and discussed in this chapter, plus any additional items we may have missed or items that you consider necessary to suit your individual style. In the larger department, you may be fortunate to have enough money in the budget to have a fully-equipped crime scene van or truck (Figure 3.1).

In that case, your equipment and supply list will include the kit, plus additional pieces of equipment, such as ladders, lighting, generators, and a refrigerator to preserve perishable items, and other conveniences. The regular crime scene kit (Figure 3.2) should be compact and capable of being carried in the trunk of a police cruiser.

Figure 3.1 Minivans are excellent for use as crime scene investigation vehicles because they have plenty of room for tools and evidence.

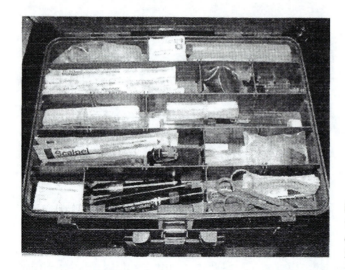

Figure 3.2   Fishing tackle boxes are excellent for making a field CSI kit.

THE IDEAL CRIME SCENE KIT

When stocking your kit, use this chapter as a basis for developing your checklist of essential items. The list does not list items in order of importance.

1. Traffic flares and cyalume wands for traffic diversion at street or highway scenes. Flares can be used to close off a traffic lane or sidewalk, or they can be used as nighttime hand signals. Barricades and cones should be in the storeroom at headquarters or in the CSI van.

2. Yellow plastic tape with or without "POLICE LINE DO NOT CROSS" lettering for designating the boundaries and restricting access to the scene. If you have a large population of people whose first language is not English, use tape printed in one or more of those languages.

3. Lights. A variety of lighting devices such as penlights, flashlights, floodlights, and battery-powered lanterns with red and amber lenses to serve as warning or stoplights.

4. Small portable generator for alternating current and an ample supply of batteries of various sizes for the direct current powered lights, and converters to accommodate variations in power sources.

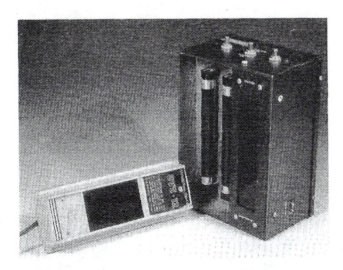

Figure 3.3 Ultraviolet lights are used to look for many types of trace evidence.

Figure 3.4 A possy box like this one serves not only as a clipboard but also as a place to store film, forms, and other tools.

5. Ultraviolet and infrared lights for examining trace evidence at the scene, such as latent prints on multicolored surfaces, fluids that fluoresce under ultraviolet light, and other substances that reveal themselves under infrared lights (Figure 3.3).

6. Report forms, spiral bound notebook, and ballpoint pen with black ink.

7. Clipboard with graph paper and pencils, and templates used for drawing items such as vehicles, furniture, and other items commonly depicted in crime and accident scene sketches (Figure 3.4).

Figure 3.5   Large number placards are helpful to mark and identify evidence at a crime scene.

Figure 3.6   Rulers and scales of all sizes are vital to show size and position of evidence. Some scales are magnetic or come as stickers. The L-shaped ruler is vital when photographing shoe prints. All long tape measures should be metal in order to assure that no stretching occurs.

8. Chalk, marking pens, and other marking devices, including markers for wet surfaces, and spray paint.

9. Numbered and lettered tags and placards and tented cards to locate certain items of evidence (Figure 3.5).

10. Steel measuring tape and wood or plastic ruler. Avoid the use of cloth measuring tapes, which stretch or shrink (Figure 3.6).

11. Evidence cards and labels with accurate ruler printed along the edge.

Figure 3.7   A good 35mm single lens reflex (SLR) camera with a zoom lens and powerful flash is probably one of the crime scene investigator's best tools.

12. Compass for determining true north, which should appear in all sketches and photographs when possible. A north arrow imprinted on a 3 × 5 card and placed in the scene where possible will aid the viewer in establishing directions in the scene.

13. Polaroid and/or digital camera for immediate feedback on your photographs, and to serve as a backup in case some of the more sophisticated camera equipment does not work.

14. 35mm single lens reflex (SLR) camera for most, if not all, of your still photos of the scene, as well as tripods, various lenses, and accessories for a variety of photo situations (Figure 3.7).

15. High-quality and high-speed film.

16. Fingerprint camera for one-to-one close-up of fingerprints and other trace evidence.

17. Video camcorder. If you are working alone, the voice recorder feature will enhance your ability to record the crime scene both visually and orally as you keep a running dialogue while you

go through the scene. If you do not wish to use the sound feature, turn it off before you start recording to avoid having embarrassing comments and other sounds come out later on, which might be made by those not aware that the sound is rolling. Date and time feature should be correct if you use it.

18. Gloves. Heavy rubber gloves for working around electricity, heavy work gloves for lifting and other heavy work, and thin latex gloves for most of work handling evidence. Carry several pairs of latex gloves, as they should be changed frequently to avoid cross-contaminating items you handle, such as blood-covered items.

19. Plastic shoe covers, or "booties." These shoe covers should be used particularly if the crime scene involves shoe impressions or deposits of body fluids or other materials that might be altered with the introduction of your own shoeprint or those of your fellow investigators.

20. Jumpsuit or coveralls made of cotton or other lint-free material to wear over—or instead of—your street clothing while at the crime scene.

21. Cord, rope, string, wire, wire ties, and packing tape.

22. Staplers, staples, thumbtacks, transparent tape, and paper clips for fastening and sealing objects and containers.

23. Bottle of alcohol and/or 15 percent bleach solution for hand washing and for instruments such as knives, calipers, and other evidence-collecting devices.

24. Moist antibacterial towelettes, individually wrapped, for quick cleanup when soap and water are not immediately available. These convenient wipes can also be used for washing off tools and cutting instruments (Figure 3.8).

25. Paper towels and cleansing tissues.

26. Knife, scalpel, X-acto knife and blades, and scissors.

27. Mirrors, including a dental mirror for peering under and behind objects that cannot be moved, or inside hard-to-reach places (Figure 3.9).

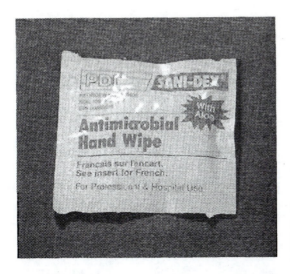

Figure 3.8 Antibacterial wipes are used when disinfecting your hands after working with biohazardous evidence.

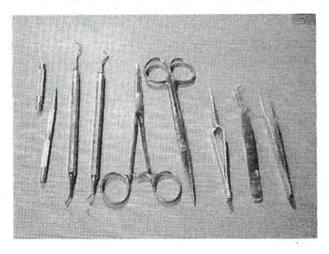

Figure 3.9 Dental and medical tools are excellent to have in a CSI kit to mark and collect evidence.

28. Magnets for retrieving small metal objects from hard-to-reach places.

29. Tweezers and grabbing devices with long handles to pick up objects otherwise out of reach.

30. Brushes of various shapes and sizes for sweeping and cleaning.

31. Syringes, pipettes, and turkey basters for collecting or dispensing liquids.

Figure 3.10   Different-size glass jars and vials are crucial in preserving small items of evidence, especially when they are in a liquid form.

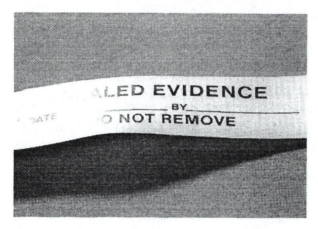

Figure 3.11   Evidence seals like this are placed on evidence bags, boxes, or even cars to help with the chain of custody.

32. Glass vials, paper bags, plastic bags, canisters, bottles, boxes, and other containers for evidence (Figure 3.10).

33. Tapes and labels for securing evidence in containers and for identifying evidence. Gummed labels may also be used for sealing some containers. A broken seal would indicate that the package had been opened or tampered with (Figure 3.11).

34. Cotton balls and styrofoam "popcorn" for cushioning items in packing.

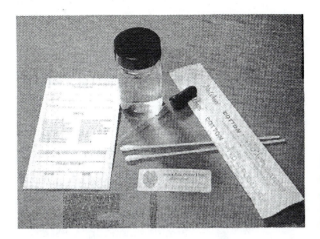

Figure 3.12 A blood collection kit should contain distilled water, sterile swabs, and proper identification labels.

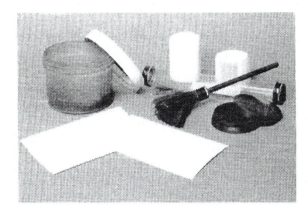

Figure 3.13a A basic print kit should contain a brush, black powder in a wide-mouth jar, lifting tape in various widths, latent lift cards, and a pocket ink pad.

35. Sterile cotton swabs, weigh paper and swatches, and distilled water for lifting dried traces of blood and other traces from absorbent surfaces, such as concrete or asphalt (Figure 3.12).

36. Silicone, microsil, traxtone, and plaster casting materials, including rubber bowls for mixing the materials. Carry a couple gallons of bottled water in case tap water is not available at the scene.

37. Fingerprint powders, including magna powder, Super Glue® (cyanoacrylate ester), and other materials for developing and lifting latent prints (Figure 3.13a, Figure 3.13b, and Figure 3.13c).

38. Report forms, cards, tags, envelopes, and paper to fold into bindles for powders that might be evidence.

Figure 3.13b When out on a scene where it may not be possible to collect the evidence, a portable fuming wand can be used to develop fingerprints with cyanoacrylate ester (Super Glue®).

Figure 3.13c These fingerprints were developed on paper using black magna powder.

39. Vials with reagents provided by the lab for field tests of substances suspected of being blood, drugs, or other controlled substances.

40. Containers with saline and distilled-water solution for collecting and preserving substances, such as blood, semen, and other body fluids.

41. Water and nourishment items for your thirst and hunger in the event you are going to be on the scene for long periods of time with no breaks.

Figure 3.14   A loop, commonly used by fingerprint examiners when comparing unknown fingerprints to a set of known fingerprints to a set of known inked impressions.

42. Magnifying glass and jeweler's loop for close-up examination of engravings, prints, trace evidence, and jewelry (Figure 3.14).

43. Corrugated boxes and large paper grocery bags for transportation of large items of evidence or many separately-packaged items to be packed in the larger containers for convenience in transporting and prevention of cross-contamination.

44. Metal scribe and engraving tool for marking items of evidence with your logo and other essential identifying data.

45. Self-sealing plastic bags for small items.

46. Evidence tape and tags for sealing and identifying evidence.

47. Printed routing forms for each item of evidence for initial identification and to document each step along the way in its continuity of custody.

SUMMARY

In this chapter we have attempted to make as complete a list as possible for your basic crime scene investigation kit. We suggest that you use it when putting your kit together and when you prepare your inventory list.

SUGGESTED OUTSIDE PROJECTS

1. Visit your local police department and discuss the inventory list with the officer in charge of crime scene investigations. Make all the necessary corrections that will make the list more functional.

2. Draw up a list of items that should be included in a crime scene investigation van or truck. Visit a local department that has such a vehicle used solely for crime scene investigations. Compare how it is equipped with your list of how you believe such a vehicle should be equipped.

DISCUSSION QUESTIONS

1. Is there a better type of highway warning device than the traditional railroad flare?

2. What is the advantage of using a steel ruler versus a cloth measuring tape?

3. To what extent, if any, is digital photography used in the police agencies in your neighborhood?

4. Describe a scenario in which it would be wise to use a camcorder for liability protection.

5. List and discuss any additional items that should be included in the list presented in this chapter.

6. Would you recommend placing a "north" arrow in each scene before taking each photograph at the crime scene?

7. What is the technical name of Super Glue®, and how is it used to develop fingerprints?

8. What information should an evidence card contain?

9. What is a "reagent," and for what type of substance would you use it?

10. What type of camera is best for crime scene photography?

Chapter Four
Roles at the Crime Scene

INTRODUCTION

Crime scenes, like crime scene investigators, come in all shapes and sizes. Many scenes, perhaps even the majority, will involve you and maybe a police officer. Sometimes you will be alone. And sometimes, it may seem as if the scene could not possibly contain any more people. Serious crime scenes usually require the efforts of a number of people who respond to perform their particular tasks. While these people often are from the same agency, there are times when multiple agencies are involved. Sometimes, they are not working in a cohesive effort. Regardless of who is at the scene or their reason for being there, it is critical that a positive working relationship be established to ensure the scene is processed without damaging evidence or hindering its discovery.

In this chapter, we introduce you to the people you will see at one time or another at a crime scene. Whether these individuals actually enter the crime scene is determined by the scene supervisor and/or the officer in charge of the investigation (which could be you) who determines if they are authorized to do so. For example, our list includes a field supervisor. Just because a person holds that title, it does not mean he or she has a valid reason for being in every scene. Supervisors and other department members of all ranks and job titles often respond to a crime scene out of curiosity. That is not a valid reason to enter a crime scene, and you should politely direct the unauthorized individuals to leave.

POLICE OFFICERS/DEPUTIES

Assigned patrol officers are usually the first to arrive and initially establish the parameters of most crime scenes. Their job is to secure the scene, treat the injured, arrest offenders, and safeguard evidence. They are often the ones that request CSI personnel and/or detectives respond to the scene. One patrol officer, generally the first to arrive, is in charge of the scene until relieved by someone of higher authority, or the officer may continue with the investigation to a logical cut-off point, when a follow-up investigator will resume the investigation at a later time. That officer will continue with the investigation until it reaches a successful conclusion or a dead-end, as many investigations do.

FIELD SUPERVISORS

Sometimes a patrol sergeant or lieutenant will supervise serious or large crime scenes involving a large number of personnel. The supervisor ensures that ample personnel and resources are present and assigned, and that the scene has been properly contained. He or she may supervise tactical operations involving the capture of suspects, but he or she does not conduct the actual investigation. Depending on the individual department's policies and procedures, the investigation is handled by crime scene investigators and field officers or detectives.

SCRIBE OR RECORDER

One person at the scene should be responsible for protecting the integrity of the scene and for maintaining the log. Every individual who sets foot within the boundaries of the crime scene must sign the log book with the scribe as witness. The person's name, rank, and job assignment, as well as the exact time of arrival and departure, should all be entered in the log.

When fingerprints and shoe impressions are collected, it may be necessary to take exemplar impressions from all the individuals who were on the scene to eliminate them from the field of suspects. Every person who entered the scene should also be required to prepare a report, which will be checked later against the log to verify that all reports are submitted. One lieutenant known to one of the authors was on a murder scene for no apparent reason other than to get a look at the macabre scene. During his tour of the crime scene, he picked up several spent .22 caliber shells in the rubber soles and heels of his shoes. When he handed them to the crime scene investigator, he had no idea where they had been when he stepped on them. Unfortunately, "tourist" officers are not entirely uncommon and they should be invited to leave. This is sometimes difficult when the tourist is a ranking officer who should know better but who feels that rank has its privileges and rules were made for others.

DETECTIVES/INVESTIGATORS

While some departments have detectives assigned to patrol, most are assigned to a separate division. When a serious crime occurs, detectives are often called to respond to the scene to handle the case. Detectives usually respond in "plain clothes." CSI officers often work closely with detectives to "read" the scene and process evidence. Some detectives are more inclined to work in partnership with the CSI officer, and other detectives are more apt to direct the CSI officers to collect or process what they deem is important. Ideally, you will develop a mutual relationship that brings the skills and experience of both of your professions to improve the chances of solving a crime. Your relationships may also be prescribed in detail in a manual of regulations.

VICTIMS

In homicide or assault cases, the victim is the central element in the crime scene. In a homicide, there is no question that the victim must be left where found for much of the investigation for photographs, measurements for sketches, and the arrival of the coroner, who is responsible for the custody of the body and immediate personal effects. In cases where the victim is injured and in need of immediate medical attention, your primary objective is to see to the victim's care. If, however, the victim has not been moved prior to your arrival and the injuries do not require immediate attention, photograph him or her in place and make accurate notes and measurements so that you may reconstruct the crime scene as accurately as possible.

Once the victim has been removed from the scene for medical treatment, he or she will have to be interviewed later at the hospital or another place removed from the immediate scene. You do not want the victim to be reintroduced into the crime scene unless absolutely necessary, such as for a reenactment of the event, which should be done after you have completed the initial phase of the investigation and the scene will no longer be compromised.

In property crimes, such as burglary, theft, or robbery, the victim may be the only living source that you have to direct you to items that have been moved or touched, and for other aspects of your investigation. Be careful to instruct the victim not to touch anything and to move only where you direct it is safe to do so without compromising the scene.

In cases when you do not need the victim directly at the scene, keep him or her away from the scene once removed, but nearby for elimination fingerprints and shoe impressions, comparing them with impressions left behind by the perpetrator(s). Make sure you treat the victim with utmost respect and courtesy. This is a very critical stage of victim contact, as any discourtesy or inattention to the victim may lead to a victim's later non-cooperation, reluctance, or unwillingness to testify or otherwise participate in the investigation and eventual prosecution of the perpetrator(s).

How you and your colleagues handle the victims, show the appropriate amount of empathy and compassion for their losses, and attend to their need for direction to trauma counseling by a chaplain or victim advocate may have a direct impact on the eventual outcome of the case. If a victim's perception of the police and the prosecutors is one of disinterest in seeing that he or she get the justice that they deserve, you may be wasting your time because you have lost your best and most important ally: the victim.

You may be following up on a crime that had been reported to a crime report center a day or two earlier. You are probably the first, and possibly the last, representative of the police department that the victim sees. When you show up at the victim's home or place of business, this is your opportunity to make or lose points for your department. You must be polite and empathetic, yet be mindful of your purpose for being on the scene. While you are conducting your investigation, one way to keep the victims out from underfoot is to put them to work. Have them search their records for serial numbers of items that have been stolen, locate vehicle registration papers, and make a list of items that have been stolen. They should also accompany you, without touching anything unless necessary, and point out objects that have been moved, removed, or changed in appearance as a result of the crime. Also, have them round up friends and neighbors who might be witnesses to the crime.

NEWS MEDIA REPRESENTATIVES

You should expect the media to be present at any crime scene, but whether they will actually show up depends on a number of factors. Most crime scenes are just not newsworthy enough to warrant much attention. This is because crime in general is not an unusual event, and most people are pretty much used to it. On the other hand, you will find a crime where the suspect or victim is a celebrity and you get an overabundance of media coverage. They will be coming out of the woodwork, on rooftops, on tall ladders overlooking the scene, in helicopters above, or in any vantage point where they might get a spectacular view to show at the five o'clock news broadcast or to hit the headlines in the morning paper.

During your investigations, always conduct yourself as though the media were looking over your shoulder, but keep them away from the scene so as not to interfere with your work. While you are doing CSI work, it is not your responsibility to keep the media informed as to what you are doing or how you are doing it. Since media camera and soundpersons and reporters have no business within the parameters of the scene, make sure that they do not compromise the integrity of the scene, and refer them to your department's designated media information officer (MIO). In less-spectacular situations, a supervisor at the location usually will handle media relations, and in more unusual cases, a permanently-assigned media relations officer will be dispatched to the scene.

In some cases, such as a homicide, be careful to shield the body from the inquiring eyes of bystanders and inquisitive camera and video lenses. It may be necessary to cover the body with a blanket or tent until the coroner arrives, and then shield other critical evidence in a similar manner. You are going to be dealing with people who are very tenaciously doing their job, and they may try to intimidate or cajole you to "help them out" with an exclusive view or comment.

ATTORNEYS

Prosecuting attorneys may show up in cases they believe that will be very important or complicated. Usually, unless you run across a novice, the prosecutor has enough respect for the integrity of a crime scene and the importance of evidence that they will stand aside and take notes, asking a critical question occasionally, but never directing the investigation. Attorneys do not have that authority. If your supervisor advises you otherwise, then do as directed, but be sure to report that information in your reports.

Occasionally, an attorney will show up at the crime scene looking for clients to represent. This type of "ambulance chaser" is usually an unscrupulous and unethical individual and should be directed to leave or be arrested for obstructing justice. Sometimes you may have a suspect in custody and his or her defense attorney shows up. This person has absolutely no authority to interfere with the investigation or to be on the scene, so the attorney should be invited to move a safe distance away so as not to interfere with the investigation. The rules of discovery, as discussed earlier, are in effect, and the prosecution will share with the defense all information that is going to be used in the trial. The attorney will have access to all reports and may examine all the evidence later at an appropriate time after you have concluded your investigation. You are under no obligation to communicate with the attorney; that will be handled by the prosecutor.

CHAPLAINS

Many police departments have established chaplain programs that serve their communities. These programs are an excellent resource when dealing with the tragedy surrounding many crime scenes. Most police chaplain programs seek clergy who are formally trained in crisis management and counseling. They can be a significant comfort to victims, witnesses, and those who work these scenes. Most police chaplains do not represent a particular faith while "on-duty" but provide generic services unless specifically requested.

Police chaplains are trained to know their responsibilities and limitations when responding to a crime scene. They are often under the direction of the sworn officer with whom they ride. Chaplains will not enter the actual scene unless at the direction of the officer in charge, such as in a case where a seriously-injured victim may be near death and in need of spiritual counseling. If other members of the clergy arrive, they should remain outside of the scene and referred to the officer or supervisor in charge.

VICTIM ADVOCATES

There are several types of advocates that might arrive at a crime scene. Some are officially affiliated with the police department or court and have no access to a crime scene until the investigation is complete. Advocates might also be from community support groups or shelters. They are most likely there in a sincere effort to assist the victim and family members, but they are not to be admitted into the scene or allowed to contact victims until the conclusion of the investigation at the scene (and sometimes, not even then if victims and witnesses are taken to the department for further interviews). Victim advocates, if properly managed, can be a great resource and a source of comfort for persons needing their services.

CORONER

The coroner will respond to a wide variety of deaths that occur outside of a hospital (and is also there if the death is not related to a known medical condition or is suspected of being caused by criminal or negligent acts). If the deceased had not been under medical care for a specified period of time, it may be an obvious natural cause or disease situation, but the coroner will still handle the deceased. The coroner will certainly respond to crime scenes where someone has been killed. It is generally a crime to move a body or to go though the person's effects without the authorization of the coroner. Exceptions are where steps are being taken to render medical attention and the person has not yet been declared dead, when searching for medic alert jewelry, or to identify the victim.

The requirement that a body not be disturbed is one that should be explained to family and friends of the deceased (and sometimes to an angry crowd). Police or medics usually cover bodies after they have been declared dead, and they remain that way, wherever they were found, until the coroner's arrival. Because it often takes some time for the coroner to arrive, people can become angry or frustrated that the body is being left in place. Once the coroner has thoroughly examined the body (and this usually includes taking photographs and collecting personal items or clothing), the body will be taken to the morgue or to a designated location where the autopsy will be performed. In some cases when no autopsy is necessary, the coroner might release the body directly to a funeral home, and a medical doctor will sign the death certificate.

OTHERS

There might be other persons at a crime scene, depending on the uniqueness of the scene, department policy and procedure, and jurisdictional differences. Some scenes are likely to attract the "brass" as well, and they should be put to work on a specific detail or asked to stay out of the immediate scene. The goal of all people at the scene is to work in an organized fashion that accommodates the needs of each of the various roles in an efficient and expeditious manner. After you have worked a particular jurisdiction for a period of time, you will know these various persons on a first-name basis. Many long-term friendships have developed at crime scenes by professionals seeking to work together to make a difference for their communities.

SUMMARY

The players at the crime scene have their well-defined respective roles to play, and interact with each other to complete the crime scene investigation with competency and timeliness. It is probably the most crucial stage of the investigation, and a well-performed initial investigation will determine the successful conclusion all the way through to the conviction of the accused. This success is largely dependent on the skillful and professional work of the people who play the roles at the scene.

Some crimes are reported to a dispatch center and the crime scene investigator is the first, and sometimes the only, person to actually meet the victim in person until the investigation is well on its way. The crime scene investigator is an ambassador of good will in addition to an inspector of inanimate objects he or she encounters at the scene. You must apply your interactive skills and be a good listener when you meet with the victim, and be sure to explain the process to him or her so that they will understand that you and your department have their best interests at heart. That will assure that they will feel included in the process.

SUGGESTED OUTSIDE PROJECTS

1. Prepare a general order creating the position of media relations officer (MRO) and prescribe the guidelines for that person when meeting with media at crime scenes.

2. Write a position paper on how the crime scene investigator should deal with the crime victims in a variety of circumstances that he or she will encounter during his or her career.

DISCUSSION QUESTIONS

1. Under what conditions would a field supervisor be in charge of a crime scene investigation?

2. Who is usually in charge of a crime scene investigation?

3. Is there ever a situation when a news photographer might be invited onto a crime scene?

4. What is the role of the media information officer (MIO) at the scene of a crime investigation?

5. Does your local department have regularly-assigned police chaplains? What is their role at crime scenes?

6. Of what value to the investigator is the victim advocate?

7. Who is in charge of the body of the deceased?

8. Who has the authority to declare a person dead?

9. What is the best way to handle high-ranking officers who act as "tourists" and have no official role to perform at a crime scene?

10. How can a CSI officer make a victim feel included in the investigation process?

Chapter Five
The Initial Response

INTRODUCTION

You perform your first steps in the process of crime scene investigation long before you are dispatched to the scene. This involves making sure you have a complete inventory of equipment and supplies and that all are in working order. It is quite embarrassing to arrive unprepared at the scene of a crime and have to explain why you need to return to the station. Once properly equipped, you are ready to respond.

There is an old, but wise, adage that says you can't help at a scene if you don't get there. This refers to the understandable, but dangerous, practice of driving rapidly to a crime scene without due regard for those on the road. Traffic collisions are all too common in law enforcement, and most are completely unnecessary. The "hot call" over the radio that causes officers to take chances are rarely so serious that it justifies the risk of a collision. This is especially true when responding to a crime scene. While a timely response is important, the few extra minutes it takes to drive safely to a scene will not likely affect the evidence. A collision, on the other hand, might mean you don't arrive at all. That will certainly be a problem.

How and when you get to the scene can depend on your job category and can affect your well-being. Crime scene investigators generally fall into two categories: Sworn and non-sworn. The category you find yourself in (or the category you aspire to) determines how you might respond.

Sworn officers are peace officers who are typically armed and perform crime scene investigation (CSI) as a full-time or ancillary assignment. Non-sworn personnel are civilians who are rarely armed and who do not have the academy and advanced officer training or equipment afforded the police officer. The non-sworn employee has the sole (and permanently-assigned) responsibility for investigating crime scenes and working in the identification and/or crime laboratory. Any promotions will usually be within the same job category.

Sworn CSI officers may or may not be part of the initial response team assigned to the scene. It is important to distinguish between crimes in progress and scenes that are "cold." Non-sworn personnel should not respond directly to an in-progress crime scene unless specific safeguards have been established to protect them. This sometimes entails a command post or designated area for CSI and other units to respond to before entering the actual scene. Responding to a scene that still contains suspects is dangerous for the sworn officer. For the non-sworn, it is foolhardy. Always wait until sworn officers have declared the scene safe before entering.

SUGGESTED PROCEDURE

Whether sworn or non-sworn, the following suggested guidelines can assist you when you are assigned to respond to the crime scene:

1. Acknowledge the call. Wherever you are or whatever you are doing at the time of receiving the call, be sure to let the dispatcher and other field units know the location from which you are coming and your estimated time of arrival. Be aware that if you, or more likely, another officer, is responding Code-3 (lights and siren), you must take additional precautions to ensure your safe arrival. You can assume that other officers will also be responding, and perhaps fire and medical personnel as well. This can create dangerous conditions when more than one unit is responding Code-3 (red light and siren).

2. Get the available details. What is the nature of the crime as reported to the department? Is there any immediate danger to arriving personnel? Is there a hostage situation? Are the suspects still at or near the scene? Are there any injuries to victims? What other help is on the way, such as paramedics, fire department, public works, or others? Are there any descriptions of fleeing suspects or vehicles? Do not wait to find out these details until you arrive at the scene, as then it may be too late.

3. Request a description of the premises if you are not familiar with them. There may be tricky access problems to that particular building or neighborhood, such as streets that are inaccessible, closed, under construction, or congested because of

media or emergency vehicles at the scene. The building may have roof access or additional doors through which you may enter instead of using the main entrance.

4. Visualize your arrival and plan of action. While en route to the scene, visualize the scene as reported to you and as you anticipate your arrival. Mentally note how you are going to stake out the boundaries of the crime scene if officers on the scene have not done so already. Anticipate the presence of witnesses, onlookers, and representatives of the media. After you arrive, you will, no doubt, have to change some of your plans, but at least you will be mentally prepared to carry out that exercise. Always keep an open mind to all contingencies.

5. Survey the scene and surrounding area when you arrive. When responding to the crime scene, be alert for evidence on the perimeter. Depending on the type of incident, you should look for different things. For example, a residential burglary might not suggest much evidence away from the scene, but a kidnapping accomplished with a vehicle might. As you get close to the scene, look for vehicles, items, and persons associated with the crime. Remember though, if you are not the sworn officer assigned to the call, you not should engage suspects or suspicious vehicles and places. Your responsibility is to investigate the crime scene. Report your findings to sworn officers and be a good witness.

6. Assess whether the scene has been completely contained. It is not uncommon to have evidence moved, damaged, or even destroyed by vehicles entering the scene. Be very careful when driving close to the scene. Although it is the responsibility of the initial officers on scene to establish a safe perimeter—usually with ubiquitous crime scene tape—the scene is not always as large as it should be. As an example, shell casings from bullets are commonly found beyond the initial containment area established by responding officers in their hurry to control the chaotic events surrounding a shooting. Blood trails and discarded or dropped contraband are other examples of evidence that can lie beyond the initial confines of the scene.

7. Assure that the scene is adequately "taped off." If the task of establishing the crime scene goes to you, it is good to remember

the advice of old-time detectives that a crime scene can rarely be too large. It can always be made smaller, but it is difficult to enlarge a scene beyond what is initially established. You should carry rolls of police tape to quickly establish or re-establish the "police line," which lawfully prevents access to the scene by unauthorized personnel. Tape can be tied to anything convenient, including street signs, trees, and police cars. It may be necessary to request additional personnel to secure the scene. Once the scene has been secured, more permanent devices such as wooden barriers can be erected if necessary.

8. At least one officer should be assigned as the scribe, or recorder, to ensure that only authorized personnel enter the scene. The scribe maintains the scene log by recording the identity of all who enter the scene and the exact times of their arrival and departure.

9. Survey the scene. Although it is not likely to be your primary responsibility, if there are injured persons present, you might be called upon to render aid. Both sworn and non-sworn field personnel are generally trained and expected to perform first aid. If you are the first on the scene, or if additional help is needed, this will become part of your duties until relieved. The protection of life always supersedes the protection of property or evidence.

10. Look around for people and objects your instinct tells you are out of place. After committing a crime of almost any category, the perpetrator may come back and hang around, watching the investigators at work. Just because a person is not running away from the scene does not mean that he or she is an innocent bystander. Lookouts for burglars may actually appear to be a couple of lovers "making out" in a car near the scene, or the ice cream vendor with his pushcart, or even a lady walking her dog. In short, be suspicious of everyone, and report your observations to the officer in charge of the investigation or the officer serving as scribe. If something appears to be completely out of order, call for a follow-up unit to check it out.

11. Communicate, communicate, communicate. Keep in constant touch with the dispatcher and your fellow officers to keep them abreast of every aspect of the situation as it develops. This does not mean you keep up a running dialogue of inane

gobbledygook. Radio time is generally at a premium, but you should broadcast your arrival and any immediate information needed by those still responding. If no further assistance is required, that should also be promptly reported.

12. Locate and separate witnesses before you start your crime scene investigation if you are the first to arrive. An officer should be assigned to keep track of witnesses until the assigned investigator questions each one. Witnesses should be kept apart as much as possible because you want to get individual statements, not "jury statements" by the person with the stronger personality convincing the others that only his or her account of the events is the correct one. While witnesses are sometimes used to stand guard over evidence or to keep others away from the scene until more officers can respond, this practice should be used only when absolutely necessary to avoid changing the witness's perspective on what occurred.

13. Locate and protect transient or short-lived evidence. When weather conditions are less than ideal, you may have to take care to preserve this type of evidence before you do anything else, because any delay may result in the permanent loss of the evidence. For example, a wet shoe print on a dry tile floor will soon dry and disappear. Footprints on the sidewalk from a wet lawn will soon evaporate. What appears to be a spilled liquid may actually be blood or some other bodily fluid that needs collection and analysis, but which may be wiped up by a fastidious housekeeper unless you locate, isolate, and collect it first.

14. Determine the true nature and scope of the crime. Do this by examining the scene, listening to the victims and witnesses, and making your own assessment in consultation with your fellow officers on the scene. Was a crime committed? Are the elements present? Are the explanations consistent with the evidence? Be aware that it is not unusual for people to make false criminal reports for many different reasons, such as defrauding an insurer or causing trouble for an enemy.

15. Cooperate. The crime scene can be a busy and confusing place, with persons from a variety of agencies thrust together in a small space. Investigators, officers, supervisors, and coroners are just some of the people that are frequently at crime scenes. It is important to work together in a cooperative fashion to ensure

that each person's role is conducted efficiently and effectively. It is your responsibility as part of the team to take advantage of all the help you can get from others and to provide your share of help in return. The old saying, "It's amazing how much good work gets done if it does not matter who gets the credit" applies to the crime investigation team. Your good work will be recognized through your reports and your successful presentation of evidence in the courtroom.

16. The media poses its own challenges to those at a crime scene. While reporters, camera operators, and other members of the crew cannot enter the crime scene itself, they are frequently present at the perimeter. The media has a legitimate right to report crime, and they will report something whether you cooperate with them or not. One problem is that if someone from your department who has information about the investigation doesn't talk to them, someone else will and they might not paint a positive image of your agency. It is wise to designate an area for the media that is reasonably close to the scene, but not so close as to impede the investigation. A single spokesperson, such as the media information officer (MIO), should also be the one to provide all accounts of the events. Never underestimate the media. They are there to get information and will stop at little to do so. There are no such things as "off the record" statements. Also, be aware that the cameras and microphones used by today's media are extremely powerful and often invisible and can pick up images and conversation from tremendous distances. Always be aware that your words and gestures are being captured. For example, an image of two officers standing around the scene of a horrible homicide shown laughing and slapping each other's backs may actually be two old friends who have not seen each other for several months. To people who do not know what is really happening, it may appear as though the officers are cracking jokes about the death.

17. Allow nonessential people to enter the scene only after you release it when your investigation is complete. You are in charge of the crime scene. Once you release the scene, you will never be able to go back and find it in the same condition. And

should you return and find additional evidence, it is always subject to the defense attorney's reasonable assertion that someone put it there or that the scene was so poorly handled in the first place that nothing can be trusted. It may also be necessary for investigators to get a search warrant if the scene has been released.

SUMMARY

Accepting the assignment to investigate the crime scene and getting to that scene quickly and safely are crucial to the success of the investigation. Your responsibility as a part of the investigative team is to work with the other investigators as a team member, observing and reporting everything that comes to your attention that may help in solving the case. In this chapter, we have gone through a step-by-step procedure of what to do, from the time you first receive the call to go to the scene until you have arrived and begun your part of the investigation.

SUGGESTED OUTSIDE PROJECTS

1. Set up a ride-along with a crime scene investigation officer in your local police or sheriff's department. If possible, make two or three separate tours lasting a full eight- or ten-hour shift each. Write a report on your observations and include an evaluation of the work performance of the officers involved.

2. Write an essay on how officers can mess up a crime scene investigation by not following the prescribed procedures. An example might be that one of the witnesses is actually the suspect who returned to the scene as the officers arrived but was able to give faulty information to the officers and mislead their investigation. In this example, an officer who had observed that person arrive after the officers arrived failed to give that information to the officers taking the report.

DISCUSSION QUESTIONS

1. When you are out in the field, how should you communicate acknowledgment of the assignment to investigate a crime scene?

2. Is it possible that a reported burglary might prove to have been no crime at all? Give an example of such a false or mistaken report of a crime.

3. What value would a plot map of the area surrounding the crime scene have for the responding officers to the crime scene?

4. For a business burglary call, how would blueprints of the building help you when you respond to a call to investigate the crime?

5. If you had the opportunity to save the life of a critically-injured victim but it would mean destroying critical evidence, what would you do?

6. Why should witnesses be separated before giving their statements?

7. In your department, does the crime scene investigator usually question witnesses?

8. Describe three different types of short-lived or transient evidence, and explain why it is so important to identify and handle such evidence early in your investigation.

9. How would you mark off a crime scene if it were a robbery inside a convenience market? A burglary residence?

10. What would you add to the list presented in this chapter?

Chapter Six
The Crime Scene Search

INTRODUCTION

Whatever you are searching for, you must do it systematically and thoroughly. Additionally, when you are searching a crime scene and many onlookers are nearby, you must appear to know what you are doing. If you carry out your search in a haphazard and careless manner, you will cause irreparable damage to your reputation and that of your department. A sloppy search indicates that the searcher is probably sloppy in everything he or she does.

The community policing programs that involve your department and the public have a very positive effect because the public is more involved, but a cautionary note is that those people are watching their officers more carefully, and they are more likely to recognize sloppy police work. The ubiquitous media, especially those presenting "breaking news," will be nearby to record your activity for posterity, and many armchair detectives will critique your work every time your act is shown on local news programs. A word of advice: Be thorough and be professional.

As the crime scene investigator, do not begin to search or process the scene when a suspect may still be present. If you are the primary investigating officer who is also responsible for CSI, you need to first devote your full attention to searching for suspects who might still be on the premises. Once you determine that suspects are in custody or have left the scene, then you can concentrate on the collection of evidence. It is, of course, prudent to remember that it is possible to miss a suspect during a search, or a suspect may return to the scene while you are processing the scene. In that eventuality, it is wise to have another officer on the scene while you are devoting your attention to the crime scene investigation.

SEARCH WARRANT SEARCHES

Search warrant searches will be rare for crime scene searches, they are usually for a return visit after the initial search has been completed. When you are acting on a search warrant your search will be limited to searching only those places described in the warrant, and only for items that have been listed as possible or probable in those places consistent with the search. For example, you don't look into dresser drawers for stolen auto tires and wheels. However, if your search is consistent with what you hope to find, and you come across other items that you believe to be contraband, guard the "treasure" against destruction or concealment and secure a new warrant to search for more contraband of the nature of your new discovery. As you have learned in the academy and in your criminal procedures classes, a search warrant is not a hunting or fishing license, and it has many restrictions.

PLAN YOUR SEARCH

All searches require that you proceed according to an organized and coordinated plan. There are different kinds of searches, depending on what you are looking for, such as searches for people (missing and lost children and adults, and suspects of all ages and genders) and searches for objects. You may be searching the premises where a burglar has taken away stolen objects and left behind evidence. You may be searching an office building for bombs purported to have been planted on the premises. In all searches you are looking for evidence of all types. Planning is your key to greater success in finding what you are looking for, as well as many items you had no idea you would find. Whether you work alone or with other searchers, draw a plan on paper and apportion the search so that each area is searched at least twice, and each time by a different person. Draw your search plan, assign searchers, and check off each area when the search is complete. If curious onlookers are nearby, post a guard to watch the searched areas to prevent contamination or evidence planting.

INTERIOR SEARCHES

Try to arrange for optimum lighting conditions, utilize available lights at the scene, bring in more flood lamps with portable generators, and use your battery-operated flashlights as well. If you are searching a building where the electricity is off, your only available lighting will probably be your flashlights and portable floods. Under these conditions, when you move from a lighted area where your eyes are conditioned to the light into a dark room or area, stop for a few seconds when you enter the dark and let your eyes adjust to the light change. The rods and cones of your eyes reverse functions when going from dark to light and vice versa, and the more dramatic the change, the longer the transition time.

Wear gloves for your search. If you believe there is the possibility of a suspect still being on the premises, you may choose to move with your weapon to a ready position. In those situations it is also wise to open each door by slamming it open until it strikes the wall or doorstop. If you hear a loud "Ugh" when you slam the door open, you have probably located a suspect hiding behind that door. In most crime scene searches, you or your colleagues have probably already cleared the area of any suspects, so it will not be necessary to move with a weapon in your hand or to slam doors open. You have now moved on to the evidence search phase of the investigation.

As you move from room to room or from one section of the search to another, stop frequently and listen for sounds, try to identify odors, and absorb the atmosphere of the scene. Sounds such as air conditioning or heaters turning on and off, or the foundation settling, and odors, such as perfume, cigar, or pipe smoke, and aftershave lotion may prove valuable to your investigation later. For example, a person confessing to the crime may at some time state that the air conditioner was on full blast and made him shiver. As for odors, you may recognize the odors on the suspect's person as being similar to those you smell earlier during your crime scene search.

Take Polaroid photos or start videorecording the scene as you enter and move around the scene to get an overall view before you start your intensive search. If you have neither a Polaroid camera nor a camcorder, use a voice-activated tape recorder or take good notes. These will be your initial observations. You will later begin using your 35mm SLR camera for the more detailed evidence photos that we will cover in Chapter Nine. If you have a notepad in hand, make a rough sketch of the crime scene and the general area for orientation purposes. You will prepare more detailed sketches later. These photos and rough sketches may help you reconstruct the scene in your mind when you are preparing your reports, and sometimes the initial photos may show certain items that may not show up later in your more detailed photographs. It may lead you to discover that something has possibly contaminated the scene or someone just inadvertently moved something. In the celebrated Jeffrey McDonald murder case several years ago, it was revealed that one of the ambulance drivers picked up and pocketed an item at the scene, believed to be a wallet belonging to McDonald.

Even though you are wearing gloves, touch nothing that you believe might bear trace evidence until you are sure that touching will not wipe away fingerprints or other traces. Shine a light obliquely across the surface of the floor and other flat surfaces before you walk on them to search for footprints or shoe prints in the dust that has settled since the last time the surface was dusted. Use the oblique light procedure over all surfaces that might have been disturbed. Sometimes undisturbed dust may yield information also. For example, one of the authors was taking a burglary report from an auto parts shop owner, who listed dozens of items that had been stolen, but about a month's accumulation of undisturbed dust was on the shelves where the victim claimed the merchandise had been stored. Then it was pointed out to the victim that if merchandise had been on those shelves, the merchandise and not the shelves would be covered with dust. The owner then admitted he was "padding" the report a little for his insurance claim. It is reasonable to assume that he probably dusted his shelves more frequently after that.

Divide the room or area into halves or quadrants, depending on the number of people you have involved in the search, and assign individuals or teams to each section. Next, divide the room into levels at which the search will be performed, such as one-third of the wall from the floor up, then the second one-third, and finally the rest of the way to the ceiling, followed by the spaces above the ceiling or false ceiling and crawl hole. Later, when each officer or team of officers has completed their part of the search, switch searchers and repeat the process. It is not unusual for one person to miss something that another person will find. As you know, sometimes we have blind spots where we look at something yet do not see it. Has it ever happened to you that a close friend comes within your visual range at a conference, for example, and didn't see that person until perhaps a half-hour later, and your excuse was "I didn't see you come in"? In the more serious crimes, a secondary search should be considered mandatory, and preferably at a time when the lighting conditions are at an optimum level.

Ceiling Area

Look for false ceilings, and search the area between that structure and the real ceiling, and the attic where there are accessible crawl spaces. Burglars have been known to climb up into crawl holes that one would not imagine could bear such weight and bulk. The moral here is to search even the most illogical places for people and contraband, so your search is truly more thorough than if you were to search only the obvious places. Search inside the ceiling light fixtures and ducts for air conditioning, ventilation, and heating systems. Sound or speaker systems, power conduits, other pipes, and enclosed areas should be given meticulous attention. Look behind and inside moldings and frames if they are loose or appear to have been disturbed. Search any facade or other object that appears to be part of the room design but might be hollow and hide contraband.

Windows and Door Frames

Look for access points to hollow cores of doors and framing that have been disturbed or that could possibly conceal small hidden items, such as bindles of drugs or folded paper. Curtain and drape rods are good hiding places.

Walls

The spaces between walls are extremely good hiding places. Sometimes a false wall can conceal an entire room that has been sealed off with plaster and wallboard. If you think there might be such a hidden room, take outside measurements of the structure and compare that with inside measurements. If you discover an unexplained difference of several feet, it could well be that a sealed closet space that has been designated as a hiding space, which is perhaps accessible from the attic or a crawl hole in the ceiling of the basement. Switch plates, plug plates, and spaces behind photos and other wall hangings provide access to the walls. Merely tapping on the wall will produce a hollow sound because most walls are hollow. Look around the edges of the wall, such as at the ceiling and floor and door and window frames. In very critical searches, it may be necessary to tear out part of the wall.

Floors

Check the floor carefully for any loose boards, recently-installed tiles or carpeting, or recent repair work to the floor or its covering. Color differences of floor covering may indicate that stains have been removed. You may search any area that might have contained bloodstains with tests that are described in Chapter Seven. In a murder case several years ago, the murderer decided to break up with his girlfriend. When she objected to such an abrupt end to their relationship, he acceded to a final fling, but he wanted it to be a threesome with another woman participating. They had their *menage à trois* with the second woman videotaping a sex act between the two who were breaking up, during which the man tortured and murdered the victim. This was all on tape. Afterward, the videographer handed the tape to the killer and went home. Some time later, the killer was questioned about the disappearance of his former girlfriend, then eventually arrested and prosecuted for her murder. The third party in the sex scene who took the pictures testified to what had happened that fateful night and told about the tape. The police could not find the tape and relied only on that witness's account of the murder. The defendant testified that he was innocent and knew nothing of his former lover's whereabouts. The defense then brought up enough evidence of alcoholism and mental instability of the prosecution's star witness that the jury voted for acquittal of the murderer.

A couple of years after the murder, the freed killer, who had already been in jeopardy and found not guilty, sold his house, where the murder had occurred. The new owners decided to remodel, and when they started tearing up flooring and repairing holes in the walls they found the missing tape. They played it on their VCR, saw the murder take place on the tape, and turned the tape over to the FBI, who turned it over to the local prosecuting attorney. Because the killer had already been declared not guilty, he could not be tried again for the murder due to the double jeopardy rule of the Fifth Amendment. But, because he had testified during his trial that he knew nothing of the murder, he was prosecuted and convicted for perjury. It was no consolation to the victim's survivors, but the man did serve a few years in prison and partially paid for his crime. All this because the officers who searched the premises missed a most valuable piece of evidence: the tape.

Miscellaneous

Building plans and blueprints may reveal valuable information about the original structure compared with its current configuration. Doors, windows, and stairways may have been eliminated or covered over. In a recent case in southern California, a newly-poured patio floor was dug up by narcotics officers and revealed a cache of more than a million dollars in cash. Consider also the cold war scare when people built bomb shelters in their backyards or under their houses, which by now have fallen into disrepair and may have been closed or forgotten.

Insulation materials serve as excellent camouflage. Recently-hung wallpaper on only one wall, which looked like a sloppy job at that, revealed a very valuable stolen painting hidden under the wallpaper. Move bookcases, inspect floor openings, and objects covering damaged or stained carpeting. You will then conduct detailed searches of the furniture, inside and under drawers, spaces behind drawers, inside and under mattresses, even hollow spaces under waterbeds. The possibilities are endless.

EXTERIOR SEARCHES

Once you and your colleagues have established the parameters of the crime scene and search areas, divide each area into workable portions and delegate each subarea to yourself and your colleagues, who are working either solo or in teams of two. If you are conducting the search by yourself, sketch out the entire area, break it into workable subareas, then search one subarea at a time, checking off on your sketch each part of the search area as you complete that part of the search.

You may choose to use any method you believe best for each individual search, such as a spiral, quadrants, ever-expanding or contracting circles, or back and forth in a straight line in a pattern as one follows when mowing a lawn. What you call it is of lesser importance than how thoroughly you conduct your search. Even when you are working alone, go back and search again, changing your method so as to maximize the chances of finding something you might have missed the first time. You not only must be efficient, but also you must present the image that you know what you are doing. This is true especially when you have people watching you work, such as that news photographer in a tree nearby, or some Monday morning quarterback who will tell everyone within earshot how sloppy you were when looking for evidence. It may sound a little paranoid, but believe us, what you do and how you do your job reflect on other people's assessment of your department. You do not want your operation to be called a "cesspool of incompetence." In other words, you must not only know what you are doing, but you must appear as though you know what you are doing.

If the weather is working against you, such as rain, snow, or high winds, you are probably going to change the sequence of your investigation so that you may search for those items that are most likely to be destroyed or altered. Shoe prints in a mud puddle or pools of blood that will be washed away unless collected immediately will take precedence over evidence that can wait until you have taken care of the short-lived evidence. If you are conducting your search on a street, a highway, or a heavily-traveled sidewalk during rush hour, you will want to plan your search so that your investigation will not suffer yet will get the traffic moving as soon as possible.

There is no sense or reason where people choose hiding places. For that reason, you must expect to find people and objects where one would least likely find them. Desperate people can fit into places so small that it takes the fire department and its jaws of life to get them out. People have been found in trash compactors (a nine-year-old boy), air-conditioning and heating ducts, chimneys, kitchen and bathroom cabinets, even desk or dresser drawers. Even when you are looking for larger items, consider that the person who hid them has possibly dismantled them and hidden their parts in several places. A postal inspector once told the story that a soldier during the Korean War sent a souvenir of an enemy's confiscated gun home, but not all in one piece. As the story goes, an alert postal clerk discovered a single piece of the gun. When the soldier sent the last piece, the postal inspector put all the separate pieces together and reconstructed the whole gun. He then charged the soldier with sending a firearm through the mails. Even though the story sounds a little "fishy," it does make the point that people do ingenious things to skirt the law.

If it does not complicate your investigation, have someone familiar with the place to be searched, possibly an employee or tenant, accompany you while you search for items that are missing or that have been left behind by the perpetrator. Be cautious when listening to claims about certain items stolen or moved, and do not accept at face value every word that person tells you. He or she may have a secret agenda, which might include misleading the investigation or exaggerating his or her losses to defraud the insurer. Some people play burglars and thieves to steal their cars or merchandise so that they can collect the insurance and split their earnings with the people who allegedly victimized them.

SEARCHES FOR BOMBS

Searches for suspected bombs or phoned-in bomb threats should be left to the specialists who are trained and equipped for such searches. But, as a crime scene investigator, you may find yourself the first one on the scene and searching for suspicious objects until the bomb squad arrives. Be careful to leave in place any object that you suspect might be a bomb, evacuate the area, and stand by until the experts arrive. If the suspected object is in a building, evacuate the entire building. If you do conduct such a preliminary search, take along someone who is familiar with the building and its contents to advise you of objects disturbed or perhaps a package left on the premises that was not there earlier. Parcel deliveries, including packages that arrived by a postal carrier, should be handled as though they were bombs until the bomb squad has cleared them.

When searching for a bomb or similar device, do not use any radio equipment, turn on or off any light switches, or operate any device that might spark and set off a device of some sort. Do not allow anyone to smoke, and avoid inserting and pulling out electric plugs. Some explosive devices have spring-wound clocks for timing and may be heard ticking if you are searching in absolute silence. If and when you find what you recognize as a bomb or what you suspect might be a bomb, and once you have verified that the bomb squad is on its way to the scene, withdraw from the area and make sure the surrounding area has been evacuated. After the bomb has been removed and/or neutralized, then continue your crime scene search.

THE SEARCH CONTINUES

If practical, put plastic covers over your shoes, wear gloves to avoid leaving impressions of your own at the scene, and continue your search. We have conveniently forgotten the name of the author, but one writer of an investigation text recommends that you keep your hands in your pockets while searching a crime scene. This is neither wise nor practical, as evidence can be collected only by moving and collecting things. Your responsibility is to determine if a crime has, in fact, been committed and to conduct a thorough investigation. Keep an open mind throughout the entire time you are on the premises, and avoid forming any preconceived notions about the outcome of your search. If you have a fixed objective, you may find only what you expect to find during your search. Sometimes claims made by crime victims may not be borne out by the facts. If your investigation is thorough, the evidence will speak for itself and either verify or disprove the statements made by the victims.

As you continue the process of investigating, stop occasionally and conceptualize the crime as it might have happened. What would be the likely point of entry? Exit? What route of travel did the perpetrator(s) take while committing the crime? Imagine that you are in the perpetrator's shoes and how you would have carried out the action. Consider the timing. How much can be accomplished in the time "window" when the crime must have occurred? For example, in an armed robbery of a gold vault, the two owners of the company stated that they were held up at gunpoint and tied up. Then several million dollars' worth of gold bricks were removed from the vault in 20 minutes by two men who used a three-quarter-ton pickup truck to cart away the loot. Gold is heavy, as the officers knew. All they did was add up the tons of gold that had allegedly been stolen, then estimate that a pickup truck of that size would have had to make several trips over a couple of hours to cart all that gold away. After pointing this out to the victims when questioning them separately, one of the victims confessed that actually they had only about a half dozen bricks in all in their vault, which they showed to the owners who wanted to look at their gold. They used the same gold bricks to show all the people and did not expect anyone to take their gold out of the vault because gold has to be assayed and weighed each time it is moved. Handling gold causes small particles to be scraped off with fingernails or by such objects as rings or bracelets, and consequently handling reduces its value. The two vault owners panicked when they received a surprise notification from one of their customers, who became suspicious of their activities and told them that he had gone to the police to investigate what he believed to be a major scam. They feared that the police would come with a search warrant and find that they had been selling the same few gold bricks many times over, and that there were actually only a half dozen gold bricks in the entire building. The vault owners were subsequently convicted for major felony fraud and the misdemeanor charge of filing a false police report was dropped.

In order to avoid allegations of incompetence or dishonesty, be sure to document your search very carefully with accurate notes, photographs, and fellow officers paying attention to each other throughout the investigation. Do not overlook the possibility of using a videographer for the express purpose of liability protection, as covered earlier. You will want to document discrepancies between what victims and witnesses describe happened and what did or did not happen. For example, a witness may distinctly remember having seen the culprit crawl in through the window. When you examine the window, you will see that the glass has been broken, and jagged pieces of the glass still sticking up in the frame, but no blood or snagged clothing on the jagged edges of the glass or on the windowsill, which would surely be there if someone had crawled through that window. Your photos or video will show this discrepancy without your having to editorialize that the reporting party has probably lied.

Sometimes a so-called "victim" will try to convince you that a window was broken from the outside and entry was made though that window. Your investigation shows that the window was broken from the inside, because it had been raining during the past few hours, and there are no muddy footprints in the flowerbed below the window, and there are no muddy scuff marks on the outside wall, which would have been placed there by a person climbing in through the window.

It is not usual for a bona fide crime to be enhanced by victims who magnify their losses, either intentionally or unintentionally. Under extreme emotional stress, three assailants may appear as five, or a man, who is five foot, three inches, may seem to be much taller and heavier. Some victims are embarrassed to say that they were beat up by someone smaller and who might appear weaker than they are. Some victims exaggerate their losses so that the insurance will pay them for their entire loss and also cover their deductible amount, or to replace worn-out tools that they would rather the insurance company buy for them. Other victims make simple errors in describing the event and calculating their losses.

RECORDING THE SEARCH

We have already mentioned the use of recording devices, such as a tape recorder, video camcorder, Polaroid camera, and other cameras. When your investigation team is large enough, one of the members of the team should

Figure 6.1 Documentation and notes are crucial during the course of your crime scene investigation.

be the scribe. Otherwise, you are the scribe along with your other duties. Every action taken by the team members should be written down exactly as it happens, and whenever a discovery of some new information or evidence is made, the scribe should record the time, exact location, description of the find, and precisely who made the discovery (Figure 6.1).

The scribe should also keep a log to record arrivals and departures of all persons at the scene for any reason whatsoever. If a supervisor just drops by at 8:47 A.M. to check on the progress of the investigation, the time and name of that supervisor should be entered on the log. You should take photos of their shoes or their fingerprints if they have touched anything during their visit to the scene. Include all persons, because sometime later it may be discovered that one of those people may have left shoe impressions at the scene (Figure 6.2).

The scribe's log will be incorporated into the completed package of reports. Some crime reports and supplemental reports add up to thousands of pages before the case finally goes to court. In addition to the scribe's log, each participant involved in the investigation will be required to complete an individual report with a complete account of exactly what he or she did and might have found and all the details of his or her participation. The officer assigned as principal investigator of the case will

Figure 6.2   Each officer who enters or leaves a scene should be logged in and out. That officer should also document his or her role or purpose at the scene.

have the responsibility of collecting and coordinating all of those reports, and the principal investigator puts them together so that they will have continuity and clarity for those who will read them. All participants should later read through the reports of their individual actions to check for the accuracy of their contributions.

TRANSIENT OR SHORT-LIVED EVIDENCE

Be careful to identify and protect transient evidence that is not likely to last long because of weather conditions such as rain, snow, or warming sunlight, or because of vehicular or foot traffic that is likely to destroy the evidence if it is not addressed immediately (Figure 6.3). Skid marks on a heavily-traveled roadway will soon blend in with previous and subsequent skid marks and may not be distinguishable from each other. Shoe or foot impressions in dust will blow away with the next strong gust of wind. Wet prints on a dry floor will dry as the sun rises. The wet marks should be noted and sketched, and photographed when first observed, or they will be lost forever. In the rain, muddy shoe prints might wash away. Sometimes you run across the well-meaning person who will start cleaning up the mess at the scene even before you have completed your investigation. It is not unusual for sex crime victims to destroy the evidence of the attack on their own bodies by bathing or douching, and putting stained bedclothes

Figure 6.3 Wet shoe prints coming off of a wet grass area onto concrete are an example of transient evidence. These shoe prints will evaporate and must be photographed immediately or they will disappear.

in the washing machine. These victims are probably not even thinking of the harm they are causing to your investigation because of their personal emotional trauma.

These items of transient evidence may not prove to be your most crucial evidence, but when you are searching the scene and collecting all available evidence, you may not be in a position to know which items of evidence are best and which are not. Meticulously and completely collect all items that are, or that might be, evidence, and then the evidence itself will often tell you what role it will play in your case.

CONDITIONS RELATED TO THE CRIME

Although they may not be counted as evidence, certain circumstances may help you determine the nature of the crime, the time of day, and perhaps something personal about the perpetrator, such as taste in food or preferences in radio or television shows. Here are some of the things you should be aware of while conducting your search.

1. Discarded candy and gum wrappers, cigarette and cigar butts or ashes, sales slips and receipts that might have fallen out of the perpetrator's pockets during the crime.

2. Doors that are locked or unlocked, which are different than how the occupant left them before the crime.

3. Is there evidence of damage or destruction of the door or the lock that would indicate a forcible entry?

4. If doors or windows were damaged, was the damage done from the inside or the outside? This may indicate whether it is a point of exit or entry.

5. Was entry made with use of a key? Follow-up investigators will find out who had keys.

6. Is there evidence that a lock was picked, as indicated by metal shavings and broken pieces of a lock pick?

7. Are there small pieces of metal on the premises, possibly from a tool that the perpetrator took away from the scene?

8. Are the windows open or closed? Is the weather outside consistent with this? On a cold day, and usually at night for security reasons, the windows are closed and locked by the occupants.

9. Are the shades or drapes open or closed? Their position may indicate that the people inside like dark interiors during the daytime or that it was nighttime and the window coverings were closed for privacy. Some nudists and other people who are allergic to sunlight keep their windows covered day and night. Some burglars close the blinds and shades so that they may work where people outside cannot see them.

10. If a window or door has been broken and the debris on the sill and surrounding area is undisturbed, you may surmise that nobody could have gone through that opening without cutting himself or herself and/or disturbing the debris.

11. Are the lights on or off? Which lights may indicate whether a person went into the kitchen or used the bathroom? The status of the lights may also give you a clue as to whether the crime was committed during the day or night.

12. Specific lighting during any time of the day might indicate what the victim was doing at the time of the crime, such as working at a desk with the desk light on. This also might indicate that a thief might have turned on a desk light to see better when rifling through the desk drawers. Something like this

might indicate that the perpetrator knew the location of his or her objective, which might point suspicion toward someone familiar with the premises.

13. What is the status of the heating and air conditioning? Some systems are designed to keep the ambient temperature constant, alternating heat and air, but most are set at one position or the other. Air conditioning on at full blast might indicate that the occupants last touched the controls during the heat of the day, or at night. Some burglars like to work in comfort and may set the controls themselves.

14. How about the food preparation areas in the kitchen? What meal was the last one eaten or prepared by the occupants? Are the dishes and cups left in the same condition as they were seen last by the victims? Perhaps the perpetrator(s) had a bite to eat to sustain themselves during their exploits. Check the kitchen sink and dishwasher for their contents to see if you get any hints about the *modus operandi* or identity of the culprits.

15. Is there an indication that perhaps guests were expected or had arrived, and were the guests possibly involved in the crime? Do the number of place settings equal the number of residents? This is especially important information to have if the residents have been murdered.

16. Can you detect any identifiable odors, such as perfumes, tobacco smoke, or medications, such as mentholated chest rub, and other substances that are foreign to this particular place of business or residence?

17. Check the sinks in the kitchen, bathrooms, and laundry room if you have a blood-related crime, such as a homicide or assault. Sometimes the assailant might attempt to wash blood off of tools or weapons. Even though the sink may appear to be clean, the elbow-shaped trap beneath the sink may contain valuable evidence because the perpetrator did not let the water run long enough to clear the pipes.

18. A toilet that has not been flushed completely may yield such evidence as cigarette butts or human waste deposited by the perpetrator, which may lead to determination of blood type or DNA of the perpetrator.

19. What is the condition of the bedding in the bedrooms? In sexual attack cases, you will collect all bedding to search for the presence of body fluids, hairs and fibers, and other evidence to substantiate the charges.

20. What is the state of dress or undress of the victims of assault or homicide victims? A rape suspect, for example, may claim that the sex was consensual, while the torn clothing of the victim may prove that extreme force was used.

21. Look at clocks and watches around the premises, and on those worn by the victims and suspects. A wall plug may have been pulled loose during the commission of a crime, or the time showing on a watch worn by a witness may be incorrect, and statements made may be crucially connected to his or her reference to the time on that watch or clock.

22. The "star 69" feature on a telephone will possibly call the phone number of the last party who called the residence or business where the crime occurred. Or you may choose to press the "redial" button to find out if the intruder made at least one phone call while on the premises and to whom that call was made.

23. If a cellular phone or pager was stolen in the crime, call the number of that unit and find out if anyone answers. Lost units are also found that way by calling the number and hearing the ring or buzz and leading you to its location. A car theft victim called the cell phone in his car. The person who answered was a friend waiting for the car thief to get out of class. A brief conversation led the victim and the local police to a high school in another city, where the car thief was arrested and the car recovered without damage.

24. Small areas, such as stairways, foyers, and hallways, may reveal items that have dropped out of an intruder's pockets. Have you sometimes taken your car keys out of your pocket and accidentally also removed coins or some other items at the same time?

25. Was the place ransacked by a person who was looking for anything of value, or did the intruder know exactly what he or she was looking for? This may identify the culprit as a member or friend of the family instead of a stranger.

26. If you have one, ask your tour guide through the crime scene if there is anything at all out of the ordinary, supporting our theory of transference.

SUMMARY

The search is one of the most important parts of any crime investigation. No matter how hard you try to do it better later, the first time you search must be your best and may be the only chance to conduct a full search. Missed evidence and crucial bits of data will be lost forever because of deliberate or accidental efforts of the occupants of the premises, whether interior or exterior, to clean up after the crime. Victims will have to clean up before resuming their lives at that location, and for them, the sooner the better. Outside, many things will be changed by gardeners and cleanup crews for the resumption of normalcy, whatever that might be.

Be precise and thorough in your search, and keep an open mind. If you are looking for whatever may present itself to you, you are more likely to find it than if you have a preconceived idea about what you are going to find. It is sort of like saying: "If only I have two good pieces of evidence I can solve this case." You find the two items you were looking for, then stop. That is certainly no way to conduct an investigation. You can never collect too much evidence. Let the facts tell you what happened rather than shaping the facts to fit your hypothesis.

SUGGESTED OUTSIDE PROJECTS

1. Discuss this chapter with an experienced crime scene investigation specialist from your local police department. Get his views on what we have written here. Then, rewrite the chapter, as you believe it should have been written.

2. With your fellow students, set up an imaginary crime scene and hide at least 8 items, which you designate as evidence. Give a list of those items to the team of students who are going to search and see if they find them all. Switch teams and repeat until all have had a chance to do their own search.

DISCUSSION QUESTIONS

1. When you are entering a room or area that is darker than the one you are leaving, what is suggested that you do before you enter the new place?

2. Why slam a door open all the way to the doorstop before entering a room?

3. What is the primary purpose for wearing gloves and shoe covers when conducting a crime scene search?

4. What is transient evidence? Give an example of transient evidence.

5. Give a couple of examples of how you might suspect that a victim is exaggerating his or her loss.

6. What are the advantages of having two officers search a crime scene as a team?

7. Why would you have a second search by a different team if the first one were as thorough as it should be?

8. What is the function of a scribe?

9. Describe three or four different patterns of search when you are searching a room in which a crime occurred.

10. What should you do if you come across an object you believe to be a bomb while you are searching an office on the 10th floor of a building?

Chapter Seven
Evidence Collection

INTRODUCTION

When you are searching for evidence, you may ask: "What is evidence?" That is an excellent question to start out this chapter. The answer is not quite so simple. There are actually two answers, one practical and the other academic. The practical answer is that we don't really know what is and is not evidence in a case until after we have collected every available item and bit of information that relates to a case and then analyzed everything and presented it to the prosecuting attorney. The attorney who is going to prosecute the case is the one who determines what is and is not evidence for this specific case, what is not relevant or material to the case, and what witnesses are not competent to testify for one reason or another. The academic definition is, "Any species of proof, or probative matter, legally presented at the trial of an issue, by the act of the parties and through the medium of witnesses, records, documents, concrete objects, and so on, for the purpose of inducing belief in the minds of the court or jury as to their contention." Not only must the judge admit the evidence into the trial if it meets the tests of legality and constitutionality, but in the end, the jury must accept it as proving a fact. Review the discussion of evidence in Chapter One before you continue with this lesson.

It is important to note the words "legally presented" in this definition. There are state and federal rules of evidence and constitutional safeguards protecting the residents and guests of this country against unreasonable violations of their personal and property privacy, and there are rules protecting their right not to bear witness against themselves. In order to be able to legally present evidence you have collected, you must also show through testimony and documentation that there was a constant chain of custody from the time it was first discovered until it is presented in court.

In this chapter, we will list and discuss some of the many types of physical evidence you might find at the crime scene; how to collect it, preserve it, and transport it to the laboratory or evidence locker, and how to present the evidence in court.

TIRE IMPRESSIONS

Tire manufacturers design and patent the treads on their products in distinctive patterns, which are exclusive to their brands only. A Goodyear tire tread will never look like that of a Bridgestone or a Winston tire tread, and vice versa. Many large laboratories, particularly those of the Federal Bureau of Investigation and many of the state laboratories, maintain files on tire patterns for the current year as well as files on tire patterns that go back many years.

To collect tire impressions for evidentiary purposes, locate them on your sketch, indicate the length of each one, and number or letter them in sequence if there is more than one impression. Next, photograph the impressions from an angle where you can include all impressions in the one photo; if there is more than one impression, depict their entire length. Take a series of photos of each impression from end to end, including a ruler in the photo so that you may enlarge each photo 1 to 1 (actual size), and so that the photos may be placed side by side to show the entire length of the impression.

When you locate a vehicle that holds the tires that you believe made the impressions in question, remove the wheels and roll their prints. To do this you will want to have impressions of the entire circumference of each tire in question. Using butcher paper or newsprint approximately ten feet long, printers' ink, and a roller, roll ink on the tire tread all the way around where "the rubber meets the road," to paraphrase an old saying. Then roll the entire circumference of the tire onto the paper as you would roll a fingerprint. Compare this exemplar of the suspected tire with the photographs and casts taken at the crime scene.

SHOE, BOOT, AND FOOTPRINTS

Shoe manufacturers, especially the ones that produce higher-quality products, place distinctive designs and logos on the heels and soles of their shoes and boots. In some case you will find that even the heel and toe patterns are different from all others. From the impression you find in pliable material, such as mud or wax, you may find the patterns we mention plus distinctive wear patterns, cuts, bruise marks, and imperfections that are unique to only one garment and its owner. You may determine the approximate size of the shoe or boot, but in pliable material and under vari-

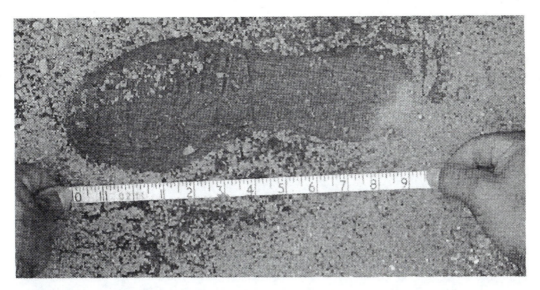

Figure 7.1   Always show exact measurements of actual impressions. Courtesy of County Sheriff's Office, Penobscot County, Maine.

able weather conditions, it will probably not be possible to discern exact sizes. However, if the impression looks like size 14, you can be sure that not many people wear size 14 (see Figure 7.1).

A footprint will also reveal the approximate size of shoe that person would wear, and there may be something unique about the shape of the foot or configuration of the toes that would aid in identifying the person who left the prints. People who are heavy or who carry heavy loads tend to make deeper impressions with their heels, and people who are running or walking fast will be lighter on their heels than on their toes. The stride pattern will show a taller person and/or one who is running and taking longer strides than if walking. The stride pattern also will have a pattern. Watch runway models in a fashion show. You will notice that for the greatest effect to show off their fashions, they walk by taking each step directly in front of the other instead of forward and side by side, as does the average walker. Size and stride patterns of the impressions may give you a hint as to the age and gender of the person who made the impression, with females and younger persons making smaller impressions and closer stride patterns than males and older persons.

People trained in the military service are likely to lead off by stepping first each time with the same foot, either right or left. A person walking with a limp will make a deeper impression with the stronger foot that bears the greater weight, and a cane or crutches may also leave an impression (Figure 7.2).

Figure 7.2   This partial shoe print impression was removed from a countertop using an electrostatic dust print lifter.

Measure the impressions and sketch them before taking photographs of individual impressions, the entire series of impressions, if any, and photos showing the stride pattern. Casting will be covered in a separate chapter.

When shoe, boot, and footprints are left on dusty surfaces, or when wet prints are left on dry surfaces, you may be able to sketch and photograph only, except that you may find footprints made by shoeless persons that display the same as palm and fingerprints. The experts may testify about footprints matching with the same authority as fingerprints. As for boots and shoes, the FBI and many other laboratories keep up-to-date files on logos, designs, and patterns of as many manufacturers' boots and shoes that they can find, and they keep adding to their files as often as possible.

BLOOD AND BLOODSTAINS

Whenever you have a personal crime, such as rape, assault, criminal homicide, or kidnapping, you are likely to find blood and bloodstains at or near the scene. It is not unusual to find blood also at property crimes. The perpetrator may have injured himself or herself while entering the place, or while prying open containers or moving objects around, or perhaps by having a nosebleed as a result of extreme emotional pressure or bumping up against a hard object. Wherever you find broken glass or sharp objects, you

Figure 7.3 This illustration shows that as a droplet of blood hits a surface, it makes a teardrop shape and then slowly thins out. By understanding this effect, one can determine the direction of travel of the bleeder.

are likely to find blood or other body fluids. Some people urinate or defecate when they are under extreme emotional stress. In a series of burglaries investigated by one of the authors, we found feces on a neighbor who wanted to make a statement about being a misfit among the other kids on the block.

The first step when finding blood or stains is to photograph them in their place, undisturbed, and to place them in your rough sketch. You may wish to make a quick determination whether the substance is blood, which is usually determined visually and by its distinctive odor, and for certain reasons, it may be important to determine whether it is from an animal or a human. Using prepared vials of reagent, it is fast and easy to conduct these tests, although you will not usually bother with these determinations until later in the lab.

The quantity of blood may show how profusely a person has bled at the scene, and the degree to which it has coagulated may indicate how recently the blood was deposited at that location. The droplets of blood will show whether the bleeder was moving, in what direction, and perhaps whether the movement was fast or slow. A large drop followed by smaller droplets indicates that the person was moving in the direction pointed by the ever-diminishing size of the droplets, which makes the pattern look like a tadpole. A thinner "tadpole-like" group of spots would indicate that the bleeder was moving faster than if the pattern looked like a fatter tadpole. The blood falling to the surface causes the splash pattern to point in the direction that the bleeder was moving (Figure 7.3). The spatter pattern may also lead an expert to testify as to an estimated height of the bleeder.

Figure 7.4 Bloodstain tests like this MacPhail's reagent are useful as a presumption test to determine if a liquid or stain is in fact blood.

Among the many reagents (usually a mixture including phenolpthalein or benzedine) used to determine if substance is blood, Benzedine is seldom used, since it has been determined to be a carcinogen. When the phenolpthalein is introduced to the substance believed to be blood, it will change color to a dark pink. Horseradish, potatoes, and other vegetables may also turn pink when mixed with the same reagent, but those foods are not likely to be confused with blood. The test is presumptive, not positive, but you may collect the substance with the expectation that it will test out as blood in the laboratory later (Figure 7.4).

Another test to determine the presence of blood on a surface when its presence is not readily visible is to spray a luminol reagent where you expect that you might find blood. In a dark room or area, the luminol will make blood luminesce, therefore confirming your expectations of the presence of blood. This is particularly valuable when the floor or carpeting or upholstery has been washed or dry cleaned and the perpetrator believes he or she has destroyed all evidence of his or her crime. Blood will show up with luminol sometimes even after a car has been professionally detailed or the surface is believed to have been thoroughly cleaned (although not really), breaking down another defense claim that there was no bloodshed.

Now that you have photographed the blood drops and stains and you have verified that they are blood, your next step is to collect them.

Whenever possible, always strive to collect blood in its natural wet state, but if it is dry already, or for some reason you must let it dry before collecting it, be very careful to let it dry in a natural atmosphere. Avoid using such drying instruments as a hair dryer to speed up the process. That works well on hair, but not on bloodstains.

When the blood is wet, your objective is to keep it in its liquid condition. Use a clean glass vial. If the blood appears to be congealing, drop a little drop of a saline solution onto the blood before drawing it up through the pipette. Your laboratory will provide you with the saline solution, but if you run out, you may make your own by mixing one teaspoonful of salt and one quart of distilled water. When you are not using it, keep the container tightly sealed to keep out contaminants. When you have collected as much of the wet blood as possible, seal the container and refrigerate it as soon as you can.

Collect partially-dry bloodstains in two steps. First, collect the wet portion with a pipette and place it in a glass vial to keep it in its liquid state. Second, go to another task or wait for a couple minutes and let the blood dry completely. Then collect it as you take other dried blood samples. Be sure to label both the dry and wet portions of that sample to establish that they were from the same stain.

Collect dried blood by using either of two different methods. If the stain is on a nonporous surface, use a scalpel or X-acto knife to scrape as much of the entire stain as possible, placing the scrapings onto a dry square of clean paper that you will fold into a bindle to completely encase the material. You may use a clean plastic bag for the dried blood samples, but some of the material may get lost in the corners of the bag. The bindle has been used more traditionally. (A bindle is a square of paper onto which a dry powder is placed, then the paper is folded in such a way that the powder cannot leak out.) After you have scraped all the dried blood off the surface of the host material, scrape off the surface itself and take it to the laboratory for analysis. It may contain waxes, cleaners, polish, or detergent that has mixed with the blood and which may be important to the chemist to isolate from the blood when performing the analysis.

If the blood has soaked into a porous surface, such as concrete, carpeting, or upholstered furniture, for example, you will have to liquefy the stain in order to collect it. To prepare the stain for collection, use tweezers and dip a small cotton square, swatch, or cotton swab into a clean saline solution. Be careful to separate the cotton swatches so as to avoid having two or more stick together. A defense attorney may try to blow up the significance of your counting 20 swatches then producing more or less during the trial. Little "glitches" like this in your presentation may destroy your credibility in the eyes of a juror or two, no matter how inconsequential your miscount actually is. Place the wet swatch onto the stain and allow it to soak up as much of the stain as possible. Use as many swatches as necessary until no more of the stain will soak up into a swatch. Place each set of swatches that you use to soak up each of the stains onto separate sheets of clean, dry paper, which you will fold into bindles. (Bindles have been used

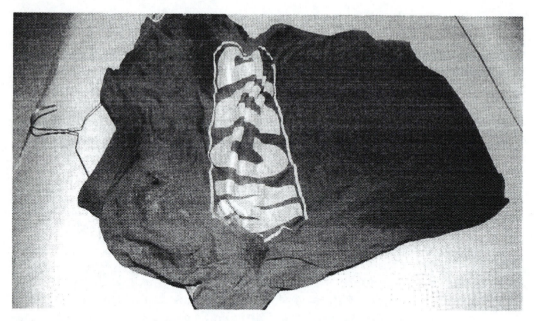

Figure 7.5   To preserve clothing that is saturated with blood, place it on a hanger and wrap it with paper. This will prevent transfer of blood from one area of the clothing to another.

for dozens of years by pharmacists to package individual doses of heroin or dilaudid for sufferers of "soldiers disease" or doses of morphine, which had a trade name of "Mrs. Dover's Powders" around the turn of the century.) Give each set of swatches that represent a bloodstain a number that corresponds with the number assigned to the stain in your sketch and photographs. To transport these collected samples, place all the bindles into a large paper bag and transport them together to the laboratory. When you later get those individual packets, or bindles, containing the blood-soaked swatches, open them up, separate the swatches, and allow them to dry naturally (without using a hair dryer) in a box or ventilated container which can be closed and locked for security purposes while drying.

Bloody clothing and bedding, and other similar materials bearing wet blood, should be hung up to dry at the scene before transporting, if possible (Figure 7.5).

If items must be transported while wet, spread them out onto a flat piece of cardboard, then label and transport them without folding or wadding up the material. If you place a wet, bloody piece of material in a closed container, mold and putrefaction will be begin almost immediately, which will destroy or diminish the evidentiary value of the blood sample

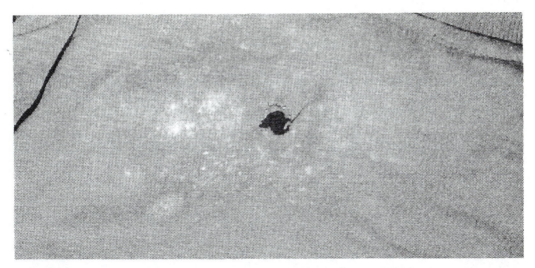

Figure 7.6 If bloody clothes are not properly dried, mold may begin to grow, as in this picture.

(Figure 7.6). In a sex crime, there might also be semen along with the bloodstains that you will want to preserve as you find it. Folding or packaging such material in a closed container may destroy any spermatozoa that might be present. When you get the wet materials to the laboratory, place them in a secure place and arrange them so that they may air dry.

Blood analysis will tell the analysts that a particular bloodstain conclusively did not come from a specified individual or that it probably did originate with a specified individual. It will also determine if the stains were from more than one owner. The basic classification system of typing blood as O, A, B, or AB isolates certain percentages of the population. Let's say that blood stains found at the scene are identified as O, B, and A. The two victims have types O and B. We might guess that a third person, possibly the suspect, has type A blood. But that obviously does not narrow down the field of suspects very much, because millions of people have type A blood. The typing procedure goes far beyond the four basic types, of course, but the real breakthrough in forensic science has been the determination of the genetic code of the person who has that type A blood.

It is possible to determine an individual's DNA, or deoxyribonucleic acid, not only from blood samples but also from many other body fluids and tissues, including hair, if the follicle is attached. The probabilities of narrowing down the list of suspects are phenomenally greater. Except for identical twins, DNA researchers have estimated that the chance of any two people in the world having identical DNA is anywhere from 1 in 200,000 to 1 in 5 billion (approximately the current world population). Once a suspect is located and in custody, a DNA test can confirm that you probably have the correct suspect. For the past few years, many laboratories have been maintaining files on the DNA of people who are being convicted of very serious crimes, including murder, rape, and aggravated assaults. News reports already have informed us that comparison of those individuals' genetic codes with current and past unsolved crimes are leading to the solution of crimes that otherwise would be classified as virtually unsolved.

In addition to blood type and genetic code, analysis of blood and other body fluids may provide information about alcohol and drug intake, and some diseases, which may lead the investigation to the suspect's family doctor or rehabilitation center. When collecting blood samples, take the maximum amount of samples possible. Do not make the mistake of taking just a few samples with the expectation that what you have is enough and any more would be a waste of time collecting and analyzing it. One spot that you miss may be the one spot that identifies a second or third person's injury at the scene. You cannot collect too much blood.

LIQUIDS OTHER THAN BLOOD

All liquids other than blood believed to have evidentiary value should be collected, packaged, and transported in the same manner as blood evidence. If it is wet when you find it, keep it wet, if possible. If it is dry, scrape it up or soak it up and package it the same as you would blood. Many body fluids of most people, including urine and feces, will reveal their blood types and genetic code. A recent case in the Los Angeles area illustrated this point very clearly. A high school teacher reported that several students had attacked her by throwing feces on her, and she presented the soiled clothing as proof of the attack. She was eventually convicted of making a false crime report, because the feces on her clothing was analyzed for DNA and proved to be her own. The prosecutor surmised that somehow she had soiled herself but was too embarrassed to admit what had really happened.

FINGERPRINTS

In any place where there are people, you are bound to find fingerprints. Residents in a house or employees in an office do not clean their prints off of every object they touch. At a crime scene, you will usually find many fingerprints, and sometimes they have been left there by the perpetrator(s). If you find absolutely no prints whatsoever, that in itself is suspicious, because innocent people have no reason to wipe their fingerprints off of ob-

jects they touch except to conceal their presence there. We will cover fingerprints in Chapter Nine.

WEAPONS

When one hears the word "weapon," the first vision that pops into the mind
is of a gun or a knife. For the purpose of this book, and for crime scene investigation in general, a weapon is any instrument or device that is used to attack
a person or animal. Besides guns and knives, weapons you will collect include
automobiles, motorcycles, bicycles, water hoses, sticks, stones, clubs, baseball
bats, golf clubs, books, chairs, kitchen utensils, pencils, and pens, to name a
few. Whenever you discover any item that might have been used as a weapon
in the crime you are investigating, photograph it in place, draw its location in
your sketch, and assign it an appropriate evidence number or letter. While
you are wearing gloves, lift the object carefully with a pencil, a hook, or a grip-
ping device to avoid destroying any fingerprints or other traces of evidence
that might be on the weapon. Place the weapon onto a clean sheet of paper or
cardboard or into a box, and wrap it in such way that it cannot be inadvertently touched or disturbed while in transit to the evidence locker or laboratory. In your notes, describe the weapon and its overall condition.

Knives

Describe the brand name, if any, the type (hunting, pocket, switchblade,
etc.), overall length, blade length, color of the handle, and a general description of the knife, including its apparent condition. Describe any material that may be sticking to the knife.

Guns

Is the gun a semi-automatic pistol or a revolver? Is it a shotgun or a rifle, and
what kind of action does it have? What is the overall size of the gun, and what
is the barrel length? What is the gauge or caliber? List the name of the manufacturer, the model, and the number. Describe the gun's apparent condition
and whether it is loaded or unloaded. Describe the grips or stock. Describe
the location of the bullets; whether there are any in the chamber, cylinder, or
clip; and whether any had been fired. Describe the location of bullets and
shell casings. If bullets are in the cylinder of a revolver, inscribe a number to
each receptacle, and list which bullet or shell casing is in which space. All the
bullets may be the same, or they may be of more than one brand.

The caliber of a gun is inscribed on the frame, and some are measured
in hundredths or thousands of an inch, such as .22, .25, .32, .38, .45, .357, or
.405. The caliber of some guns is measured in millimeters, such as 9mm,
which is the same as .38 caliber, or 7.65mm, which is the same as .32 caliber.

Shotguns are measured by gauge, such as 12 or 16. Rifles have a caliber, such as .30, but they also may be designated as a 30-06, which means that it was first manufactured on 1906.

If a gun has been fired, look for the bullet holes and the shell casings. A semi-automatic pistol extracts and throws out each shell after it has been fired, whereas the bullets in a revolver are removed with the aid of an ejector after the entire cylinder has been emptied. Extractor marks and ejector marks are different, and ballistics will note that difference. Merely finding five or six empty shells on the floor at a shooting scene is not proof that a semi-automatic weapon was fired, as the gun may have been a revolver and the shooter ejected the spent rounds to reload.

Indicate on your sketch the location of all shell casings. Place markers, such as tented numbers, next to each one, and photograph them in place. A ballistics expert may be able to determine the location of the shooter by studying the final destination of extracted casings. Loosely defined, ballistics is the study of missiles in flight, and sometimes it is possible to determine the location of a shooter by starting with its final resting place, which may be the body of a victim, and tracing its flight pattern. For example, a .22 caliber bullet struck a man driving his car along the Interstate 405 freeway through the city of Costa Mesa, California. A ballistics expert was able to pinpoint the probable location from which the bullet was fired. Police officers questioned the resident of the house, and he admitted that he did accidentally fire his .22 rifle while standing in his backyard at the same time as the victim received the wound. Comparison of the rifle and the bullet verified that, in fact, they matched. The house was nearly a mile from the freeway, yet the bullet still had enough strength to penetrate the victim's arm.

The trajectory of a bullet can also sometimes be determined with laser light projected from the point of impact. When the trajectory involves short distances, rods are placed into the holes to show the angle. This is commonly used for automobiles, buildings, and even people (Figure 7.7).

When picking up a gun, hold it by its checkered grips or other part where fingerprints and other traces may not be found (while wearing gloves, of course). Unload the gun, following the procedure for cataloging the location of the bullets covered previously. We do not recommend picking up a gun by sticking a pencil into the barrel, because that might alter the rifling or disturb the residue in the barrel. Try moving a handgun by placing a pen in the trigger guard and carrying it that way.

When handling any firearm, you must always assume it is loaded until proven otherwise. Never insert your finger or any object into the trigger housing until you know it is not loaded. Be especially cautious about handling semi-automatic or automatic firearms. The bullets for these weapons

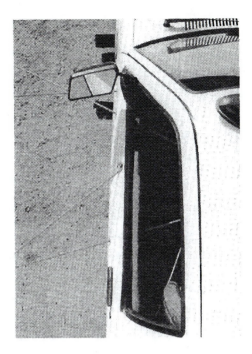

Figure 7.7 Wooden dowels are placed through bullet holes to show a bullet's path or trajectory.

are commonly fed from a magazine. Removing the magazine does not mean that the weapon is empty; there may be an additional bullet in the gun chamber. If you are not familiar with weapons, you should not be handling them. Even experienced police officers sometimes come across unusual weapons they are not familiar with, sometimes with tragic results.

It is dangerous to package a loaded gun as evidence, and therefore guns should be emptied where they are located, except when absolutely essential for evidentiary purposes that it remain loaded; you may never encounter such a time when it must remain loaded. Seek assistance from a firearms expert if you have any doubts about how to handle any firearm safely. Always aim the weapon in a safe direction, and never point the muzzle at anything you are not willing to destroy. When dealing with a revolver, mark along each side of the cylinder that is directly below the hammer. This will show what position the cylinder was in when you found it. Open the cylinder and count the number of bullets—if any—that are there. Carefully removed the bullets and package them for later analysis. Leave the cylinder open when packaging to make clear that the weapon is empty. With a semi-automatic weapon, there may be a round in the chamber that must be carefully removed and packaged. After the chamber is clear, lock the slide to the rear and leave it in the open position. Make sure the magazine is out of the weapon and then package it.

Figure 7.8
The test-fired
bullet is
preserved
exactly as it
fired from the
gun.

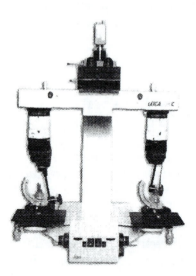

Figure 7.9 Comparison microscope used to
compare known object with the suspect object,
such as a bullet, to see if there is a match.

When you locate any expended bullets or shell casings, always carefully package them to avoid damaging them. Each bullet and casing should be packaged separately. Bullets and casings are composed of soft metals that can easily be scratched. When a bullet is fired, the harder metal parts of the gun leave impressions on the bullet and shell casing. These can be analyzed later and compared to show that a particular bullet was fired from a particular weapon. (Figures 7.8, 7.9, 7.10).

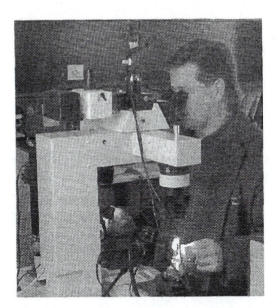

Figure 7.10 Comparing test-fired bullet with bullet taken from a victim.

Clubs, Sticks, and Other Objects Used as Weapons

Handle all objects that have been used or might have been used as weapons with the same care as you would handle guns and knives. Avoid handling any part of the object where you might find fingerprints or other traces, and do not disturb anything that looks as though it may be human hair, blood, tissue, or bone fragments. Include the location of the object in your sketch, photograph it in place before moving it, then pack and transport each item separately before placing it in a large package that you will use to transport the evidence to the evidence locker or laboratory. Describe the object, including its measurements, and write in your notes the apparent condition of the weapon as you found it.

OTHER EVIDENCE

Tool Marks and Impressions

Chapter Nine is devoted to a detailed discussion of tool marks, impressions, and the various ways to preserve them. As with weapons and, as a matter of procedure, all items of evidence, draw the objects or assign them a number, or both, and indicate their exact location. Photograph them in place before moving, and be sure to thoroughly describe the objects, their apparent condition, and what relationship they appear to have to the crime under investigation.

Hairs

Experts can determine whether a hair is from an animal or human, its possible racial origin (a person of mixed race may show one heritage more pronounced than another), the age range, possibly the gender, and sometimes the part of the body where the hair had been growing. Certain drugs and narcotics in the owner's body also may show up in a hair analysis, in addition to what type of hair spray a person uses. Particles found adhering to the cuticle, or outside scaly surface of the hair may reveal dirt or hay on the farmer, sand on a person who frequents the beach, or dried cement on a concrete worker.

The analyst may be able to make an educated guess as to the owner's gender and approximate age by the hair's length and evidence of grooming, hair coloring, bleach, and conditioner. Closer examination may also show if the hair has pulled out or if it fell out, was cut or broken, was damaged by a blunt force injury, and whether blood or tissue is present in microscopic amounts. If the hair has been pulled out at the roots, the criminalist may determine the owner's blood type and DNA.

Search for hairs on clothing, weapons, or the bodies of victims and suspects is a painstaking task, and it must be done with strong light, magnifying glasses, tweezers to pick up the hairs, and a great deal of patience. Whether you find a single strand of hair or a handful, indicate in your sketch the location where you find it, photograph it in place, and collect and transport it the same as you would any other evidence.

When you find hair believed to be evidence at the crime scene, it will be a matter of routine for hair samples to be collected of all suspects and possibly of some of the investigators at the scene for identification and elimination purposes. As a crime scene investigator, it is doubtful that you will be involved in this process during the initial investigation. However, you might be required to collect such samples as a follow-up assignment. When you take samples, collect at least one hundred hairs from at least four quadrants of the head. Draw a chart and indicate which hairs you remove from each quadrant. Pull a few hairs with follicles attached from each section and cut the rest. If you are going to compare hairs from areas other than the head, cut and pull several hairs from each of these areas of the suspect's body and indicate on your chart the location from where each set of hairs was harvested. In sex crimes, the pubic hairs from victim and suspect will be combed to look for foreign hair, because in such a violent contact, there is likely to be an exchange of pubic hairs.

Fibers

Fibers may be animal, vegetable, mineral, synthetic, or a combination of two or more of those materials. You may find single fibers on the scene, on the victim, and on the suspect or in his or her vehicle or home. The fibers you find may be attached to buttons or in torn parts of clothing, as if the victim tore them from an attacker's clothing. A nail, a tree or shrub branch, or other sharp object at the scene could have snagged the fibers without the perpetrator being aware that the material had been torn. A violent crime victim might be found in a car trunk or in a location other than where the attack took place, and this can be established by the discovery of carpet fibers on the body and clothing of the victim that are later found to have come from the assailant's living room. You may find a single strand of fiber, or a large piece of material consisting of thousands of strands, and either find may be the one piece of evidence that will make the case and solidify a conviction of the accused.

If many different strands of material are found at a single location, sketch, photograph, and record them as found and then label and package them in the cluster as found. When many strands of fibers are found at different locations, handle each one as a separate item of evidence, numbering or lettering them separately, packaging and transporting them in separate containers to the laboratory. As with other small items of evidence, use tweezers to handle the fibers, and, of course, wear your rubber gloves. Remember to change gloves frequently, particularly when you move from one type of evidence to another, to avoid the risk of transferring evidence, as well as to avoid criticism for sloppy work. It is better to change gloves too often than too seldom. Keep patches of cloth together so that the criminalist may count the warp and the woof (number of threads in each direction) per square inch.

The expert can identify the manufacturer of the material not only by the weave (warp and woof) of the material but also by the texture and quality. Some colors are used exclusively by certain manufacturers, as are specific styles and designs. The weave of a piece of cloth that you find at the crime scene may match the distinctive color and quality of an article of clothing found on a person suspected of committing the crime. The torn piece and the large article with the piece missing may actually be matched mechanically by demonstrating the fit as you would fit together two pieces of a jigsaw puzzle. Sometimes, in a crime such as a vehicle striking a victim, the impression of the victim's clothing is imprinted onto the painted surface of the vehicle. There are also likely to be small fragments of the material embedded in the paint.

Glass and Glass Fragments

Whenever you have broken glass at the crime scene, you are likely to find particles of the glass spread out over a wide area within "flying distance" of the window, mirror, or other glass object that was broken. The explosive nature of the breaking glass itself, plus the force that was used to break the glass, will result in glass particles flying onto the skin and clothing of the person breaking the glass and onto people nearby. It is common for people to get cut by the flying glass as well, particularly if the person breaks the glass with a fist, an elbow, or a foot, for example. Auto safety glass is actually two sheets of glass bound together pretty much like a wadded up piece of plastic, with all the glass adhering to the plastic. Some types of glass crumble into what appears to be very, very small pebbles of glass, but most glass breaks into shards and slivers when broken.

When you find a broken panel or sheet of glass, try to keep the larger parts intact as you find them, and collect the many small parts so that the lab technician may attempt to piece the broken parts together like a jigsaw puzzle. The pieces may have come from a single piece of glass or more than one. Also, you are likely to find shards and small particles of glass on the clothing and in the hair of the person who broke the glass and on any bystanders there at the time. Sometimes small particles of glass are found in the lab when the criminalist vacuums the suspect's clothing. The criminalist will also be able to match glass particles by their physical content, sometimes the manufacturer, whether the glass came from a car headlamp or window, and many other characteristics of the glass. When you find broken glass and glass particles, locate them in your sketch and notes, photograph them in place, then collect them. Pieces that are found away from the immediate area of the broken source should be packaged and labeled separately, as they may have come from a different source.

It is possible to determine the sequence of bullet holes and whether the bullet came from inside or outside of a pane of glass. When a bullet or similar missile enters the pane of glass, it may shatter the pane completely, or it will make a hole the approximate size of the missile when it enters, then it will take more of the glass with it as it comes out the other side, the hole resembling a cone. See Figure 7.11. Energy causes fractures that radiate outward from the

Figure 7.11
Casing
comparison
made with
comparison
microscope.

bullet hole, fractures that continue for varying distances, depending on the velocity of the bullet, and then move back toward the original location and beyond, in a motion similar to the waves in the ocean. This force on the glass causes fractures that run perpendicular to the radial fractures, giving the glass the appearance of a spider web. See Figures 7.12 and 7.13.

A second bullet will cause radial and concentric fractures similar to the first shot, but subsequent radial fractures will stop at the place where the

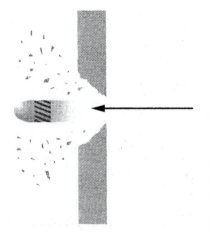

Figure 7.12   This illustration of a bullet going through glass shows that the entrance hole is smaller than the exit hole. This is helpful when determining direction of travel.

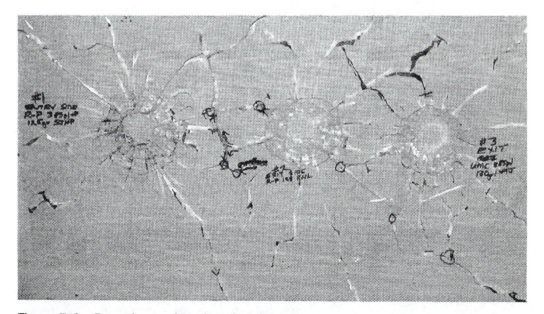

Figure 7.13   By understanding that glass fractures never cross one another, you can determine the sequence in which bullet holes were made.

earlier one passed. One radial fracture will not cross over an earlier one. Careful examination will show the sequence of the shots fired (Figure 7.14).

If larger pieces are broken out of a frame, it will be possible to photograph the various pieces of glass, make transparencies of the photos, and move them around to try for a mechanical match. A broken pane of glass may have been caused by a blow to the surface (Figure 7.15), or sometimes a smoldering fire sucking in as much oxygen as it needs will actually cause windows to break inward so as to feed the fire's need for oxygen.

Figure 7.14   In this photograph, there are three glass fractures that stop when they intersect with another fracture. This indicates that these fractures were secondary to one another.

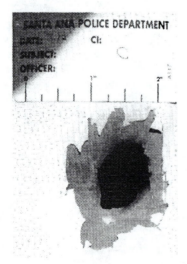

Figure 7.15   By understanding bullet impact, you can determine the approximate angle from which this bullet originated.

Soils, Rocks, and Minerals

Certain regions and neighborhoods have soils, rocks, and minerals that are unique to the area. Raw, undisturbed land that has not been excavated or developed will be easier to locate by its soil characteristics than developed land, which has been cleared and stripped of its rock formations then had a variety of topsoils added from many different parts of the country. In this second type of neighborhood, the developers may have brought in only one or two types of soil then used a particular type of sod and grass, and treated it with specific brands of fertilizer and pesticide. This treatment of the soil may result in such an individual character that some landscape architects may recognize the neighborhood almost immediately by its unique combination of materials.

When soil and rocks are found adhering to the tread of shoes and tires, clothing, or the underside of a vehicle, they may have been picked up at a crime scene and transported by the suspect. These materials may be just the evidence you need to place that person and/or his or her vehicle at the crime scene. Ownership is not enough. You must then prove that the suspect was wearing the shoes or driving the vehicle at the time of the crime. When you find tire or shoe imprints at the scene, take samples of the soil where you find the impressions. From about four different compass points from the impressions that you have photographed and cast, collect three or four tablespoonfuls of the soil and whatever other ingredients it contains. Place each sample in a separate plastic bag, seal the bags, and label them for the laboratory. These samples will be compared with the residue that you remove from the shoe or tire treads of the suspect.

Paint

Every paint manufacturer uses essentially the same ingredients to make its paints, but each has coloring materials and other additives that are copyrighted and unique. Each model of car each year is a different color. The colors are not plain blue or red or yellow, but "robin's egg blue" or "bullfighter flag red" or "sunrise yellow." Even the whites of one car to another are slightly different and may be distinguished by an expert in the laboratory. The same variations occur between manufacturers of paints for all other purposes as well. When you want to match a specific color at the paint store, you bring in a sample and the clerk will mix it for you. When you take a sample to the laboratory, the criminalist will match the exact same color by referring to the color charts of the manufacturers, which they keep on file and continuously update as new colors are created.

When you pick up chips of paint at the scene or scrape off a sample from a surface that has been struck by a car, such as another car or a building, indicate on your sketch exactly where you found it and photograph it in place. Then package and transport it as any other item of evidence. Several scrapings from a single location may be placed in the same bag or paper bindle, but samples found at different locations should be bagged separately. Take paint scrapings from a vehicle that also has paint transfer from another vehicle, as the damage has already been done. In other cases, choose a part of the car where the removal of the paint is not going to destroy the outward appearance of the car, such as on the underside of a door or interior of a trunk. Scrape all the way down to the bare metal, which will probably reveal several layers of paint and primer in the same sequence as when the car was painted at different times. Going down to the original color on a piece of the car left at the scene of a hit-and-run collision, for example, will lead to identification of the make and model of the suspect vehicle.

Liquids

Collect liquids with a bulb and syringe or a turkey baster, and try to keep liquids in the liquid state by sealing the container. Alcoholic beverages must be sealed in a glass or metal container so that the alcohol will not evaporate. In order to avoid diluting the beverage further, be sure to remove any ice cubes that might be in the drink. Refrigerate liquids, but do not freeze liquid evidence.

The components of flammable liquids, such as those that have been used to start arson fires, can be identified in the laboratory. Sometimes it is possible not only to say that the liquid is gasoline, but that it is 87 octane Shell gasoline (or other brand). Sometimes the incendiary material found at the fire scene can be compared with the contents of a can of gasoline found at the suspect's home, and the expert may state with assurance that the gasoline used to start the fire probably came from the can at the home of the suspect.

Other liquids can be identified and may prove to be valuable evidence in an investigation or case. A glass of soda might be used to show a suspect's taste for a particular brand of soda. A beverage containing medication may give the criminalist a clue as to a medical problem that the owner of the beverage may have and may indirectly lead to a suspect through his or her medical records.

Wood

Wood may be identified by species, such as oak, elm, ash, and so forth. A piece of wood found at the scene of a crime may be a broken piece of a certain type of tool, such as a hammer or axe handle. Two broken pieces of wood may be matched mechanically (jigsaw method), by species, or by how they are treated with stain or varnish. Wood chips or sawdust tracked into the crime scene may indicate that the perpetrator came from a construction site or was perhaps working in a shop at home. Also, the scene of the crime may have sawdust from recent construction work, and the perpetrator may have taken some away from the scene on his or her clothing or between shoe or tire treads. Photograph, catalog, and handle as other pieces of dry evidence in case the wood or sawdust might later prove to be relevant to the case.

Documents

Crimes involving documentary evidence usually originate in the home or office. They involve forgery, fraud, embezzlement, theft by trick and device, false representation, and many others. What you are looking for, of course, depends on the crime, but writing, typing, and printing instruments may yield clues to help solve the crime (Figure 7.16). Documents have to be written or printed. Pens, pencils, typewriters, computers, notebooks, and paper are all items worth close scrutiny.

Sophisticated crime schemes may be found on computer programs, with forms, letters, and other information in the program. A computer expert can sometimes have success in cracking the code and getting by gates with formulas for figuring out passwords. Typewriter ribbons and the surface of the

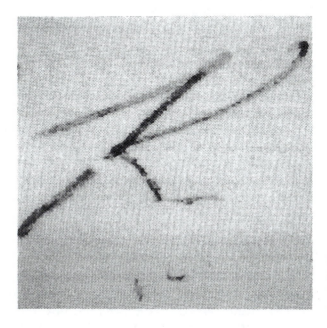

Figure 7.16   In this illustration, correction fluid has been used to cover up some writing.

roller, or platen, may be impressed with the text from a recently-typewritten document that may be so unique that particular items can be identified as the instruments that were used to produce certain incriminating documents.

Forged and fraudulent checks, loan documents and securities, extortion notes, and threatening letters all originated with some person, and with the aid of certain instruments. The objective is to connect the documents with the instruments and their makers. Sometimes the suspect has shredded, torn up, or burned documents that are needed for evidence. Collect the shredder and the wastebasket containing the shredded document or parts of the shredded document. Burned documents may hold together in the charred state until you touch them and then crumble into ashes. Photograph them as you find any of these items before you attempt to handle them in any way. If you place a solid piece of cardboard underneath the charred document and lightly spray it with a fixative, such as hair spray, you may be able to hold it together. If you are successful so far, make sure you have photographs of the document in its present state just in case it falls apart as you proceed. Also, if you are able to keep it intact so far, consider the feasibility of covering the document with a sheet of clear plastic to add to its stability. Place the document in a box so that it will not be disturbed further until it gets to the lab. The lab technician will probably attempt to place the charred document between two pieces of glass for further analysis.

Checks, checkbooks, and documents that appear to belong to someone other than the occupant of the business or house may be forgeries. If the owner or occupant of the premises is present, ask for a statement of ownership, and record the responses that person gives you. Include in your report the data about where you found the documents and other materials, and handle them the same as any other evidence.

When the victim claims that his or her name, logo, and other personal identifying data, such as checks or credit cards or letterheads, have been forged for the unlawful use of another person, have that person sign an affidavit of forgery. This will probably best be done later by a follow-up investigator or in the prosecuting attorney's office. You will also need exemplars of the victim's and the suspect's writing, typing, printing, and so forth, as applicable to the particular case under investigation, which you should secure as quickly as possible.

Preparation of the Exemplar

Depending on the crime, you will want to get a sample of the suspect's writing. Your department may have a standard form that it uses, but we suggest that you make your own form, customized to the specific crime. For example, in a highly-publicized Colorado murder case, which is still under investigation at the time of writing this chapter and which will continue for years, the victim's family found a ransom note and turned it over to the investigators. The one thing you should not do is to hand a suspect a copy of the note and have him or her copy it. Not only are the handwriting experts looking to compare the handwriting, but they are also looking for grammatical structure, spelling, punctuation, and overall composition. By letting the suspect look at the original while trying not to copy it, you would be destroying the value of having that person prepare an exemplar at all. Dictate the words you want the person to write, but do not spell the words or dictate the punctuation as though you were dictating a business letter. If you had a dyslexic suspect and a ransom note with numerous misspelled words, you certainly would not want to spell words that you dictate to the suspect.

Miscellaneous Trace Evidence

During your crime scene investigation you will come across something that we have not covered in this text but that your police officer senses tell you might have some evidentiary value. Whenever you do come across such an item, photograph it in place, record it in your report, and process it as evidence. As the investigation proceeds, many of the items that you collect may prove to be of value to the case, and many others will lead to dead ends. It is better to collect too much evidence than too little. In the final analysis, you may have done a better job collecting more evidence than you need than if you missed a crucial item that is lost forever once you have left the crime scene. See Figure 7.17.

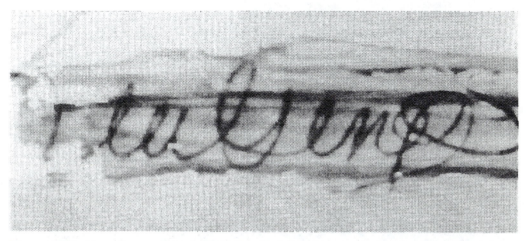

Figure 7.17 By using a strong back light, the ink underneath the correction fluid can be read.

PACKAGING AND LABELING EVIDENCE

In this chapter we have discussed some of the methods for collecting and preserving evidence. In addition to those instructions we have already covered, here are some basic guidelines: If the item is large enough and there is space on the object where you can inscribe your logo or other identifying data without destroying the monetary or evidentiary value, do so directly on the object. Smaller items cannot be marked directly, and you must place them in suitable containers (Figure 7.18). In all cases, attach an evidence label to the object itself or to the container, listing the number or letter designation of the item, date, time, case number, your logo or initial, and to whom or in what locker you placed the item. Containers are glass vials, paper bags, self-sealing plastic bags, new paint cans for flammable liquids, boxes made of wood or cardboard with string to hold items in place, and packing Styrofoam "popcorn" to keep items from moving about while in transit. Place your logo on the container and attach the evidence tag.

Figure 7.18 Proper care must be taken when handling and packaging evidence.

CHAIN OF CUSTODY

We have covered the chain of custody procedure earlier in the text, but just a word to remind you that from the moment the evidence is collected until the moment it is introduced in court as evidence, there must be an unbroken chain of custody of every item of evidence. This is extremely crucial to every case.

SUMMARY

As you can see, evidence comes in many shapes and guises, sometimes presenting itself to you when you do not even recognize it as evidence. Consider the type of crime you are investigating and seek out those items of evidence to prove each element of the *corpus delicti*, then look for whatever else you can find that might be even remotely related to the case. Sometimes one crime is committed to cover another, such as arson to conceal a murder, or a so-called "victim" may fabricate a crime story and then create a crime scene to back it up. Your investigation is to determine what crime, if any, took place, and to collect as much evidence as possible to establish the facts. Remember that you can never collect too much evidence.

SUGGESTED OUTSIDE PROJECTS

1. Create your own file of tire designs. Go to the various dealers and ask for brochures with photographs of tire treads, and take photographs of as many different tread designs as you can find. Continue this project for six to eight weeks. (After you complete the course, continue updating this file as each new design comes out.)

2. From your imaginary crime scene, collect and package the following items that represent evidence: an alcoholic beverage containing ice cubes, paint scrapings from the interior of a car's trunk, a knife, a gun, a screwdriver or hammer, a torn piece of clothing, several strands of hair, and a wet article of clothing. Photograph them as you have them packaged, and attach evidence tags on each.

3. Place a printed document on a non-flammable surface and set the document on fire. After it has cooled down, photograph it in place. Then, use whatever means possible to preserve the

document intact for evidence, using hair spray to hold it together and a plastic sheet to cover it. After you have mastered the process, write a report to the authors, advising us what worked best for you.

DISCUSSION QUESTIONS

1. Describe the process of chain of custody and why it is important to a crime scene investigation.

2. When you find a dried bloodstain, how do you remove it from the surface?

3. How do you transport dried blood to the lab for analysis?

4. What do the letters DNA stand for?

5. Of what value is DNA evidence to a rape investigation?

6. What is a *stride pattern* and what can it tell the experienced investigator?

7. On a pliable surface, lay down your own stride pattern and explain how it helps to determine your height and weight.

8. From what body materials or parts may the laboratory determine a person's DNA?

9. Can blood type be used to identify a suspect positively? Why? Why not?

10. In this country, what is the most common blood type?

11. When you find trace evidence at the scene, what is the principal reason for you to photograph it before attempting to collect it?

12. How do you identify trace evidence in your photographs?

13. How do you keep blood in its liquid state in a glass bottle or jar?

14. Explain the radial and concentric fractures in glass.

15. How can you tell that one bullet hole in a window was made before another one?

Chapter Eight
Evidence by Type of Crime

INTRODUCTION

In the preceding chapter we covered evidence by type and category and methods of collecting the evidence. In this chapter we approach the subject from the aspect of what one might find in different types of crimes. In addition to what one must regard as evidence, there are other discoveries you might make during your investigation that may not be admissible in court but that still help isolate and identify the perpetrators. For example, as we noted earlier in the text, food missing from a refrigerator may indicate that a burglar has a taste for cottage cheese and leftovers; but that fact, in itself, does not prove guilt. What it does tell you, however, is that eating on the job may be part of the perpetrator's *modus operandi* and is a behavior pattern that shows up in every crime that he or she commits. You might even start calling this culprit "the hungry burglar." In this chapter, we will make a few suggestions to aid in your investigation.

CRIMES AGAINST PERSONS

Criminal Homicide

For many officers, investigators, and crime scene investigators, homicide is the ultimate crime scene. There is no denying the importance of properly working a scene where a person has been killed. Despite the clear severity of the crime, however, most homicides are solved. In fact, homicide has one of the highest clearance rates of reported crime. This is largely due to the unpleasant fact that most victims of homicide are killed by someone close to them. And while television and novels are full of stories of murderous intrigue, most murder is the result of a sudden explosion of thoughtless rage.

Emerging in the 1980s was a growing trend of random homicide that posed new challenges to the homicide investigator. Homicide was no longer just the "mom-and-pop" variety, that is, committed mostly by members or friends of the family or business partners to collect life insurance premiums, or as revenge for past transgressions. Drive-by shootings began to dominate the headlines, and the traditional links between suspect and victim have become increasingly blurred or non-existent. Bodies also began to be found on street corners, parks, and alleyways with little if any indication of motive. The majority of these "random" killings were gang-on-gang violence fueled by persons obsessed with gang culture and battles over drug turf. Thankfully, recent years have brought about significant reductions in gang violence and homicide in particular, thanks to aggressive enforcement by the police with the help of the public, harsh adjudication by the courts, and effective follow-up by probation and parole officers.

Serial killers do exist and can be especially difficult to identify, as many move from city to city to conceal their trail. Through the use of improved communication and databases like the FBI's Violent Criminal Apprehension Program (VICAP), detailed information about killers is compiled from agencies throughout the country so it can be analyzed for commonalities leading to a profile of the offender. The CSI officer plays a critical role in recognizing and reporting what may appear to be innocuous information that, once compiled, leads to the apprehension of a killer.

The most obvious item you should hope to find at the scene of a homicide is the weapon or other means with which the perpetrator committed the act. When you first observe the body of the deceased, be careful not to hastily decide what type of weapon caused the wounds. All wounds are not what they appear to be. For example, what looks to be a small-caliber bullet hole actually may have been made with a stiletto or an ice pick, or perhaps even a screwdriver; whereas a blunt force wound may tear the skin in such a way so as to appear as though it were made with a knife. Assume nothing while searching for weapons, and collect all objects that even remotely suggest that they have any relationship to the crime. You should not limit your imagination, or you will miss crucial evidence.

Never move anything at the scene until photographs and a sketch have been obtained. Oftentimes, there is a question as to whether the death is the result of homicide or suicide. In fact, there are other possibilities, including accidental causes, natural causes, and undetermined causes. Many murderers attempt to conceal their actions by altering the scene to make it appear as if the victim took his or her own life. You might find it surprising that in some cases, family members have altered suicide scenes to make it look like a murder took place. It is critical, therefore, that every detail of the scene is documented to assist investigators and pathologists in determining the cause of death. It has been shown, for example, that some apparent suicides were actually homicides, because the victim could not have fired a weapon in a manner consistent with the evidence located at the scene. This evidence included the trajectory of the bullet, the blood spatter pattern, and the distance of the weapon to the victim based on the discharge of gunpowder.

Careful interviewing also is essential in a suicide case. This is not usually the responsibility of the crime scene investigator, but there will be times when you will be required to conduct the interviews. Family members, friends, and co-workers should be questioned about the victim's attitude, demeanor, and plans for the future. Actions during the few days prior to death are extremely important. In a recent case, a young female was found dead by her mother on the floor of her bedroom. The girl had a trash bag tied around her head and neck with the cord to a pair of headphones. There were no signs of forced entry into the home, and her parents reported nothing unusual had occurred during the night when the death apparently occurred. The positioning of the bag over the girl's head raised the question as to whether her death was a homicide.

Investigators learned from the victim's older sister that she had confided in her about an Internet relationship that the victim had via Email with a male in another state. The male professed his love for the girl, and in an effort to surprise him, the victim traveled to his home only to discover he was involved in another relationship. The despondent victim returned home several days before her death. Her mother confirmed her daughter had been depressed, but not to the degree where she feared for her safety. The male, meanwhile, was very upset with the girl for her surprise visit, and he sent a series of venomous messages that ruthlessly degraded her.

The night of her death, the girl told her mother she was walking to a nearby store to purchase pain relievers for a headache. She returned later and retired early to her room saying she did not feel well. The CSI officer and investigator located a bag from the store and a receipt for several bottles of sleeping pills in the girl's wastebasket. The empty bottles of pills and an empty bottle of wine were also in the trash. The girl's mother recognized the wine as being the brand they kept in the house. She further led the investigator to the garage where a box of trash bags matched the style found on the girl's head. The girl's sister was able to locate the Emails that had apparently left the girl with no hope to live. As in many cases of suicide, the victim did not leave a note, but the evidence located at the scene established that her death was at her own hand. These findings were later supported by an autopsy.

When suicide notes are found at a scene, they must be carefully preserved for later analysis. Fingerprint and handwriting analysis may be done to corroborate that the victim wrote the note. Always be alert for secondary impressions left on the object upon which the note was written. This is commonly found when notepads are used.

When it appears likely that a homicide has occurred, you of course want to determine who did it. Again, many times the victims knew their killers. Homicides occur during disputes, family fights, bar fights, and somewhat inexplicably, among friends enjoying a beer (until a beer is kicked over, or someone makes a disparaging comment, or someone does some other act that for some reason leads to violence). In these instances, the killer may already be in custody or investigators are pursuing him. When you confront a true "whodunit," it helps to learn about the victim, their activities, and their relationships with other persons.

Homicide investigators typically work backwards from the time of the death and contact all persons who knew the victim. A thorough background investigation is done to look for motives that might involve pending lawsuits or criminal cases, persons in need of money, the presence of a large will or insurance policies, disputes, and the lifestyle of the victim. When processing the scene, be alert for anything that might suggest a possible motive.

At a homicide, as at any death scene, you will be working with the coroner. Only the coroner is authorized to move the body, so be sure and wait for his arrival before collecting evidence from the body itself. It is a good idea to consult with the coroner and coordinate your investigation with him to avoid unnecessary duplication or disagreements.

Homicide investigations are conducted in a slow and methodical fashion. You should be prepared to be at a homicide scene for several hours. Remember to double-check everything you do to ensure accuracy. A homicide case might take years to come to trial and will be meticulously scrutinized. Your memory of exactly what you did at the scene might be unreliable over time, so you will have to rely on the accuracy of your notes and your report. There will be no opportunity to go back and correct any errors.

Many homicides end up having been committed by relatives or friends of the victims. Although proof of a motive is not necessary to prove the elements of a crime, it will certainly help focus the investigation if the reason for the crime were known. Some of the questions an investigator should ask himself or herself are: Who would benefit most by this death? Or who wanted to see this person dead? Was there a great amount of money, a long-standing hatred, or a desire for revenge that motivated this murder? Is there a new love in the suspected killer's life with a third party in the way of this blossoming love? Is there a sizable insurance policy, and if so, who is the beneficiary?

Look for threatening letters or diary entries that might indicate a problem relationship, such as broken marriages or relationships, philandering spouses, or jealous lovers. Telephone and address books might provide names and other information about friends, relatives, or business associates. Telephone bills that list long-distance phone calls may lead to the discovery of people the victim may have called regarding his or her fears of impending doom. Personal papers and correspondence will provide names and addresses of others who may have some information about the victim's life, for example, if the victim had testified against someone in a criminal trial that led to a conviction, leading investigators to determine if the murder is in retaliation for the testimony.

Are there signs of violence on the premises, such as broken lamps, overturned furniture, or other disturbed furniture? Does everything in the place look too neat, as though it had been cleaned up, including removal of latent prints from the scene that should be there, such as on jewelry, clothing, or other personal items belonging to the victim? Some perpetrators make a habit of collecting souvenirs to remind them of their crimes for their morbid sense of sentimentality. Cannibals like Jeffrey Dahmer collect body parts and keep them in the refrigerator and in other places around their houses because it creates some sort of a bond between perpetrator and victim long after death.

There are still other questions that can be asked about a homicide scene. Was there a forced entry and/or exit indicating that the perpetrator did not have a key? Or was entry made by invitation of the victim, or by someone who had a key to the premises? Someone who had ever borrowed or had temporary possession of a key and returned it could still have made a copy quite easily. Did the victim appear to have known the perpetrator, indicated by such things as two or three cocktail glasses or beer bottles, or more than one serving for a meal served at the approximate time of the murder? Did the killer(s) leave anything behind at the scene, such as an article of clothing or other personal item that had not been at the scene before the crime? A spouse or a frequent visitor may provide you with this kind of information.

If the victim shows signs of life, the first officer(s) on the scene may have had to damage or destroy evidence in order to administer first aid, but that is just something you have to take in stride. If the victim is still at the scene and you have already determined that death has, in fact, occurred, take photographs of the victim in the position he or she was found. Only the coroner, a medical examiner, a paramedic, or other qualified individual may pronounce death. You may see that the victim is dead by the absence of pulse and respiration (which are presumptive signs of death, but not positive), as well as *livor mortis* (postmortem lividity), *rigor mortis*, decomposition, and other positive signs of death. After you have completed photographing and sketching the body in place as it was found, the coroner will then take custody of the body. The body is the jurisdictional responsibility of the coroner, but the crime investigation is the responsibility of your department. The coroner's people will not remove the body from the scene until you and your colleagues have finished the part of the investigation that requires that you keep the body in place.

Sometimes the perpetrator makes a homicide appear as though a death were a suicide or an accident. For that reason, you should approach every dead body case as though it were a criminal homicide until the investigation determines that the death was not caused by the "criminal act of another," as the coroner would classify such a death. There are times when even an accidental death turns out to have been the result of someone's negligence, at which time it becomes a criminal case again. A phony doctor who performs an illegal surgery, for example, is committing murder if the patient dies.

Assault

In many cases, felony and misdemeanor assaults are distinguished by the weapon used to commit the crime. Use of a gun or a knife in assaults classifies them as felonies, whereas assaults with such weapons as baseball bats, automobiles, and other objects may be either felonies or misdemeanors, depending on the nature of the injuries the victim sustains. Some assaults may be listed as felonies or misdemeanors depending on the investigating officers' initial evaluation of the injuries sustained by the victim. They may be reclassified later as the more or less serious crime, depending on what the doctors say after they have taken X-rays and conducted a preliminary examination of the victim.

Assaults range from "simple" assault (pushing, shoving, punching) to "aggravated" or "felonious" assaults that usually include a weapon or result in serious injury. Cases involving the latter often pose more difficulties for the crime scene investigator than does a homicide scene. The reason for this is that homicide scenes are static. To be blunt, the victim isn't going anywhere. You usually have ample time to process a homicide scene.

An assault scene, though, is often chaotic. People are injured—sometimes severely—and providing medical care must be a priority. Responding medical personnel can trample evidence and disturb the scene. Often the victim will be transported to a hospital, and that means there is a second location to which you will have to respond.

It is not uncommon to encounter assault victims who are uncooperative. Many assaults occur between family members, friends, and acquaintances, and victims often do not want the suspect arrested. In these instances, CSI can be important to help determine what occurred. Witness statements are often essential to these investigations.

Keep in mind when dealing with the scene of a serious assault that you might be working a homicide scene and just don't know it yet. Many victims die enroute or at the hospital, and even injuries that appear to be not life-threatening can result in death (sometimes even a considerable time after the assault). Always treat a serious assault case with care.

Until you know what weapon was used to inflict an injury, look for any weapon or device that the perpetrator might have used. Some articles may have blood, hair, or tissue attached and should certainly be considered suspect. Photograph the suspected weapon and collect it as described in Chapter Seven.

Sometimes it is not possible to determine the exact nature and extent of the crime during the initial phase of the investigation. Many victims and witnesses are shocked and confused or are uncooperative. Maybe they are not sure about what happened, or perhaps a loved one inflicted the wounds and you have a reluctant witness. Another problem you will have determining the extent of a victim's injuries is that some people have a high or low threshold of pain, whereas others have a tendency to exaggerate or minimize their pain.

Robbery

Robbery takes many forms, but it always involves the taking of property from another by force or fear. This could be the result of a bully asking to "borrow" money (with an implied threat of injury for non-compliance), or the more recognizable form of confronting a bank teller with a gun. At the "nutrition bar," where all the snack machines are located near the school cafeteria, the bully who forcibly takes money from another child is committing a robbery. Although he or she does not use a weapon, we call that a "strong-arm robbery." Regardless of whether the bully actually assaults the victim beyond the forceful grabbing and holding, or how much money is taken from the victim, it is still a robbery. A carjacking, which involves taking a vehicle from its driver by force and/or fear, is also considered a robbery. From a CSI perspective, you are generally asked to assist with identifying the offender. Although most demands by robbers for money or property are made verbally, those robbing banks often use notes. Notes need to be processed for fingerprints, watermarks, and, of course, handwriting. Areas the robber may have touched—countertops, doors, cash registers—need to be processed for latent fingerprints.

More and more businesses use video surveillance systems to deter robberies and to help identify those who commit them. Always ask if such a system exists, as not all systems are clearly visible. It is very important to obtain the videotape, as most tapes are erased over rather quickly if left in the store. Some surveillance systems use specialized video equipment that might not allow the videotape to be played on a standard machine. Older systems use 35mm cameras to photograph the suspect by triggering the camera with a remote device (often caused by removing the cash tray from the register). These images are not as time-sensitive to collect, but in most cases, the film should be collected and the camera reset right away in the event of another robbery.

When photographs or video of a suspect are not available, a forensic artist is sometimes employed to create a composite of what the suspect looks like. Sophisticated computer software programs even allow non-artists to generate composites based on witness accounts of the suspect's description.

Have the victims and witnesses repeat verbatim, if possible, the words used by the suspect while committing the crime. Sometimes a witness may recognize a foreign or regional accent, and some robbers use exactly the same words when committing their robberies, perhaps because they think it brings them luck, or because it works so well in getting results. Some robbers ask for a specific object or amount of money, which is that robber's trademark, and some even apologize and try to explain why they are committing the crime.

A recent series of robberies in Santa Ana involved a man who not only asked for cigarettes in addition to money, but he was angered if a clerk did not hand him his favorite brand. When the suspect was eventually arrested, he not only had several packages of this brand of cigarette on his person, but bags of this brand in his residence. The same suspect was caught on videotape during several robberies, but he committed a dozen more robberies where there were no cameras. About half of the victims in those cases could not identify the suspect from a photo line-up, but because of his clothing, his specific demands for money and cigarettes, and his method of operation were so distinct, he was successfully charged with all of the robberies.

Robbery cases can be challenging because the scenes are often well traveled by others. This is especially true in commercial robberies, where the business may still be in full operation when you arrive. Look for tiny details that can make the difference. Remember that discarded cigarette butts, candy, or other "trash" might contain clues, including the suspect's DNA, or maybe there is the demand note he wadded up and tossed once outside the business. Sound farfetched? Well, it's perhaps a long shot, but when you consider that many robbers first pose as customers while they "case" a business, they sometimes handle and leave behind products they touch, like a can of beer, a magazine, and so forth. Find that item and you might find your robber.

Look for the weapon that was used or that the suspect threatened to use at or near the scene. Some robbers discard the weapon so as to be unarmed if stopped by officers for questioning, whereas others retain it as a souvenir to remember the moment and to use again.

We have a tendency to give some robbers nicknames based on their behavior, such as "the gentlemen robber," "the robber with the sick baby," or "the lunch bucket bandit" because the robber carries a child's lunchbox to carry his loot. These monickers help investigators tie a string of robberies together by *modus operandi* and facilitate the robbers' arrest because it is sometimes possible to anticipate a robbery. Then they place surveillance on a prospective place of business, or they dress up an officer as a decoy to trap the perpetrators (we said "trap," not "entrap," you will note).

Child Abuse

When we speak of child abuse, we generally include sexual, physical, emotional abuse, and neglect. Physical abuse and neglect are the most prevalent (or at least most reported) forms of child abuse and are probably the easiest to investigate. That is not to say, however, that it is a simple thing to do. The most common defense against a charge of physical abuse is that the incident was accidental. Careful documentation of the scene is essential to determine how an injury was sustained. Complicating matters is the fact that many of these cases are not reported when and where they occurred but rather later at schools or hospitals. In order to do a complete investigation, the location where the injury occurred needs to be processed for evidence. This may require a search warrant.

Once at the scene where the injury took place, you will need to carefully photograph and sketch the surroundings. Depending on the type of injury and the account of how the injury is alleged to have happened, look for ways to corroborate or disprove the explanation. A tragic but common form of abuse involves placing a child in scalding bathwater. A common defense is that the child entered the bathtub while the caretaker was momentarily distracted (usually by a phone call). It is important to measure the height of the tub walls (could the child climb in without assistance) the height and types of the water controls (could the child reach and adjust the water) and how hot the water heater is set for. The water should also be allowed to run at its hottest setting and then measured. Because water heaters are set differently, you will have to measure each tubful to learn how hot the water can get. Using an immersion thermometer, direct the hot water to run at the immersion line on the thermometer. Measure and record (both in writing and with photographs) the temperature of the hot water in five-second intervals (this usually involves an assistant). Continue measuring until the water temperature has been constant for 30 seconds. Take an additional measurement underwater at the center of the tub to determine the temperature in the bath. Repeat the process with both the hot and cold water turned on together and continue until a constant temperature has been maintained for 30 seconds.

Another test is to have the parent or caretaker who ran the bath demonstrate for you how he or she filled the tub at the time of the incident. Ask the person to use the same amount of water at the same temperature that was used when the child was injured. Note the depth of the water and measure the temperature in the same manner previously described.

Doctors will be able to use that information to determine how long the child's exposure to the water would have had to be to sustain the injury. This can sometimes substantiate or disprove the explanation provided by the caretaker.

Another common scalding injury involves children reaching up to pull a pan containing scalding hot liquid off of the stove. These accidents do occur. Unfortunately, so do intentional acts of cruelty. Always measure the height of the stovetop. Could the child have reached high enough to reach the pan?

When objects are used to injure a child, they often leave patterns that can identify what was used. Belts are common instruments of abuse and often leave marks. These marks can be matched up with belts worn or kept in the home. The diameter of the belt might be consistent with one in possession of the suspect. Sometimes holes in the belt or the buckle leave a distinctive pattern on the skin. Electrical cords leave characteristic loops when folded and used to injure. Belts and cords and other flexible objects will leave "wrap-around" injuries that literally wrap around the victim's body leaving clear evidence that a flexible object was used. This can allow you to distinguish between injuries caused by falling or bumping into a solid object (as is often the explanation given by the offender) and one caused by a cord or similar flexible object that are typically used to punish. When photographing injuries, always use a color bar to show that the colors in the processed photographs are accurate. This can be critical when using the color of bruises to determine when an injury occurred.

A child abuser sometimes makes bite marks on the victim, and if the injury is observed soon enough, a cast can be made to preserve the suspect's tooth marks. These can later be analyzed by a forensic dentist who can make a comparison as accurately as a fingerprint examiner. Even bruises left by biting can be measured to determine the bite radius of the suspect. While not as precise, this evidence can greatly narrow the range of suspects by eliminating those with a bite radius that is inconsistent with the pattern.

Sexual abuse of a child is sometimes identified by the presence of sexual disease. The presence of gonorrhea, vaginal warts, and other sexually transmitted diseases is a clear sign of sexual abuse. Sexual assault suspects are often identified by their blood type and increasingly by their DNA. Don't be surprised to find that the majority of child abuse—including sexual abuse—occurs in the victim's home and is by someone the child knows. Because access to a child is generally limited, this biological evidence usually identifies the suspect from those few persons that could have committed the crime. More detailed evidence is collected by medical doctors who use specialized equipment to locate evidence of sexual trauma and penetration. Officers and CSI personnel should not be conducting investigations that involve an examination of the victim's genitals. Photographs of these areas can be taken in conjunction with a medical examination by a physician.

Neglect cases often involve unfit living conditions. A child must be provided with basic necessities of life, including reasonable shelter, clothing, and food. It is important to remember that these are basic conditions and not necessarily what you would consider minimal. It is not a crime to be poor or homeless, and these circumstances alone do not constitute child abuse. When examining where a child lives, look for evidence of proper sanitation. Is there running water? Is there a functioning toilet? Examine the kitchen for fresh food. Does the refrigerator work? Is any of the food spoiled? What is the overall level of cleanliness? While a dirty house is not necessarily unfit, it should not have obvious hazards to health, such as rotting food, human or animal feces, or insect or rodent infestation. Unfit homes often contain evidence of extensive drug and alcohol abuse, and sometimes this is accessible to children living there. Photographs are critical when documenting incidents of neglect. See Figures 8.1, 8.2, and 8.3.

When dealing with child victims, reassure them that they have done nothing wrong. Children often feel guilty about what has occurred or because they have identified the perpetrator. Child abusers frequently threaten their victims with harm, or harm to their family, if they tell on the abuser. The actual interviewers of child victims should be left to those

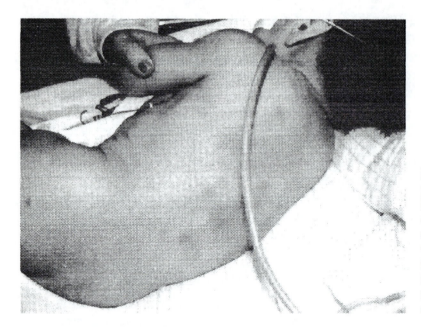

Figure 8.1 When photographing bruises, note the different colors or stages of healing that the bruises are in. This can be an indicator of repeated and ongoing abuse.

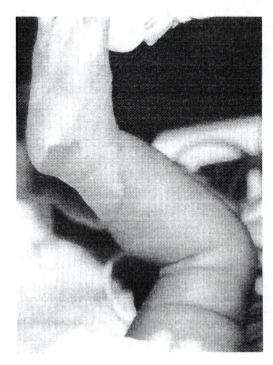

Figure 8.2 The different degrees of blistering and peeling skin can indicate the degrees of burns as in the case of child abuse.

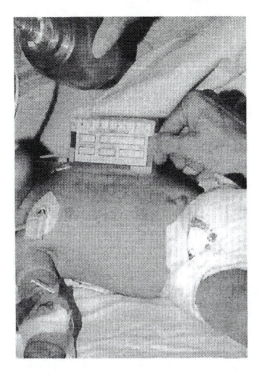

Figure 8.3   Often internal injuries cannot be documented. In such a case, photograph any external injuries that may coincide with internal injuries.

specially trained to do so. If you must ask questions, be sure and ask children open-ended questions like, "What happened?" Never ask a child a leading question like, "Your daddy did this, didn't he?" These questions are too suggestive for young minds and will damage and perhaps destroy the criminal case. The most important thing you can do for a child who has been victimized is to let them know they are safe.

Pay close attention to the child's room. An abused child sometimes takes out his or her anger on toys or personal objects because the person who abused them—perhaps a parent or older sibling—is so much bigger, stronger, and authoritative. The child may keep a journal or diary documenting the occasions of abuse. Corporal punishment is not, in itself, against the law. In many cultures it is normal for parents or elders to spank or slap children to discipline them. What is against the law is when the punishment goes "over the line," whatever that boundary is in the eyes of the investigator and eventually the courts and juries.

Question the child and the parents and other persons involved separately. Never question a child whom you think may have been abused in the presence of his or her parent. This practice prevents any hint of undue pressure on the child to change the story about how certain injuries were inflicted. As the crime scene investigator you may not be the person to handle the questioning. But in case you are, it may be better just to get the bare essentials about the nature of the injuries, and leave the in-depth interview about how the injuries happened for the juvenile experts to handle. Your responsibility is to take photographs of the places where the injuries took place, make an accurate sketch, and report all of the evidence that you find that either substantiates or disproves a parent's story about how the injuries occurred. For example, a doctor can usually tell whether a child fell and broke an arm, or whether someone broke it by twisting it, or whether a child fell down the stairs or was thrown.

Sudden Infant Death Syndrome

Sudden Infant Death Syndrome, or SIDS, is not a crime. It is a medical tragedy that remains unexplained. It is defined as the sudden and unexpected death of an infant, under one year of age, that remains unexplained after the death scene investigation, medical history, and autopsy. Law enforcement is typically called to these scenes in response to a perceived medical aid (typically a call of a baby not breathing), or because the infant has been found to have died. There has been a significant effort to improve the training of police and other first responders to be able to recognize the symptoms of SIDS and to provide for an empathetic, but thorough, response.

Where once police might have responded to the unexplained death of an infant with suspicion, they now do so with compassion and sensitivity. This is not as simple as it might sound, for despite being the leading cause of infant death, the majority of officers have never been directly exposed to a SIDS incident. In addition, physical changes to the infant's body that mimic injury, "confessions" by caregivers that they are responsible for the death, existing indicators of abuse or neglect, and concerns over the welfare of siblings, are factors often present that can significantly complicate a field assessment regarding the cause of death.

There are two factors that must be present for there to be a SIDS incident. The victim must be under one year of age, and the victim must have been sleeping when the incident occurred. It is important to understand that while sleep is a component of SIDS, it does not mean that the event occurred at night or in a crib, but that sleep of some sort was involved. This could mean, for example, that the infant died while sleeping in a car seat while being driven from one place to another. SIDS deaths occur without warning and without sound. If you were to witness a SIDS death, you would probably not notice that it had occurred. A simplistic explanation for a complex and mysterious process is that babies simply forget to breathe, but that may not be completely accurate, as pathologists and pediatricians are still trying to figure out the root cause. Without clear evidence of trauma or other reliable indicators of foul play, accident, or disease, the unexplained cause of death for an infant under one year is likely to be SIDS. That will be determined by the pathologist at the autopsy.

When parents and caregivers discover infants who have died of SIDS, they almost universally blame themselves for the death. It is not uncommon for them to tell you "I killed the baby" or similar expressions of guilt. In a SIDS death, no one is to blame, but this is little understood by the families who must encounter this tragic situation. Fortunately, through education and job-specific training, police officers today are able to quickly identify the characteristics of SIDS and handle these tragedies with the empathy and support they deserve. It is very helpful to all concerned that information about SIDS be relayed to the parents as soon as possible.

Regrettably, police officers must continue to be alert to the potential of criminal causes of death. The authors' experience is that despite the presence of grieving parents and a lack of trauma, an infant's death can be the result of criminal acts and negligence. Police have the difficult task of balancing the need for a thorough investigation with the concerns of family and others involved in the event. Officers are trained to understand that criminal causes of infant death are nevertheless rare, and any investigative steps need to be tempered with a non-accusatory approach and with the knowledge that 97% or more of these cases involve non-criminal causes of death.

Perhaps the greatest change in our response has been to allow parents access to the infant during the investigation. This ranges from being allowed to be close to the baby, to allowing parents to actually hold their infant (some states preclude the officer from offering the latter without authorization from the coroner). Coming directly from the recommendations of SIDS parents, this practice greatly eases the emotional burden for survivors at the time when the final goodbye at the scene must be made.

CSI is often performed at the scene of a suspected SIDS because the exact cause of death will not be known at the time. It is impossible for anyone to correctly assess every incident of SIDS in the field. Even the final medical and forensic diagnosis takes many weeks, but officers are now well equipped to recognize the indicators of SIDS, provide a supportive yet thorough investigation, and connect survivors with support groups and other resources. It is good idea to sketch and photograph the scene and to note anything peculiar.

In about half of the SIDS cases, there will be a discharge of fluid from the nose or mouth of the infant. This often contains traces of blood and is not indicative of trauma. If this discharge got onto bedding or a similar object, collect it. It is also advisable to collect the baby's last bottle (if used) and any formula cans. While it is highly unlikely to contain anything harmful, if these items are needed for later analysis, they will have been discarded if not obtained at the time of death. When you perform CSI at a SIDS scene, always inform the parents or caregivers of what you are doing and why. Be aware that they may feel they are under suspicion and not understand that your actions are part of a routine response to SIDS. Let them know you understand that the loss of their infant is the probable result of SIDS and that SIDS cannot be predicted or prevented. Your support is extremely valuable to SIDS families and will not be forgotten.

Kidnapping

Kidnapping takes many forms and poses some unique challenges to the crime scene investigator. If there is a stereotypical form of kidnapping, it probably involves abducting and holding someone for ransom. These events do occur, but they are not the kidnappings most often seen today. In areas of the country where undocumented persons are smuggled in for money, we see "coyote" kidnappings. The term coyote is slang for the smuggler. Often the person being smuggled pays a portion of the money being charged for safe passage into the country with the remainder payable upon arrival. When the money is not paid (usually by family already at the point of destination), the person is held until the money is paid.

Other forms of kidnapping occur when a person is taken from one place to another to facilitate a crime. This frequently involves taking someone by false pretenses to a location where they are subsequently raped or robbed. Persons are taken against their will to ATM machines to withdraw money (most ATM machines have cameras). People are taken to places and abused for failing to pay debts for drugs or loans supported by criminal activity.

If you are lucky enough to have a ransom or demand note at the scene, it is, of course, a significant piece of evidence. Many demands, however, are made by telephone. If the kidnapping is still in progress, it is a good idea to attach a tape recorder to the phone. More advanced methods of tracing the call are usually done by investigators via the phone company and generally require warrants or emergency affidavits. Don't overlook the possibility of caller ID, star 69, or other such systems offered by phone companies that provide caller identification to subscribers. Believe it or not, some

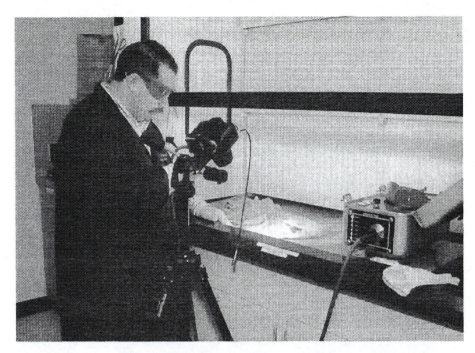

Figure 8.4   An alternate light source can be used to locate and document biological fluids, such as semen, which will fluoresce. Photographs then can be taken showing the location of the evidence.

criminals fail to think of such things, and more than one has been the unfortunate recipient of a team of police officers who simply cross-traced the criminal's phone number to his address.

Vehicles are often used to commit kidnappings and can be a wealth of evidence. Besides the obvious potential for fingerprints, vehicles should be processed for hair, fibers, and in the event of sexual assault, semen and other related fluids (Figure 8.4, Figure 8.5, Figure 8.6). Tire patterns can often be matched to the scene where the abduction took place. Items unique to the scene—dirt, rocks, and leaves—are sometimes trapped in the tread of the tires. Look in the areas below the windshield or in the beds of trucks where debris can fall.

Of course, many cases of suspected kidnappings are in fact something else. Missing adults are often gone for a variety of reasons and most are not because of criminal activity. Missing children most often turn up in the hands of a family member or friend who forgot or didn't consider notifying the parents. When children have, in fact, been taken, it is usually by

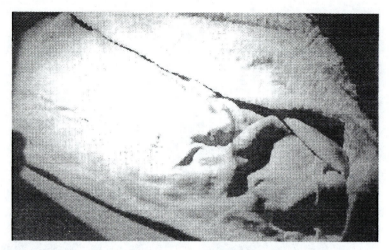

Figure 8.5   Here the evidence is seen with the light source illuminating it without any color filtration.

Figure 8.6   This is the same evidence viewed under orange filtration with the stains now made visible.

someone they know. Check to determine whether there are custody orders in place or if there is a divorce or separation where custody is in dispute. Child abduction by strangers is thankfully rare—it is generally a parent or someone working for them who are responsible.

If you get involved in a search for a child, it is critical to check the home and yard first. This tried-and-true rule has saved many an officer the time and effort (and embarrassment) of looking for a child who was home all along. It happens all the time. When you are searching, look anywhere a child can fit. This includes ice chests, washers and dryers, trash compactors, cupboards, and under beds. Outdoors, look in dumpsters, trashcans, and vehicles. Police dogs can be of great assistance when searching large areas.

Sometimes what is alleged to have been a kidnapping may not be a kidnapping at all. Regardless of what the parents or other reporting parties tell you or your colleagues, the first place you search are the premises from where the child was reportedly taken. Look in places where you might expect to find a child alive, but also look in place where you might find a dead child or where someone may have hidden the child's dismembered body parts. Do not overlook the refrigerator and freezer or the trash dumpster out back or down the street. The kidnapping actually may have been a physical or sexual abuse gone horribly wrong, and the kidnapping story is manufactured to divert the investigation somewhere other than the direction in which it should go.

If a ransom note was found, collect all the types of devices that the author might have used on the premises, including pens, pencils, typewriters, and computers. If the note was made up of words clipped out of magazines and newspapers, collect any of those items from which the clippings may have been taken. Even if you have no reason to suspect the family members of the crime, it is still possible that the kidnappers prepared the note while in the house. Your investigation may lead to a family member as the actual culprit, and what would have been done to the evidence had you not collected all these materials when you were on the premises? To take them for "elimination" purposes during your initial search would not have required a search warrant. If the note is handwritten, you will want to get hand-writing exemplars from all family members for "elimination" purposes. Do not have anyone look at or copy the ransom note to prepare the exemplar.

Domestic Violence

Crime scene investigation plays a critical role in the successful prosecution of domestic violence. Why? It is one crime where although the victim may have reported the crime, they frequently decline the subsequent prosecution. There are many reasons why domestic violence is under-reported and why victims choose not to follow through, but current thinking promotes aggressive prosecution of their abusers regardless of whether the victim cooperates. The reason domestic violence cases can be prosecuted without the victim's assistance is that crimes are committed against the State, not a particular victim. Although it is helpful (and generally required by prosecutors) to have the victim support the prosecution by providing their testimony, it is not always needed. What is needed, however, is evidence that can speak on behalf of the victim.

Regrettably, most incidents of domestic violence involve physical injury to the victim. Of course, these injuries need to be photographed, but also the suspects need to be photographed. A typical defense in these cases is that the suspect was acting in self-defense. If it can be shown that the suspect did not have visible injuries at the time of the incident, it can minimize or eliminate this defense. When both parties are injured, photographs are critical to determine who is the offender and who is the victim. Even when one person reacts in self-defense, how and to what degree they respond can determine if they are nevertheless criminally liable for their actions.

In many states, the doctrine used to determine who is prosecuted in a domestic violence case where both parties are injured is called the "dominant aggressor." If the wife slaps her husband and he responds by punching her in the face and knocking out her teeth, the man will be the one prosecuted. If a man pushes his wife to the bed and she breaks a lamp over his head, she will be deemed the dominant aggressor. As you can see, in cases of mutual abuse, the law looks to see not only who started the incident, but also who raised the level of violence with an unreasonable response. Always photograph both parties' injuries (not just close-ups) to show their relative sizes.

Victim injuries should be photographed again several days after the incident to show the true extent of injury. This is very important. Oftentimes, what looked like redness or slight swelling one day will reveal extensive bruising and damage days later. Black and swollen eyes are common injuries that are not fully visible at the time of the assault. Strangle marks on the neck can also take time to be visible. Make appointments with victims to have subsequent photographs taken.

Identify, photograph, and collect any weapons used in an assault as well as any damage done to the premises. Pay particular attention to the telephone. It is common to find that the suspect has pulled the phone from the wall to prevent the victim from calling the police. Destruction of phone lines is an additional crime. Another very important piece of evidence is the recording of the 911 phone call that is typically made in these cases to report the event. All 911 calls are recorded by the 911 Call Center, and part of the investigation will be to secure copies of the tape before it is erased (as some tapes are erased after a reasonable period of time, such as 60 days). It may be the victim or a witness (often children in the home or a neighbor) who makes the call, and it is strong evidence for the prosecution. You or the follow-up investigator should request a copy of the tape in a timely manner to prevent erasure and to assure that it will be available for presentation in court when necessary.

When a victim of domestic violence refuses to cooperate with prosecutors or takes the witness stand and denies that the crime occurred, their statements are usually impeached by the use of crime scene photographs, statements to the responding police officers, and the 911 tape. Rarely is a case lost under these circumstances.

Studies on domestic violence indicate that victims rarely report the first incident. In fact, victims may suffer such assaults a dozen times or more before finally calling the police. When they do call, most victims are frightened and unsure about their future. Abusers often warn their victims that they will injure or kill them or their family if they report the abuse. Studies show that the most dangerous time for a woman is when she tries to leave the abuser. It is important to keep these dynamics in mind when dealing with domestic violence, so that you can better understand a victim's fear and reluctance to report and prosecute their abuser.

Sex Crimes

Forcible rape or a violent child molestation come to mind when one first hears the term "sex crimes," however many sex crimes are committed by fraud, or trickery, or the victim may be unconscious while the crime is being committed. The victim may not know that what is happening is even a crime. What a child may think of as normal play with an older friend or member of the family (or even a stranger) may be a sexual molestation. But the child feels no pain and has no information that such behavior is legally and morally wrong. Therefore, unless someone else observes the behavior, or if it is revealed during a conversation with the child, it will probably go undetected, perhaps beyond the statute of limitations. Then the child grows up and learns years later that what uncle Charlie used to do with him or her was actually a molestation.

For a variety of reasons, some rape victims fail or decline to report the crime, perhaps because they erroneously feel guilty for letting themselves get into such a situation. A person in a position of power over the victim, such as an employer, may make sexual advances, and the victim will not file a criminal complaint for fear of losing his or her job or not getting a promotion. Or perhaps the boss promises him or her an increase in salary in exchange for his or her silence, and he or she may be in dire need of more money to make ends meet. Many reported rape cases are approached by defense attorneys as though the victim were actually the aggressor, and the attacker an innocent victim. "What does this have to do with crime scene investigation?" you ask. The items of evidence you need are such seemingly-innocent alcoholic beverages and hypnotic drugs, such as the "date rape" drugs. The suspect may have convinced the victim that they should go someplace in his vehicle, leaving her car behind, thereby placing her in a situation where the pressure is to "put out or walk home."

A doctor or nurse will be the only person to examine the victim and collect evidence from her body and to examine the body of the suspect for similar evidence, such as exchanged pubic hairs and body fluids, saliva, physical evidence of sexual penetration, and other related materials. Your task as crime scene investigator is to look for similar substances at the scene of the alleged sex act to determine if there was any evidence of sexual contact.

A very serious problem in a rape case is the traumatic condition of the victim, who may compulsively start cleaning the room, taking a douche and bath, and putting the bedclothes into the washing machine, all to clean away the "filth." Search for items that may have been placed in a clothes hamper or washing machine that may yield evidence of the sex act. Look for signs that a struggle may have taken place, lending credence that the act was entirely involuntary. Some rape suspects, particularly in those cases sometimes referred as date rapes, may resort to their defense that "all women fight at first before they give in."

In the child molestation case, you are looking for evidence of a sex act having taken place somewhere at or near where the child described it had occurred. If the crime took place in the suspect's place of residence, search for any photographs, movies, videotapes, or any other material that might tend to prove the suspect's preference for children rather than women his own age. You may find children's toys or clothing and other things that you might find in a child's room, such as special wallpaper or bedding. The pedophile may consider himself a child in spirit, thereby "explaining" his pedophilia.

Some rapes are committed by fraud, such as phony marriages, where there is consensual sex, but the consent is based on the belief that the marriage was lawful. Both prosecution and defense may stipulate there was consensual sex, especially if the couple had sex on more than one occasion. That type of rape is more of a document-related crime, yet still a sex crime, but the sex act is overshadowed by the fraudulent act of the perpetrator. A doctor or dentist may sexually assault or rape a victim who is under sedation and unable to resist or who might be totally unconscious at the time of the act. In addition to collecting whatever evidence is available to establish that a sex act took place, the utilization of hidden video cameras and women working undercover as decoys may lead to the suspect actually attempting to commit the rape while under surveillance or investigation. This would aid in establishing a pattern of behavior, which tends to prove that there were unlawful sex acts being committed upon unsuspecting women in the sanctity of the examining room.

In some rape or molestation cases, the perpetrator may have used "sex toys" and other paraphernalia in addition to, or instead of, his actual body parts. In that case, you have an additional crime, rape with a foreign object, or sexual battery in addition to, or instead of, rape. In a case of that nature, you must present the object that was used to commit the act, or have the victim describe the object as accurately as possible.

CRIMES AGAINST PROPERTY

<u>Arson</u>

One very important note regarding photographing a fire scene is that you must remember to open up the camera's aperture a couple of F-stops to allow more light into the camera, and your lighting is going to have to be brighter and at a different angle. Charred wood and other charred surfaces have a tendency to suck up light like a sponge sucks up water. Before you take photos at a fire scene, take a few practice shots to get used to the idea that you are not washing out the pictures so that you will have the freedom to "open up" for the fire scenes. See Figures 8.7 and 8.8.

Figure 8.7   When a person is burned, the muscles contract, causing the arms and legs to bend, as seen in this photograph. Courtesy of Sheriff's Department, San Diego, California.

Figure 8.8   Light bulbs are good indicators at an arson scene, because they tend to swell in the direction of the most intense heat, which may be a clue as to the point of origin in a fire. Courtesy of Sheriff's Department, San Diego, California.

Although much of the evidence in arson cases is destroyed by fire, well-trained fire investigators are experts in locating the point of origin, or the place where the fire started, as well as the incendiary device or material and accelerants used to start the fire and to keep it going. Charred wood may be saturated with kerosene or gasoline, a pile of oily rags might still be smoldering, and candle wax or remnants of a fuse may indicate how the fire was ignited. There may be some sort of device that sparks when set off, such as a telephone, an electric switch, or a doorbell that was placed among some highly-flammable material that started the fire. If the arsonist is the owner or a tenant of the property, you might not get the cooperation you need, but he or she may still provide valuable information by describing the condition of the place when last seen, which may be verified or refuted by other witnesses, or proven to be false by evidence you find at the scene (Figure 8.9).

A tenant or owner who starts a fire himself or herself or who hires a "torch" to do the job may replace expensive furniture and other personal treasures from the premises with junk from a thrift shop before the fire. A witness who is familiar with the premises might be able to spot this differ-

Figure 8.9 Burn patterns can show the point of origin at a fire or area of most intense heat. Courtesy of Sheriff's Department, San Diego, California.

ence, whereas you would have no idea that such a switch took place. In a cocktail lounge fire in Newport Beach a few years ago, the firefighters discovered that most of the liquor bottles in the storeroom were broken, ostensibly by the fire or the people attempting to put it out before the fire department arrived. Closer examination led the investigators to discover that the broken bottles had been full of something other than liquor when broken. The investigators discovered that the lounge owners had another place in Santa Ana, and they were able to secure a search warrant for that place. In the storeroom of the bar in Santa Ana, they found dozens of cases of liquor that had been delivered to the lounge in Newport Beach. Liquor dealers code the cases of liquor for specific destinations, the investigators discovered. The owners of the two places were convicted for bankruptcy and insurance fraud as well as for soliciting for an arson.

Another hint for the photographer is to take photos of the bystanders who are watching the firefighters and investigators at work. Perpetrators have been known to return to the scene to check on their handiwork, sometimes even pitching in and helping wherever they can. A recent Southern

California series of fires was found to have been started by a highly-respected arson investigator; the investigator was convicted for arson and murder because people died in one of the fires he started. Some fires were started in the city of San Marino, also in Southern California, a few years ago, and the investigation led to a police patrol officer who started the fires so that he could start putting them out and call the fire department. The police chief and other civic leaders had lauded the officer as a hero for saving lives by finding the fires. It turned out that he was just lonely on the graveyard watch and hungry for attention. He was encouraged to leave his police job and seek attention elsewhere.

Auto Theft

Auto theft is a growing problem across the country. In many areas, the face of auto theft is changing. While it was once common for new cars to be stolen and sold or stripped for parts, now many auto thieves are taking cars merely for quick transportation. In Southern California, for example, auto thefts have significantly increased among older cars that most owners do not expect anyone to want. Using shaved keys or easily bypassing the ignition systems, suspects take the cars for local use and leave them near their destination. Sometimes these cars are stolen several times! The police recover most of these vehicles fairly quickly.

Vehicles are identified by their license plates and a 17-digit Vehicle Identification Number (VIN) that is affixed to the dashboard or inside door pillar. Because these numbers can be removed or altered, there are secondary numbers in hidden places in most vehicles. Always closely inspect the VIN plate to see if it appears to have been altered or replaced by one taken from another vehicle. An auto theft investigator can locate and cross-check secondary numbers when needed.

Auto theft is a difficult crime to solve unless the thief is caught in the vehicle. CSI does account for a number of suspects, however, that are caught by their fingerprints. When dusting a car for prints, pay particular attention to the inside of the vehicle. In many jurisdictions, prosecutors will not charge a case if the only fingerprints you have are from the outside of the vehicle. The theory is that the suspect might have only touched the vehicle at some time and was not the one who stole it. Print the top area of the side windows where suspects pull open the door. These prints will be pointing down indicating the suspect's hand was on the inside. Print the rearview and side mirrors that a suspect might have adjusted. CDs provide a great surface for finding latent prints. Perhaps the suspect played one while driving the vehicle!

As with many crimes, suspects often develop a *modus operandi*, or M.O., that distinguished their way of doing business. It is important to document how the vehicle was entered, how the ignition was damaged or bypassed, and anything located in the car. If you find a spark plug inside a car where the window was broken, you have probably found your point of entry. These little plugs shatter a car window quickly and surprisingly quietly. Does the car contain anything that does not belong to the victim? More than a few unfortunate crooks have unwittingly left objects behind that were used to identify them. When a suspect is caught, his M.O. might be sufficient to charge him with additional auto thefts.

Criminals continue to steal cars for profit, and you might come across a "chop shop" that contains parts from a variety of stolen vehicles. Again, the use of secondary VIN numbers and sometimes after-market security numbers can be found to assist in identification. Some car owners pay professional car thieves to steal their cars so that they might collect the insurance, but you probably would not be able to find that out by investigating the crime scene. It may seem unusual, however, if the victim left the keys in the car so that the thief did not have to hot-wire it. You might also find it suspicious that a vehicle involved in a hit-and-run accident, or another crime, is suddenly being reported stolen by the owner. Again, a close examination of the ignition might reveal no damage or that the keys are still inside! Not every vehicle reported stolen is what it appears, so always conduct a thorough investigation.

You may be able to identify the perpetrator by carefully searching the recovered vehicle that had been stolen. Check the mirror and seat adjustment for a clue as to the thief's size, whether it is approximately the same as, or different from, that of the car's owner. Always look for latent prints. Some thieves do not wear gloves or wipe off their prints. The thief may have a certain taste in radio stations or may have played a particular tape or compact disc that he or she liked, which may be part of the thief's trademark. Check the ashtray, glove compartment, and console cabinet for items removed or left behind (theory or transference). Has the thief left behind any tools or articles of clothing, or perhaps picked up a passenger who left one of those objects behind without the knowledge of the thief?

Burglary

In burglary investigations, you are primarily concerned with determining where and how the suspect gained entry to the building or vehicle or other place or object, and what was taken. Although the majority of burglaries fall into the two categories of residential and commercial, you will investigate many other burglaries that involve objects other than buildings. Make a thorough examination of the exterior to identify the point of entry. Suspects often enter by forcing open doors or breaking windows, but many methods of entry are less obvious. Suspects often gain access to commercial buildings via vents and skylights. These entry points are generally not obvious from the ground. Metal roll-up doors are also frequent targets at large commercial buildings. Suspects attack these doors in various ways, including driving vehicles into them or using gas cutting torches to cut them open.

Many commercial buildings use alarm systems and are increasingly using surveillance cameras. Always inquire whether there are videotapes available after a burglary. When the suspect bypasses alarm systems, it often indicates that the burglary may be an inside job. Former and/or currently-employed disgruntled employees are potential suspects. The same holds true when the suspect was able to quickly locate safes, hidden merchandise, or otherwise take some action that required special knowledge of the business practices and the building layout. When you encounter these types of circumstances, the investigation should include discussing this possibility with a manager or supervisor who might be able to provide the name of a suspect or two. Questions would include who has keys or electronic access to doors, alarms, safes, and other authorized means of entry into the building.

Most homes are entered via unlocked doors and windows. Victims sometimes leave an extra key under the porch mat or a nearby obvious hiding place, such as a flower pot next to the door, and suspects simply locate these keys and unlock the door. When forced entry is used, suspects generally do so from the side or rear of the house in order to minimize the chances of being seen or heard by neighbors. Burglars often live in the area that they burglarize and are often seen by neighbors, but because they are familiar faces, they do not arouse anyone's suspicion. One of the problems that a burglar has is that he or she has to carry stolen items out of the house. This exposes burglars to being seen coming and going from the home. When burglars use vehicles, they will often park in the driveway of the homes they burglarize so that by looking obvious they appear normal. Every residential burglary investigation should include a search of the area for potential witnesses. Many a burglary has been solved because a neighbor saw something he or she felt was unusual but not suspicious enough to call the police.

Physical evidence at most burglary crime scenes are processed in the same manner. The point of entry is photographed and documented. The method of entry and any tools used should be noted. Any object believed to have been touched by the suspect should be dusted for fingerprints. When a tool used by the suspect leaves behind a pattern, these areas should be carefully photographed and, if possible, collected for later analysis. The city of Fountain Valley (CA) once investigated a series of residential burglaries where the suspect twisted off doorknobs with a pair of pliers. The police collected the doorknobs because the soft metal clearly showed the teeth marks from the tool used by the suspect. Eventually, the police located a suspect with a pair of pliers that were later matched in the laboratory to the doorknobs, proving that they were pried off with the same tool.

It is always a good idea at a burglary—especially a residential burglary—to seek consent from the victim before taking action that can damage the scene. While we might not hesitate to cut a wall apart to collect a bullet from a murder scene, we probably should think twice about causing damage at the scene of a burglary. We don't want to cause the victim expense that is not justified by the amount of the loss or seriousness of the crime. A typical example of this is fingerprinting. Before brushing black powder on that antique white dresser, or, worse yet, spilling powder on a white shag carpet, explain to the victim that it might not come off. Sometimes it is prudent not to fingerprint an object especially when there is no clear indication of its evidentiary value.

Victims should also be consulted about the actions of the suspect. Victims can tell you what the suspect touched or moved, what was taken, and its size. Could it be carried out in pockets, or was a vehicle necessary to transport it? Did the weight of the object require two suspects to carry? Victims might also be able to tell you if the suspect turned on lights, ate food from the home (or brought his own), used the bathroom, and how he left the residence (open rear door, unlocked front door, etc.). Victims are often able to provide very valuable investigative leads.

Some burglars know the victim. Burglars can be family members or friends who are aware of money or valuables in the home and know exactly where to find what they are looking for. Sometimes suspects believe they are owed the property they take because of an unpaid debt or some type of dispute. Many burglaries are reported after a party is held at a residence. Depending on whether the time and method of entry is clear, it may be that the "burglary" is actually a theft that took place the night of the party but was unnoticed at the time. Or, it may be that guests at the party saw objects that they later returned to steal.

Does the burglary victim have teenage children? It is not uncommon for children to bring their friends to their home only to have them steal. Does the victim have a family member that uses drugs? This is a common motive for thefts from residences and neighbors, who are not always suspicious when they see family members entering a home. Grown children often return to their parents' home to steal. That having been said, never directly accuse someone—especially a family member—of being a criminal. Ask victims if they can think of anyone who would steal from them and why. This will often lead to the victim suggesting that it might be a friend or family member.

Always secure an accurate description of the stolen items. It is especially important that serial numbers are included in the report, so that the information can be placed into stolen property databases. Victims often have to be prompted for this information, and they may not have it readily available. Be sure to explain that without a serial number, the odds of stolen property being returned to the rightful owner are very low.

The percentage of reported burglaries cleared by arrest is very low, largely because they are crimes of stealth and nobody saw any suspects. Good crime scene investigation, combined with detailed questioning of victims and neighbors, greatly increases the chances for success.

Sometimes it is possible to determine whether the intruder was familiar with the premises, or if he or she knew to look for the object taken in the burglary. Besides the dresser or cabinet drawer from which valuables were removed, was anything else disturbed? Did the intruder stumble or fall over any of the furniture, or knock over a lamp while groping around in the dark? Have books on the bookshelves been moved or removed, or have other possible hiding places for money been moved or destroyed?

Which lights were turned on or off during the intrusion, and which ones were left on? What was the method of entry? Was a tool used, or had the owner left the door or a window unlocked upon leaving the premises earlier? A friend of one of the authors recently lost a nanny, who said she was going back home to her mother country. The lady of the house went into the bedroom, took her cash box out of its hiding place, and removed the nanny's pay for the week. This friend teaches private acting classes and stores a lot or her cash in the box (possibly to avoid notifying the tax people of her considerable cash income). She bade the nanny goodbye and left the nanny in charge of her child for the last day, and when she returned home a few hours later, the nanny and the cash box were gone. Fortunately the nanny had left behind her young daughter. It was easy for the investigators to figure out who stole the box containing several thousand dollars in cash.

Outside the premises there may be signs that the burglar lingered for awhile, may have left shoe prints, discarded candy or chewing gum wrappers, or perhaps smoked a cigarette or two while waiting for his victim to leave so that he could enter during the victim's absence. Look for signs that a vehicle may have been parked nearby. Also search trash cans and dumpsters to see if the burglar discarded any of the loot, such as purses or wallets.

Theft

Many thefts are "crimes of opportunity," which involve no witnesses and no evidence. Nevertheless, work on the theory of transfer, and search for any item the perpetrator may have taken away from the scene and lost or discarded along the way. When a thief steals a purse or wallet, he or she will usually take out only the cash and credit cards and discard the rest, so that there will not be any incriminating evidence on his or her person in the event of being stopped and questioned by the police. You may be in luck and find something that belongs to the thief that he or she inadvertently left behind, or some item the thief decided to keep for sentimental reasons.

One of the best things you can do for a victim reporting the loss of their wallet or purse is to tell them to immediately contact their bank to cancel their credit card and bank accounts. Many thefts today are being committed for the sole purpose of acquiring information to be used for identity theft. Victims should carefully monitor their credit history for several months after a theft to ensure that the information was not fraudulently used. Since most purses also contain the owner's address and keys, many victims feel safer if they immediately re-key their doors as well.

Shoplifting is a common form of theft and one that more and more is being captured on store video systems. Always attempt to obtain the videotape, because within a day or so, they are usually recorded over. Shoplifters sometimes use "booster boxes" or other devices with trap door bottoms or false panels as a method to steal merchandise. Always examine bags, boxes, and clothing in the possession of anyone arrested for theft. If you find that these items have been altered to facilitate a theft, you might have also found evidence that the theft was pre-planned. This evidence of intent is used in many states to charge shoplifters with burglary, which carries a much stiffer penalty.

Pawnshops, secondhand stores, garage sales, and swap meets are some of the places follow-up investigators will look for stolen merchandise, but there is little the crime scene investigator can do in this type of crime. Some departments take reports over the telephone or have victims come into the office to make their reports because of the futility of looking for evidence. If you get involved in writing the crime report, always ask the victims if they can locate the serial numbers to their lost property or if they applied their driver's license number to any of the property (many departments have programs that encourage this, and some even loan engravers for that purpose). If a victim is unable to provide a serial number, the odds of recovering their property is very, very low.

Computer Crime

The use of computers to commit or facilitate criminal acts is growing at a rapid rate. Forgery, fraud, identity theft, pornography, and counterfeiting are just some of the crimes that might involve a computer. Even criminals who don't use a computer to commit crimes might be using one to record their activities or to talk about them with others. Computers belonging to victims are also sometimes collected as evidence because they contain information that might identify an offender (such as a stalker).

When a computer is determined to be evidence, it must be handled very carefully. Many criminals who use computers establish sophisticated techniques to protect their illicit data. It is not uncommon to have programs on a computer that will shut down or erase data if improperly accessed.

The best advice for dealing with computer systems is to get an expert in computer forensics to the scene before any action is taken. Experts offer your best chance of preserving any data that a criminal has taken steps to protect. If the computer is off, do not turn it on. If the computer is on, you should photograph the screen and note the time on the task bar. Unplug the computer from the box itself and not the wall. This is because if the computer has an uninterruptable power supply, a signal will be sent to the computer to perform a shut down procedure. Do not use the computer's on/off switch or do a system shutdown. This causes many operating systems to wipe out temporary files that may be important to the case. However, if the computer is on a network, it may have to be shut down. In that event, it is strongly recommended you consult an expert. Place evidence tape over all the drives and across the cover of the case. Then transport the computer and all peripherals (monitor, keyboard, printer, storage devices) to the lab and hold until an expert can respond. It is very simple to destroy evidence by improperly handling a suspect computer. Time is usually on your side; get an expert to examine any computers you seize as evidence.

SUMMARY

Perhaps several of the suggestions in this chapter may aid in your crime scene search. Do not be discouraged when you conduct an exhaustive search and do not find all the evidence you are looking for. In some cases, you may not find any evidence at all. What is important is that your search must be as thorough as possible and not be sloppy or unprofessional. Home run champions strike out half of the time at bat, and you are going to strike out sometimes. The point made in this chapter is to keep looking until you find little or nothing. Never approach a crime scene with a defeatist attitude that there is no use searching because you are not going to find anything. Always operate on the theory that the perpetrator leaves something at the scene and takes something away from the scene. Many times it may only be a memory or a shadow, but perhaps forensic science will be developed to the point someday that even memories and shadows may be turned into tangible evidence.

SUGGESTED OUTSIDE PROJECTS

1. Put together a sample ransom note without use of a pen, a computer, or a typewriter. Make all the words and sentences out of clippings from newspapers, magazines, and other printed sources.

2. Do some research and describe at least seven different types of devices that an arsonist might use to start a fire from a remote location. Draw sketches or diagrams of each device, and describe how it would work. You may choose to seek the assistance of someone from your local arson investigation squad.

3. Research recent child abuse cases in your jurisdiction. Explain the nature of the incidents and how the investigations led to the finding that injury was not caused by accident.

DISCUSSION QUESTIONS

1. Why is it necessary to collect all items that may have been used as a weapon in a homicide even though you have a pretty solid idea that the weapon used was the gun found next to the body?

2. Is it possible that a knife wound may actually appear at first to have been a blunt force injury?

3. According to your local police and sheriff's department, what percentage of homicides are committed by friends or members of the family?

4. What percentage of homicides are gang related?

5. If you are the first person to arrive at the scene of a homicide, what is the first thing you must do?

6. What are presumptive signs of death? Give two examples.

7. As a crime scene investigator, do you have the authority to pronounce a person dead?

8. What are positive signs of death? Give five examples.

9. In your jurisdiction, can a person commit a robbery without using a weapon? Explain.

10. Is it possible for a child to be sexually abused without knowing it? If so, give an example.

11. Can a married woman be raped by her husband in your jurisdiction?

12. Is it possible for a female to rape a male? Explain.

13. What is the difference between taking photographs at an arson scene and taking photos at a burglary scene?

14. Why are so many petty thefts not solved?

15. In the jurisdiction where you live, what percent of criminal homicides were cleared by arrest last year?

Chapter Nine
Impression Evidence

INTRODUCTION

We operate on the theory of transference; that is, we expect the perpetrator to leave something behind at the crime scene and take something away from it. It is a simple fact that a person can hardly move about the crime scene without leaving behind imprints of his or her shoes, feet, wheels (if using a wheelchair or skates), or pogo stick. Then, when the victims arrive home and the police arrive to investigate the crime, their own movements about the scene tend to obliterate those left by the perpetrators. For that reason, shoe prints are often referred to as the "missed evidence." With this evidentiary problem in mind, in a perfect world the victims would back off and call the police without entering the premises, and the officers, upon arrival, would search the floor and ground surfaces for impressions before entering. In this chapter, we discuss what may be done with impression evidence when you are fortunate enough to find some at the crime scene.

EVIDENTIARY VALUE OF IMPRESSION EVIDENCE

Shoe prints, tire prints, and other impressions can be matched "beyond all reasonable doubt" by their characteristics. (Remember only death and taxes are absolute.) Impressions found at a crime scene can be compared with shoes, socks, tires, tools, and other objects that made those impressions to such an extent that the criminalist or lab technician can declare a match with virtual certainly. As people go about their daily business of walking, driving, or using tools in their work or hobbies, all these devices wear down in unique ways. Sharp rocks, glass, or other hard foreign objects will make their distinctive marks on the softer surfaces, which will be unlike marks made on any other similar object, such as a shoe or tire. Normal and abnormal wear and tear on these objects will also be unique. When the actual object is compared to an impression suspected of having been made by that object, all of the wear patterns and cuts and gouges will create a mirror image of their characteristics on the materials with which they come in contact.

When there are a sufficient number of these identifying characteristics brought out during the comparison process, the expert will then testify as to the match. The next step is to put the perpetrator in those shoes, socks, or vehicle, or in possession of those impression-making objects. Even when there are not sufficient unique characteristics and a positive match is not possible, the impression will reveal different class comparisons, such as approximate size and/or weight of a suspect by shoe size. It is possible to determine the manufacturer by shoe or tire patterns. The pattern of impressions may reveal the length and width of a vehicle, or the approximate height of a suspect by the stride pattern and the length of the steps taken by the suspect. Deeper impressions at the heels may indicate that the person was carrying a heavy weight, and deeper impressions of the sole portion of the shoe may indicate that the suspect was running. With these bits of information, investigators (at the least) may be able to narrow down their list of possible suspects.

THE SEARCH

Give careful consideration to all contingencies while conducting your search for impressions of any kind. Some impressions may be more easily recognized, whereas other are more difficult because of the surface onto which the impressions have been made. As with your search for fingerprints and other traces, aim a flashlight across the surface at an oblique angle, which will more readily reveal any impressions that are present. Once you locate an impression, be careful to protect it until you can properly document and collect it. Cover the impression to protect it from the weather, and mark it off with tape, traffic cones, or numbered tents to keep people from stepping on or otherwise destroying the impression. Take photographs before attempting to remove or make impressions of any evidence.

PHOTOGRAPHING THE IMPRESSION

In order to obtain maximum contrast of impressions, take all of your photographs with black-and-white film. Begin by placing your camera on a tripod directly over the impression, making sure that the film plane is

Figure 9.1   Set up your camera on a tripod, making sure the film plane is parallel to the shoe print. Using oblique lighting, shoot three photographs of the shoe print while aiming the flash between the tripod legs.

precisely parallel with the surface (Figure 9.1). This is crucial to avoid distortion of the image when the photograph is produced in the darkroom. Check with your photographic expert to make sure that you are using the correct camera lens for your camera. Place an L-shaped ruler next to the impression so that it measures both the length and width of the impression. Place an identifier card alongside the impression with a north arrow to show direction as well as the case number, evidence item number, date and time of the crime, and the time you took the photograph (Figure 9.2).

The first photo should be an overall orientation shot using the flash at a normal "straight-on" angle (Figure 9.3). Because the impression is actually a three-dimensional object, use oblique lighting to cast shadows in the valleys and highlights on the peaks of the impression pattern (Figure 9.4). To do this, hold the camera flash approximately two to three feet away from the impression at about a five to ten degree angle off the ground when taking the photograph.

MAKING THE CAST

Before casting any impression, lightly mist over the entire surface with hair spray or other similar fixative (Figure 9.5). This will help to keep the fine detail of the impression from being damaged during the casting process. For

Figure 9.2 Use an L-shaped ruler to measure the shoe prints' width and length. Also include an information card with a north arrow, case number, evidence number, date, time, and your name.

Figure 9.3 Take an overall photograph of where the shoe print evidence is located to aid in orientation and direction of travel.

Figure 9.4   Using straight directional lighting, much of the detail in this shoe print is not visible.

Figure 9.5   Spray hair spray over the impression to help set it before pouring the cast.

many years the standard medium for making casts of large impressions was plaster of paris. Because plaster of paris tends to be very fragile, a better substance to use is Traxtone, which was originally created for use by dentists.

Traxtone needs no reinforcement materials as does plaster of paris, and it is easier to mix (Figure 9.6). It sets in less time than other materials, and it is a much more durable product than plaster of paris. Traxtone comes

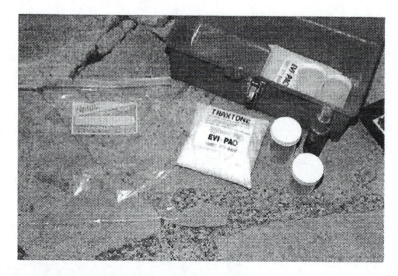

Figure 9.6
This is all that is needed to make a cast using Traxtone.

Figure 9.7   Pour the contents of one bag of Traxtone and a pre-measured amount of water into a self-sealing bag and mix.

in pre-measured plastic bags, which, when mixed with water, is just about right to cast one shoe print adequately. Pour the entire bag of Traxtone into a large self-sealing bag. Add the correct amount of water specified in the instructions and seal the bag (Figure 9.7). For your convenience, it is wise to prepare pre-measured bottles of water for this mixture. Knead the bag of Traxtone and water until the colored pigments dissolve, indicating that the mixture is ready to use (Figure 9.8).

To begin the impression, start by pouring the Traxtone from the bag just above or below the impression, or whichever part of the impression is on a higher level (Figure 9.9). Be careful not to pour the mixture directly

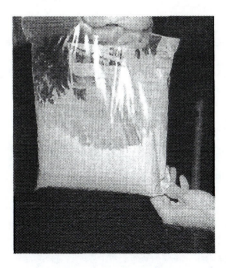

Figure 9.8 Continue mixing until all of the colored pigment indicators are dissolved and the material is a consistent green color.

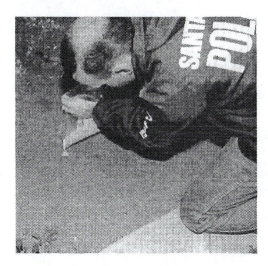

Figure 9.9 Begin pouring the Traxtone at one end of the impression. If the impression is on a slope, start at the highest end.

onto the impression or you may destroy its delicate detail (Figure 9.10). Allow the mixture to slowly work its way into the impression by pouring slightly behind it. Slowly work the mixture down the entire length of the impression until the whole impression is completely filled, pouring additional Traxtone around the outside of the impression as well.

Under normal temperatures, Traxtone will set in approximately 20 minutes, and you will then be able to remove the cast. While waiting for the cast to dry, inscribe onto its surface a north arrow, case number, evidence number, date, time, and your name or distinctive logo (Figure 9.11). Once the cast is ready to remove, do so by prying from one side, then securing it

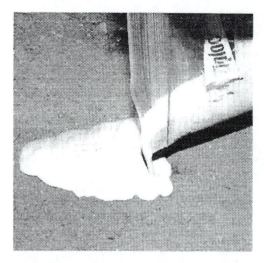

Figure 9.10   Do *not* pour directly into the impression. Let the Traxtone flow naturally to avoid damaging the fragile detail. There is no need to build a form around the impression, and no additional supports need to be added to the Traxtone.

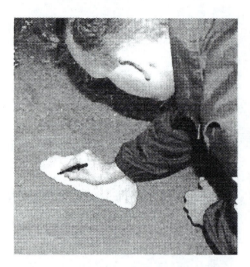

Figure 9.11   Traxtone usually sets within 20 minutes. Make sure to etch in the case number and evidence number to the top of the cast before it completely dries.

in a box with the impression side facing up. This will protect the impression from damage or wear. Do not attempt to clean dirt or other debris from the cast (Figure 9.12). That can be done later in the laboratory when the material has dried more thoroughly (Figure 9.13).

PLASTER OF PARIS

You will need the following materials: plaster of paris, water, a rubber bowl and spatula for mixing, hair spray or other fixative, thin oil, a syringe, talcum or baby powder, reinforcing materials, such as chicken wire or

Figure 9.12   Package the cast in a cardboard box like this gun box, making sure the impression side is face up. *Do not* attempt to clean the dirt from the impression in the field.

Figure 9.13   Back at the lab, the cast can be cleaned under running water using a brush. This also allows additional time for the cast to dry. Courtesy of Sheriff's Office, Penobscot County, Maine.

wooden sticks, or cut-up clothes hanger wire, and framing materials, such as wood or a corrugated box (Figure 9.14).

With the wood or corrugated-box material, build a frame around the impression to be cast (Figure 9.15). Spray the surface with light cooking spray or oil to prevent the plaster from sticking when you pour it. Mix the plaster with water to the thickness of cream, and add salt to

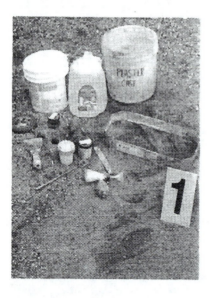

Figure 9.14   These are the tools needed to make a cast using plaster of paris. Courtesy of Sheriff's Office, Penobscot County, Maine.

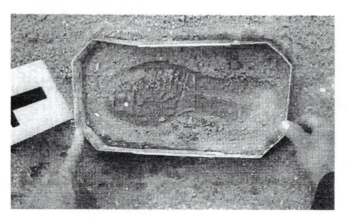

Figure 9.15   Build a form around the impression to prevent the plaster from flowing out. This will also aid in making the cast thicker, which will add strength to the cast. Courtesy of Sheriff's Office, Penobscot County, Maine.

hasten the setting process or sugar to slow it down (Figure 9.16). Slowly pour the mixture over the impression by using the spatula or a spoon, fork, or putty knife to soften the flow onto the impression to keep it from damaging or destroying the surface. After you have poured about a half-inch thickness of the mixture onto the impression, place reinforcing materials onto the surface. Pour more liquid, add more reinforcing

Figure 9.16 Mix water and plaster of paris in a container until a proper thickness is obtained. Courtesy of Sheriff's Office, Penobscot County, Maine.

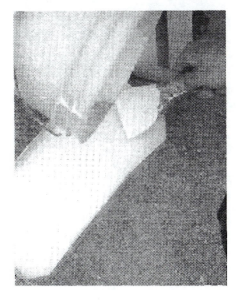

Figure 9.17 Pour the plaster of paris into the mold using a putty knife to break the fall of the plaster as it flows into the mold. Add sticks or pieces of wire to the mold to give it more strength. Courtesy of Sheriff's Office, Penobscot County, Maine.

materials, then continue filling the area to be cast (Figure 9.17). While the plaster is setting, inscribe onto the surface of the cast a north arrow, the case and evidence numbers, the date and time, and your name or distinctive logo (Figure 9.18). When the cast is dry, carefully remove it from one end, dirt and all (Figure 9.19).

Figure 9.18 Let the plaster dry. Times may vary depending on temperature and humidity. Etch in the case number and evidence number to the top side of the cast before it completely dries. Courtesy of Sheriff's Office, Penobscot County, Maine.

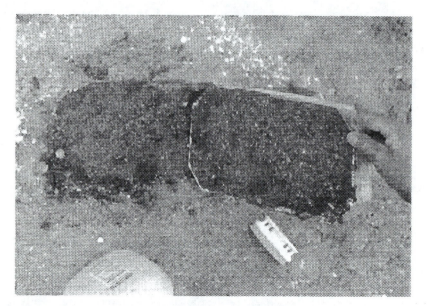

Figure 9.19 Carefully lift up the cast from one end. Book the cast in as is. *Do not* attempt to clean the dirt from the impression in the field. Courtesy of Sheriff's Office, Penobscot County, Maine.

WATER-FILLED IMPRESSIONS

If the impression is in a puddle of water you cannot drain, or if it is in snow, build a frame around the impression and sift dry plaster into the impression until the water is absorbed. Spray fixative from time to time and add reinforcement material as you go. In snow, you may find that spraying with fixative and talcum powder may help preserve the impression before you add the plaster, which has a tendency to heat up as it dries. If you can, drain

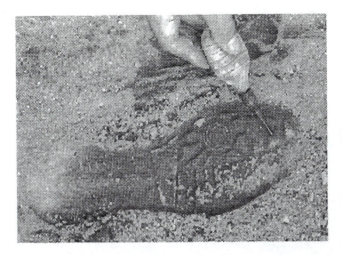

Figure 9.20 A rubber bulb or plunger can be used to remove excess water from the impression. Courtesy of Sheriff's Office, Penobscot County, Maine.

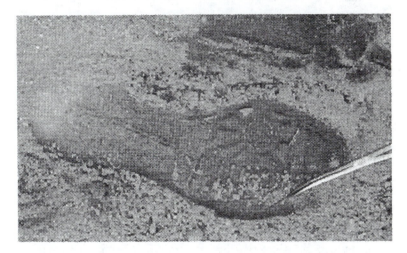

Figure 9.21 Use tweezers, forceps, or a cotton swab to remove debris from the impression. Courtesy of Sheriff's Office, Penobscot County, Maine.

the impression by cutting a channel from the impression to a lower level, which you may have to dig to allow the water to drain. Let the impression dry, using a turkey baster to help drain out the water (Figure 9.20), and carefully remove any debris from the surface with tweezers (Figure 9.21). If you have a power source nearby, you may hasten the drying process with the aid of a hair dryer, not aimed directly at the surface (the air pressure could disturb the surface of the impression). Lightly cover the impression with talcum or baby powder to help soak up some of the moisture, and

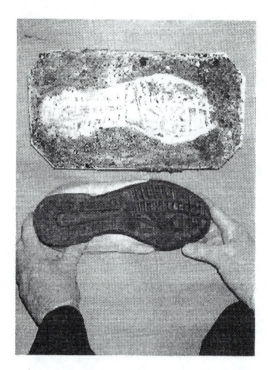

Figure 9.22 A side-by-side comparison of a cast and a suspect's shoe showing similar class characteristics. Courtesy of Sheriff's Office, Penobscot County, Maine.

alternately spray with hair spray or fixative before pouring your casting materials (Figure 9.22).

CASTING TOOL MARKS AND SMALL IMPRESSIONS

Use silicone rubber, latex rubber, microsile, moulage, or one of the compounds that dentists use for making impressions for dentures and other dental prosthetics. Build a frame around the impression to be molded to hold the mixture in and around the impression while it is introduced to the area and until it dries and can be removed intact. Mix the material according to the directions and introduce it to the impression to be cast. As the substance dries, mark the cast with a north arrow, case and evidence numbers, date and time, and your initial or logo. If the object is too small to hold all this information, place it onto an envelope and write all the necessary information on the outside of the sealed envelope, paper bag, or other container rigged to hold the item so that it will not be damaged or destroyed.

If the impression is on a door or window frame or other object that can be removed, do so and take it to the laboratory so that the cast may be made under more ideal conditions away from the crime scene, and at a more convenient time. Casts of the tools suspected of having been used to make the impressions should be made in the laboratory. Photo images of the impressions and tools that possibly made them are studied for similarities and possible matches.

Each tool is unique. Tools are designed differently by the different manufacturers and are made of a wide variety of materials. The metals used for most tools come in different degrees of hardness, depending on their function, quality, and price. New materials are being developed as we speak, such as knives made of porcelain, and some of the old materials are still used, such as rubber and hardwood mallets. Stress and wear eventually cause weakness in all tools, and the tools develop cracks, stress fractures, and degeneration from use, time, and the elements.

Whenever two objects come together by pounding, cutting, scraping, prying or rubbing, they mark each other one way or another. The harder material of the two usually makes the mark on the softer material, but some materials mark each other because they have the same hardness quotient. Tools such as hammers and mallets make impressions on the objects they strike; tools used to pry open doors and windows, such as screwdrivers, make impressions on wooden door and window frames; wire cutters used to cut through fences or to cut open padlocks and other tools used to commit crimes leave their signatures on the softer materials. At the same time, the tools themselves undergo changes from such contacts. Wood pried with a screwdriver is going to have to give way to the harder metal object, but in that door or window frame a nail or screw or similar metal object will make marks on the screwdriver. Eventually every tool develops its own distinctive "fingerprint," and then imprints a mirror image of that fingerprint onto the material it strikes, cuts, scrapes, or otherwise impresses as they meet.

When you find a tool suspected of having been used in a crime, photograph it in place, describe it completely in your report, spot its location in your sketch, and handle it carefully, preserving its condition and appearance exactly as you found it. The tool may contain particles of material it was used against, such as wood or metal shavings, blood, hairs, or fibers, so be sure not to clean it off before taking it to the lab for analysis and comparison.

Marks made by tools are called impressions (from pounding or prying) or striations (from scraping). Following are some other tools and the marks they make: A screwdriver makes scrape marks inside the mechanism when used to open a bathroom door lock. Pipe wrenches leave their marks on pipes, nuts and bolts, doorknobs, and ignition switches. Axes and hatchets leave their signatures on wood, human bones, and skins. Bolt cutters, tin snips, scissors, and shears are used to cut wires, ropes, lock hasps, and sheet metal. Whenever the crime scene search indicates which tools were possibly used, look for those types of tools and take them to the laboratory for comparison and possible matches.

In most cases, the perpetrators will bring along their own tools with which to commit the crime, having prepared themselves for the various obstacles they expect to encounter. When they have completed their work, they take the tools away with them for use another time. Sometimes a burglar will use the same "lucky tools" over and over again, as many other professionals do. As the tools wear, they may chip or leave scrapings behind. The tip of an ice pick found at the crime scene may match the shaft of a pick, or a small chip from the corner of a pry tool may match the broken tool found in the possession of a suspect loitering near the scene.

Some thieves, burglars, and assailants use whatever tools or weapons they find at the crime scene, commit the crime with them, then leave everything but their loot behind so that they will not be caught possessing incriminating tools. It is naturally more difficult to match those tools with their users. When the culprit brings tools to the scene, then leaves them behind, it may be possible to trace their ownership by brand, initials engraved or marks on them, or fingerprints left on the smooth surfaces.

When you find a mark made by the perpetrator using any of the aforementioned tools, or any others we have failed to mention, be sure to photograph them in place first, indicating their exact locations, and describe their appearance in your report. Then follow the procedure for casting the impression described earlier in this chapter. Never place a suspect tool into, onto, or against a mark that was possibly made by that tool, as that would contaminate the evidence. Once you touch the suspected tool to the mark it possibly made, you have destroyed their evidentiary value. The matches will be made by putting together photos of the corresponding tools and their suspected marks, or by comparing positive and negative molds.

Tool marks can and should be measured, but sometimes a tool makes a mark that appears larger or smaller than the tool itself. The reason for this phenomenon is that certain materials, such as wood, stretch under pressure and then retract. The result is that a mark made on a windowsill by a 5/8-inch pry tool may measure only 3/8-inch or a half inch. Impressions made on other materials, such as sheet metal or aluminum, may stretch and not retract, and the results is that the first examination may indicate that the perpetrator used a larger tool. When you describe the tool and the marks, record your exact measurements. Do not make the mistake of stating, "The pry mark was made by a tool with a 5/8-inch bite."

SUMMARY

Do not underestimate the importance of impression evidence, no matter how inconsequential it may seem. It is often difficult to recognize such evidence and time-consuming to collect it, but at the time of your investigation, it is almost impossible to differentiate between critical and non-critical evidence. Later, when you and your colleagues are putting the case together, you will realize how important such impression evidence is to the case.

SUGGESTED OUTSIDE PROJECTS

1. Create you own shoe print impressions in different types of soil, such as sand or clay. Practice photographing them with plaster of paris and Traxtone. You will find out which works best for you.

2. Using a variety of hand tools, make your own set of impressions and striation marks in different types of materials. Using different materials, make casts of those impressions.

DISCUSSION QUESTIONS

1. An impression is what form of evidence: physical, trace, or transient?

2. What are the advantages of using a digital camera for evidence photos? The disadvantages?

3. Why take impression photos in black and white instead of color?

4. Is it best to make prints or slide photos for court presentation?

5. What are the drawbacks of using plaster of paris?

6. What are the advantages of using plaster of paris for casting?

7. Describe how you would cast a footprint in a mud puddle.

8. What type of mark does a pry tool make?

9. What type of mark does a hammer make?

10. How do you light a shoe or tire impression you want to photograph?

11. What is the advantage of using Traxtone instead of plaster of paris?

12. Describe how you would package and transport a cast.

13. What is the difference between a striation and an impression, and describe what type of tool would make each.

14. Why should you not place a suspect's shoe into a print left in the mud?

15. For what types of impressions would you use silicone rubber for casting?

Chapter Ten
Fingerprints

INTRODUCTION

Fingerprints have been, and will continue to be, one of the best forms of identification available to a police investigation. Everyone has fingerprints and footprints, which serve as friction ridges, which are developed on the fetus before birth and remain until after death, barring any catastrophic scarring condition. To date, no two individuals in the world whose fingerprints are on file have ever been found to have the same fingerprints. Identical twins have the same DNA, or genetic code, but not the same fingerprints, so even they have their own unique identities.

In this chapter, we shall cover the types of fingerprints, places where fingerprints may be found at the crime scene, and the different techniques used to develop fingerprints.

THE FINGERPRINT EXPERT

As a trained crime scene investigator, you may or may not be qualified as a fingerprint expert. In this book we are operating on the assumption that you are qualified as an expert only in identifying, collecting, and preserving evidence. Other texts will address the expert qualification requirements. As with photography and other aspects of crime scene investigation, you should be careful to avoid representing yourself as an expert if you are not, as some attorneys are very talented in bursting the bubbles of officers who exaggerate their qualifications. In order to collect and preserve fingerprints efficiently for the expert in the laboratory, you do not have to be able to analyze and compare prints. However, you will be expected to have sufficient knowledge to develop good prints for the expert and to roll prints of suspects and others for elimination purposes.

WHAT ARE FINGERPRINTS?

The skin on the surfaces of the hands and feet is quite different from the skin on the rest of the body. It consists of raised portions of skin known as friction ridges that enable a person to hold objects and to stand without his or her hands and feet slipping. Without these ridges, standing and holding objects would be far more difficult. Even simple tasks such as unscrewing the cap off a mayonnaise jar would be far more difficult without the aid of those ridges.

The skin is an organ of the body that consists of two layers. The top or outer layer is called the epidermis and contains the friction ridges. Beneath the epidermis is the dermis, which is joined together by the dermal papillae. Deep in the dermis layer are the sweat glands and sweat gland ducts. These sweat ducts go up through the dermis to the epidermis, where they form sweat pores along the ridges. Throughout the day sweat comes out through the pores and onto the surface of the skin and along the ridges (Figure 10.1). Sweat consists of water, salts, oils, amino acids, fatty acids, and other materials that come from objects the hands or feet touch. When you touch an object, fingerprints are transferred onto the surface with the sweat and other materials in the pattern of the ridges. This is similar to a rubber stamp that transfers its image onto paper using black printer's ink.

From a law enforcement perspective, the unique characteristics of this friction skin make it invaluable in the identification of people. This is because the characteristics of the skin remain unchanged from the time they are formed during the twelfth week of gestation until the time of death and decomposition. Granted there are other factors to consider such as cuts, calluses, and blisters. However, unless the dermis is damaged, the epidermis will heal itself without any permanent disfiguration.

The transferred image of friction skin ridges is made with nearly invisible materials and is hard to see with the naked eye. These nearly invisible prints are called latent prints (Figure 10.2). Latent fingerprints must be made visible with the aid of chemicals, powders, digital or photo image enhancement, and sometimes with ultraviolet or infrared lighting. At the typical crime scene, if one can be considered "typical," you will have to develop these "latent" prints to make them visible so that you may collect them for identification purposes.

The second type of print is the patent print (Figure 10.3). Unlike the latent print, the patent print is visible to the naked eye. This is usually because certain materials, such as paint, grease, oil, ink, or blood is picked up

Figure 10.1 Finger-tip.

Figure 10.2a Latent print developed with black powder.

Figure 10.2b Latent print on clear plastic.

Figure 10.3 Patent print.

Figure 10.4 Plastic print.

by the friction ridges, mixed with the sweat, and printed onto the surfaces the person touches.

Next is the plastic print (Figure 10.4). This print is three-dimensional and the individual has touched some type of pliable substrate such as putty, wax, chocolate, or grease. It will be difficult to collect these by transferring onto tape as you collect the other prints, and you should photograph them before making any attempt to remove them from any surface.

The fourth type of print is the inked print (Figure 10.5). An inked print is made by applying a thin layer of black printer's ink onto the surface of the friction skin and transferring its impressions onto a card, paper, or other document to preserve as a permanent record. An example of an inked print would be one that you have placed onto a "ten print" fingerprint card designed to

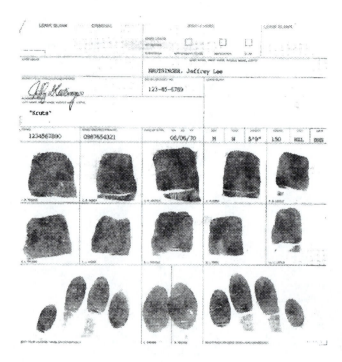

Figure 10.5 Inked set of ten prints.

record fingerprints of suspects, job applicants, and other people legitimately at a crime scene for "elimination prints," or to eliminate their prints found at the scene because they had a legitimate reason for leaving their prints there, such as being residents and guests. These prints are used for documentation, classification, comparison, and importation into a computer database as a permanent record. Unknown prints will be compared against various databases in an effort to identify their owners. And now with the growth of technology, inked prints are becoming a thing of the past. The latest automated fingerprint identification system digitizes or scans the fingerprint when it is rolled across a special sensor that reads the friction ridges and characteristics (Figure 10.6).

The layperson understands that fingerprints have patterns to them. Even as far back as prehistoric man, cave drawings have shown patterns in the skin on human fingers. But it wasn't until the late 1800s that its importance to the law enforcement community was truly realized. While there are several different types of fingerprint patterns, we will break them down into their three main classifications. First and most common is the loop pattern (Figure 10.7). Upon close examination, you will find that the friction ridges enter on one side of the finger, re-curve and exit on the same side as they entered. There is also typically one delta formation of ridges in a loop pattern. This delta pattern can be seen opposite the re-curving ridges. Loop

Figure 10.6   Live scan.

Figure 10.7   Loop pattern.

Figure 10.8   Whorl pattern.

formations will either slope to the left or right, thus being subclassified as right or left slope loops.

The second most common fingerprint pattern type is the whorl (Figure 10.8). While inexperienced defense attorneys often call them "swirl" patterns, do not be confused. This pattern type consists of friction ridges that make up a circular formation in the center of the finger. Other times there will be an S-shaped flow to the ridges. Whorl patterns typically consist of two delta formations on either side. Subclassifications of whorl patterns include, plain whorl, central pocket loop whorl and double loop whorl.

Figure 10.9   Arch pattern.

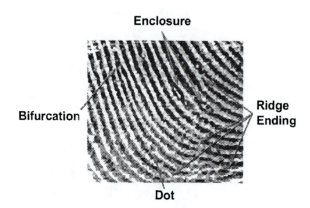

Figure 10.10   Key points the examiner will isolate, identify, and compare.

The third and least common pattern type is the arch (Figure 10.9). In an arch pattern, the friction ridges enter on one side and rise and exit on the opposite side. There is also an absence of any delta formation. Subclassifications of arch patterns include the plain arch and the tented arch. In some cases, patterns that are similar to loops are actually classified as arches. To learn more about fingerprint patterns, take the time to read a textbook that is dedicated solely to the topic.

To understand what makes an individual's fingerprint unique requires the fingerprint examiner to look even closer at the individual characteristics that are formed by the friction skin ridges. These individual characteristics are also known as points of identification, points of similarity, or minutae. For purposes of this text, we will refer to them as characteristics.

As with pattern types, there are also a variety of different types of characteristics an examiner looks for. For simplicity's sake, we will narrow down this list to three characteristics. First is the "ridge ending." This characteristic can be easily spotted at the point where a friction ridge stops or comes to an end. Next is the "bifurcation." This occurs when a single friction ridge splits or forks into two separate ridges. And lastly is the "dot." This is a short ridge that is no longer than its width. Other common characteristics include the enclosure, island, and short ridge. See Figure 10.10.

PROCESSING FOR PRINTS

Traditionally, a fingerprint comparison is done by comparing a known inked impression side-by-side to an unknown latent fingerprint. The fingerprints are magnified using a 5X magnifying loop (Figure 10.11), or en-

Figure 10.11   Typical magnifying loop.

largements of the fingerprints will be used and then marked with a red pen to show the similar characteristic. Upon first examination of a fingerprint for comparison, a qualified latent fingerprint examiner will look at the fingerprint pattern types. Once the examiner has found two similar pattern types, he or she will then look for a characteristic as a starting point. Usually this will be near the core or delta of the print since these are easy landmarks to identify. Then the counting begins. Once a similar characteristic has been located on both the known inked impression and the latent fingerprint, the examiner will look for another characteristic in the same relative position. For example, if the starting point is an upward ending ridge, the next characteristic should be the same type and the same number of ridges away. Then each additional characteristic should be plotted out to see if they occupy the same relative position to one another. The examiner will continue marking the characteristics until they have come to an opinion as to whether the prints were made by the same person.

While there is no set number of characteristics that is required to make an identification, each comparison is based on its own merit, taking into consideration the quality and clarity of the print and the experience of the examiner. In fact, many in the field are trying to get away from a system of counting points, as this can be misleading. Organizations such as Scientific Work Group on Friction Ridge Analysis, Study and Technology (SWGFAST), have been formed to work out the details "to discuss developing a consensus standards which would preserve and improve the quality of service provided by the latent print community." One thing that all examiners agree on is that if just one unexplainable characteristic exists in either the known or unknown print, then there can be no positive identification.

If you come across a scene that is completely devoid of any prints, either you have a scene untouched by human hands or feet, including those of the victims and other inhabitants of the premises, or you have a scene that has been carefully wiped clean of all prints in an effort to hide the identity of the perpetrators. In spite of all the publicity about how valuable prints are to criminal investigations, many offenders do leave their prints behind. Some perpetrators do not plan their crimes well or are interrupted by returning victims or the police, and they do not have time to think about their prints. Some criminals, believe it or not, do not even consider the possibility of being caught and are very sloppy, leaving evidence all over the place. Some criminals simply do not think. Still others will automatically assume that a witness will remain silent and cover for them because of some real or imagined bond between the witness and the perpetrator. Very close friends, relatives, or colleagues are known to develop a code of silence. That is one reason why some perpetrators are nonchalant about leaving evidence scattered all over the place.

When searching for prints, be sure to include palm and footprints, even though your agency and most others do not have classification systems for those types of prints on file. When you locate a suspect, the fingerprint expert in the lab may be able to make positive pattern matches of inked prints of suspects produced in the laboratory and those lifted at the crime scenes because of the unique characteristics of those prints.

Before processing any surface for latent prints, carefully examine the surface to make a decision as to which method you will use for developing and collecting any prints you might find. For example, porous items such as paper or cardboard can often be better processed in the laboratory using chemicals such as iodine, ninhydrin, or physical developer, to name a few. On nonporous surfaces, such as glass or metal, the basic black powder may be the best medium to use. Of course, whenever it is possible to move an object bearing a print, it is wise to take it to the lab for processing. For example, cyanoacrylate ester, also known as Super Glue, can be used in a specially-constructed airtight chamber (Figure 10.12). The cyanoacrylate ester causes the fingerprint residue to polymerize and begin building up a white layer on top of itself (Figure 10.13). This allows for the development of fingerprints that might be missed if processed using black powder alone. However for typical field purposes, powders are usually the medium of choice for processing prints.

Search all surfaces a perpetrator might have touched during the commission of the particular crime you are investigating, and even places where it would not seem logical that someone would touch. Use a strong light and shine it obliquely across the surface to see if you can detect any disturbance of dust on polished surfaces, or traces of prints. Then use the brush and powder of a color that contrasts with the color of the host surface

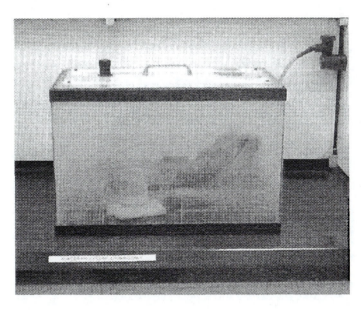

Figure 10.12 A small fish tank serves as a fuming chamber where evidence is exposed to cyanoacrylate ester.

Figure 10.13   This fingerprint was developed using cyanoacrylate ester or Super Glue. Notice how the fingerprint turns white. At this point the fingerprint can be photographed or developed more with powders or dye staining chemicals such as Sudan Black and Rhodamine 6G.

Figure 10.14   A basic black powder kit consists of black powder, application brush, lifting tape, white lift cards, and a portable inkpad.

you are dusting. While black powder is the most common, you will usually have a variety of colors and types of powders to choose from. The best host surfaces for fingerprints will be smooth and nonporous, but always try to get prints off of any object that the perpetrator may have touched. New discoveries are made every once in a while, such as prints on skin, certain cloth materials, and other surfaces before now not even attempted to take prints from in the past.

DUSTING FOR PRINTS

Having selected the appropriate powder and your favorite brush (Figure 10.14), apply a small amount of powder to your brush by lightly dabbing it into the powder. It is important not to start by putting too much powder on the print. This could potentially obliterate the print. Begin brushing lightly over an area where you believe you might find a latent print. First, picture in your mind how and where a person might have touched that particular object, and move your brush across the imaginary print until you have laid down a smooth field of powder. If nothing appears, move on to the next probable area location and repeat the process (Figure 10.15).

From a public relations standpoint, there are two considerations here. First, you must appear as though you know what you are doing, and your approach will make that impression. Second, consider the victim's property. The place may have been "trashed" by the burglar or vandal.

Figure 10.15   Use a flashlight at an oblique angle to locate disruptions in the dust and/or to visualize fingerprints.

But you need not add to the victim's loss by spilling fingerprint powder all over the place. Use the powder sparingly, and when you are dusting a space on a wall, tape a card or paper to the wall below the place you are dusting, and then fold up the two free corners of the card or paper to the wall, making a dustpan of sorts. This is particularly important when you are working in a room with a deep shag carpet of a very light color. Even when you are careful, it will take several vacuum attempts to clean up after you leave.

When you find a print, brush lightly along the same direction as the emerging ridges, at the same time reducing the amount of powder that has accumulated between the ridges (Figure 10.16). Continue applying the powder with your brush until you are satisfied that you have completely developed the print. Do not continue to brush over the print, or you will eventually rub it off. Now that you have revealed at least one print, expand your search area for additional latent prints that you might develop.

It is a good practice to photograph all prints before you attempt to lift them. While this may not be practical in all cases, it should always be an option. This especially applies to the visible (or patent) and plastic prints, as you may destroy a print while lifting it from the surface. The fingerprint technician in the lab at least will have the photograph to work with. Use the fingerprint camera, making sure that the print and the film are parallel so as to avoid distorting an enlargement of the image. If you can, collect the evidence intact and book it in the lab.

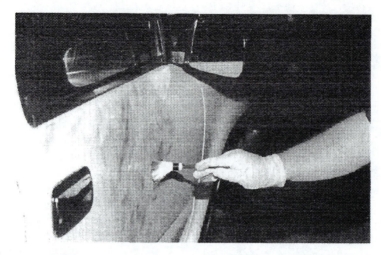

Figure 10.16   Apply a thin layer of black powder to the surface. Once fingerprints are visualized, slowly continue dusting the print until it is fully developed. Do not over powder your evidence.

LIFTING THE PRINT

Tape is the common medium to lift prints developed with black powder. Tape comes in a variety of widths in either a frosted or clear glossy finish. Now that you have photographed the print, examine it carefully to see if it can be transferred to the adhesive tape. If it is a plastic print in a gummy substance, such as partially-dried paint or grease, you may not be able to transfer it onto the tape. That's why you photographed it first. If you cannot transfer the impression, see if there is some way to remove the host object, such as a chair or table, or even a window frame or a door, depending on the importance of the print to the investigation.

Use tape free of bubbles and wide enough to cover the entire print you intend to lift. If you have several prints together, place the tape so that the edge of the tape does not end in the middle of a print. It is going to be difficult to put two strips of tape side by side to get an undisturbed print. Keep your own fingers off the sticky side of the tape that is going to lay on top of the print(s). Slowly and steadily pull the length of tape from the roll without stopping, so as to avoid leaving an accumulation of adhesive on the sticky side of the tape, which will interface with the pattern of the print.

Attach the loose end of the tape to the surface at least an inch beyond the print you are going to lift. Then carefully lay the tape down smoothly and evenly, keeping it extended so that the magnetic characteristics of the tape do not cause it to attach itself to the surface unevenly. Continue applying and smoothing the length of tape onto the surface until you have laid it

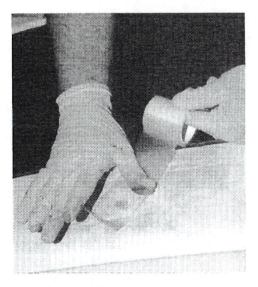

Figure 10.17   Lay down lifting tape over the print, starting at one end and then smoothing it out over the entire surface with your finger. Be sure to smooth out the tape to remove all air bubbles.

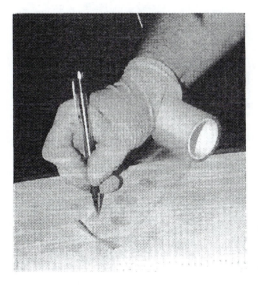

Figure 10.18   Once the tape is in place, draw an up arrow on the tape to help with orientation later. Be careful not to draw over the fingerprint.

down at least one inch beyond the print you intend to lift. Use a plastic ruler or your fingernail to smooth out the bubbles (Figure 10.17). Instead of rubbing the tape where you cannot make the tape stick to the surface, puncture the bubble with the tip of an X-acto knife and then press the tape to the surface (Figure 10.18).

Carefully and slowly remove the tape, which is now holding the impression transferred from the host surface. Keep the tape extended so that it will not double up and attach to itself and destroy the print that is now

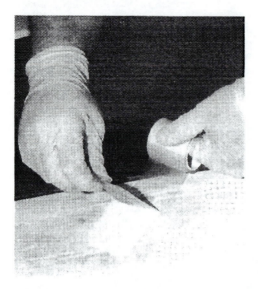

Figure 10.19   Slowly peel the lifting tape off starting at one end. Keep your hand on the other end so the tape does not stick to itself.

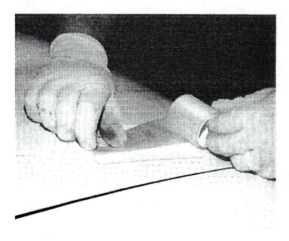

Figure 10.20   Apply the tape to the fingerprint lift card in the same way in which the tape was lifted, starting at one end and working it down to the other end to prevent air bubbles in the tape.

on it (Figure 10.19). Place a white card, or one of a contrasting color if you are not using black powder, on a flat surface so that it will not move. Check to make sure that the card will hold the entire transferred print. Attach the edge of the tape that does not contain any of the transferred print onto the edge of the card and roll the entire length of the tape onto the card (Figure 10.20). Instead of cards, your agency may use transparent plastic sheets to hold the transferred prints.

It is a good idea to draw a picture of the item of evidence and then mark it with the letter "X" to indicate where on the evidence the print was taken from. In the case of a window that was the point of entry,

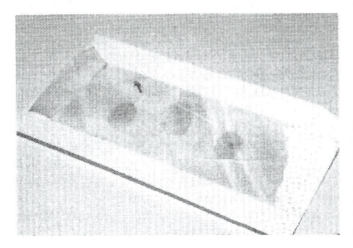

Figure 10.21 Once the lift is completed, fill out the other side of the card with a detailed description of where the print was obtained as shown in Figure 10.25.

measure the window and add those measurements to the diagram (Figure 10.21).

There will be times that when you place the print on the card, it appears to be nothing more than a black blob. However, there is still hope. Depending on the residue of the print or the amount of powder you applied, the print could be over developed. It is now time to do a multiple lift. This means lifting the same print again. To do this, begin by dusting the print as described above without adding any more powder to the brush. Watch carefully for the development of fingerprint ridges. Repeat the steps to lift and label the print. It is a good idea to put multiple lifts on the same card so they are not mistaken for another suspected fingerprint. Make sure that you write "Multiple Lift" on the card. It's also recommended that you label each tape lift with a number corresponding to the number of lift it was.

ROLLING THE EXEMPLAR, OR "ELIMINATION," PRINT

When you find fingerprints and other prints at the crime scene, your objective is to identify who put them there. Although you may actually fingerprint the perpetrator, you will be rolling prints on everyone who possibly left prints at the crime scene, which will include victims, witnesses, guests, and other people who had access to the premises. The fingerprint technician in the lab will check the prints found at the scene with prints on file of your colleagues who may have touched something during the investigation. The purpose of the elimination printing process is to take innocent persons off the list of possible suspects in the case. In the process, it is not unusual that at least one of them cannot be eliminated, and that person turns out to be a suspect.

Traditionally your department will have a special setup for fingerprinting people. On the counter will be a glass plane that you will coat with a thin layer of printers' ink, and there will be a device to hold the fingerprint cards in place. More modern facilities will use an inkless automated fingerprint identification system such as "Live-Scan" to capture these fingerprints. In the field, you will have inkpads and a portable fingerprinting kit with a flat surface and holder for the fingerprint cards. The fingerprint cards will be printed with spaces designating all ten digits and at the bottom of the cards will be spaces for the thumbs separately and all four fingers together. If you do not have printed fingerprint cards, plain cards will do. All you have to do is label each digit that you print.

Place the inkpad and cardholder on a table or other flat surface at about elbow height. Direct the subject to stand behind and slightly to your right with his or her right hand extended so that you can use your left hand for rolling the fingers separately on the ink pad and then onto the card in sequence (Figure 10.22). With your right hand, straighten out each finger as you ink and roll it, and fold the other fingers inward toward the palm out of the way (Figure 10.23). Direct the subject to relax and to let you guide the hands and fingers as you go through the procedure. An uncooperative subject or one with arthritis will be difficult to print. Do not stop the procedure until you have a complete set of legible prints. After you complete the individual thumbs and fingers, there are spaces for each thumb and all four fingers of each hand. You do not roll these. Press the thumbs one at a time onto the inkpad and then onto the card. When you simultaneously print all four fingers of each hand, place them flat onto the inkpad, and then guide them onto the card so that all four fingers lie flat on the card. You may have to turn the hand slightly so that the little finger will also print the card.

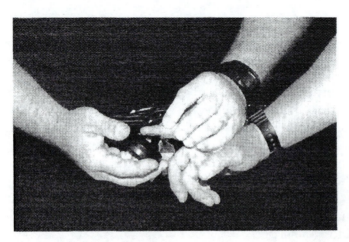

Figure 10.22 Using a pocket inker, apply a thin layer of black ink to the entire surface of the subject's finger.

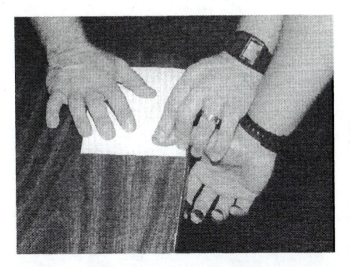

Figure 10.23 Start with the right thumb and work your way down to the little finger. Make sure to roll the print to get as much of the fingerprint detail as possible onto the card.

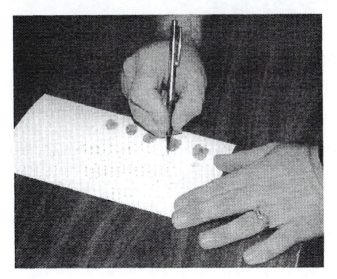

Figure 10.24 Label the fingers 1 through 10 starting with the right thumb as number 1 to the right little finger as number 5 and then the left thumb as number 6 to the left little finger as number 10.

When you roll each thumb and finger separately, be sure to ink the entire digit by rolling the entire friction ridge surface, about 180 degrees. The key is to practice so that you use just the right amount of ink and pressure to ink the digits without filling the spaces between the ridges with ink. Then use the same amount of pressure as you place each digit onto the card, and you will make a legible print. If you accidentally smudge a print, start again until all prints are clear and legible. If a digit is missing, write in "missing" in the space where the missing digit would have been printed. Fill out the front and back of the card (Figures 10.24 and 10.25).

Figure 10.25   Fill out the back of the card with the subject's name, case number, date, and time, as well as your name and badge number.

PALM AND FOOTPRINTS

Select a card or sheet of paper large enough to hold the entire impression. Ink the entire surface of the foot or palm by rolling the ink into the surface with a roller, or use an even pressure on the foot or palm while applying the ink and again while printing the impression onto the card or paper. You can also use this procedure for making impressions of shoes or socks. Instruct the person to wear the item while you apply the ink, and then have him or her step evenly onto the paper to print the impression. Be sure to have the subject remove the inked footwear after making the imprint so that you can avoid having ink all over the place.

PRINTING DECEASED OR UNCONSCIOUS PERSONS

The fingerprint technician will handle these procedures in the hospital or the morgue using a field kit. Decomposed bodies may actually require removing the fingers and soaking in a hardening solution before trying to roll the prints. If rigor mortis is present, the rigor may be broken only after the coroner or medical examiner has established the time of death.

Fingerprint Success Story

A woman was approached by a strange man who gave her a note that read: "READ CAREFULLY. We are going to an ATM machine and make a cash withdrawal. If you cooperate, you will not get hurt. Resist and you WILL become a statistic! Do as you are told and you will be on your way in about 10–15 minutes." The suspect then took the woman to an empty business office where he raped and sodomized her. The suspect then took the victim back to her car and left the note behind.

The crime scene investigator properly collected and packaged the evidence. The note was later processed with ninhydrin. As a result of the processing, latent prints were developed all over the note. Six of those fingerprints were searched through CAL-ID, which is a California-based automated fingerprint system housed in Sacramento. The search revealed a possible "hit" on five or six fingerprints in the file. An original copy of the suspect's ten prints was then ordered. That set was originally a set of applicant prints taken for a reserve officer application in 1976. Since then, the suspect had no other prints taken or arrest record. A side-by-side comparison was then made between the known inked impressions of the suspect's ten print card and the latent prints developed on the note. As a result of that comparison, 19 fingerprints were identified on the note as belonging to the suspect. The victim later made a positive identification, the suspect ended up pleading guilty, and he received a 35-year prison sentence.

SUMMARY

Fingerprints will continue to be used as a principal means of positively identifying people. For that reason it is imperative that you meticulously search every crime scene for prints left by the perpetrators, even though you will not find any at many of the scenes.

SUGGESTED OUTSIDE PROJECTS

1. Practice rolling exemplar prints of yourself or fellow students until you are able to produce clean and legible print cards.

2. Touch various types of host surfaces with your bare hands, dust for prints and lift them, then transfer them onto white cards as described in this chapter.

DISCUSSION QUESTIONS

1. When it comes to twins, why are fingerprints better for identification purposes?

2. What is the purpose for taking "elimination prints"?

3. What is a latent print, and how do you develop it for collection?

4. What is a plastic print?

5. Explain the procedure for dusting an area for prints.

6. Is it possible to identify a perpetrator with palm prints?

7. What parts of the body contain friction ridges?

8. Explain the procedure for rolling exemplar, or elimination prints.

9. Why should you photograph prints before lifting them?

10. What is the likelihood of two people in this country having identical fingerprints?

Chapter **Eleven**

Documenting the Crime:
Reports, Photographs, Videos, and Sketches

INTRODUCTION

Once you have left the crime scene and you are on your way back to the office with your evidence collection, you will probably never have a chance to go back and repeat the investigation. Even when you have the luxury of returning to an undisturbed scene for a second time to retrace your steps from beginning to end, picking up loose ends and discovering crucial evidence that you missed the first (or second or third) time, it will never be the same. There will be critics who will suggest that you went back to change evidence, or—worse yet—that you planted evidence.

Your reports, sketches, photographs, and videotapes should reinforce one another in reconstructing the entire investigation from beginning to end. Your reports will show the sequential developments of your role in the investigation process. If you could have the entire investigation videotaped from beginning to end, your written report should be almost like a transcript of the event. The photographs will show the overall scene, and then a series of photos will take the viewer on a tour through the scene, showing the dimensions and relationship of the evidence to the various other objects encountered during the investigation. Your sketch will serve as a blueprint for re-creation of the scene exactly as you found it upon your arrival. Together, all of these tools will guide all the other people involved in the investigation to a successful conclusion. Eventually they should aid in presentation of the evidence in court.

THE REPORT

In this chapter we will be dealing with your reports as a crime scene investigator. For more information on the overall reports, including the original crime report, interviewing victims and witnesses, and other follow-up reports, see *Police Field Operations*, sixth edition (Adams, Thomas F. 2004. *Police Field Operations*. 6th ed. Upper Saddle River, NJ: Prentice Hall. The report should be a step-by-step account of exactly who was involved in the search; what role each of the participants played in the investigation; what evidence was found, by whom; and what was done with each item of evidence from the moment it was picked up and prepared for transportation to the office or the laboratory, how it was handled enroute and by whom, and what time it was each step along the way.

For crime scene investigation, a voice-actuated microcassette recorder is probably the best piece of equipment to use for accurately recording the notes that you will later put in written form at the office. A notebook or clipboard and pen will get in the way when you are taking photographs and collecting and packaging evidence. You can put the recorder in a shirt pocket or hang it around your neck. You should record a running dialogue, documenting what you are doing, what you and your colleagues find, what you do not find, including your observations of other people at the scene, what they are saying, and generally every part of your investigation as it moves along.

Begin your report by entering all of the identifying data about yourself and your colleagues. If this is a standardized report form supplied by your department, it will have spaces for filling in all the essential information. Date and time of the crime, time of your arrival and departure, classification of the crime, and other essential data are recorded. You should also describe the lighting and weather conditions, the temperature, and any other information relevant to the case. You may be required by your department to start off your report with a brief summary of your investigation followed by an itemized list of evidence. Actually, this is a good practice, because it gives the prosecutor a thumbnail sketch of the status of the investigation and an idea of how to proceed with the prosecution. Follow-up investigators and supervisors may read the entire report again.

Record your first observations of the overall scene upon your arrival, the names and specific duty assignments of other officers at the scene, and especially the exact location and description of the property. An example might be: "A wood frame two-story house with an attached two-car garage in the center of a one-acre lot on the southwest corner of Sixteenth and Spruce." An example of a business address might be: "Suite 318, a six-room suite taking up the entire south half the third floor in an eight-story concrete and brick office building located approximately midblock on the north side of Chatway Street, address 1353." List names or description of people milling about the scene, and indicate whether the crime scene has been defined by barricades or warning tape or by officers protecting the scene from contamination.

Record everything you see, hear, taste, feel, and smell. Although many of those sensory experiences will not be considered of any evidentiary value, they may be useful to the officer assigned to the initial investigation or the follow-up investigators. Working on your theory of transference, record also what you do not find that one would normally expect to find. For example, one would expect to find fingerprints in a room occupied by people, but your search yields absolutely none, indicating that someone must have wiped them clean. You may see several nails or hooks on a wall with nothing hanging from them, or a knife rack missing a knife that you do not find anywhere on the premises. Your tour guide may point out to you the presence of certain tools or other items that were not in place before the crime, such as a screwdriver that does not belong to the occupant of the house, which is an example of transference.

The Search

Describe the room or area that you searched, its dimensions and general appearance, and who did the searching. Instead of stating something like "the undersigned searched . . ." or "officers searched . . ." or "Officer Villis and I searched the entire scene," record exactly what Officer Villis searched and what you searched. When something is found, report who found it and where, describing its condition and location. If a witness finds an item and turns it over to you, say so, and be sure to get the name of the witness and where you might find him or her later. It will not go over well in court if you say something like "it was found" or "an unknown person handed me the item and he said he found it on the living room floor next to the sofa." In the infamous O. J. Simpson case, criminalist Dennis Fung of the LAPD Crime Lab testified, "I collected the samples," when actually it was not he, but his junior partner who collected the samples. Sometimes an officer may erroneously say, "An item of evidence was found." "Who found what?" the judge will demand. Such errors ruin your credibility.

Evidence

Describe each item of evidence as thoroughly as you can, including its appearance and condition, such as "wet stains which appeared to be blood" or "bloodstains on the bedsheet covering the bed in the master bedroom where the victim stated the rape took place." If you state that the stains were blood, then add a statement as to how you determined it was blood if there might be any doubt, such as by a benzedine test. Otherwise your statement should be that the stains *appeared* to be blood. If you find shoe prints in a mud puddle and you drain the water as to make a cast of the impression, report that you drained the water and how you did it. Then describe the procedure you went through to photograph the impression and make a cast of the print.

Be precise in your report as to exactly who found the evidence, who made the cast, who collected the evidence and how, who packaged the evidence and how, and any other information to document the evidence collection procedure completely. After the evidence was packaged, your report should then continue with the journey of that evidence to its final destination in the lab or evidence locker. You must deal with each item of evidence in this same careful manner with great attention to detail. The integrity of your investigation and reports depends on it.

Sequence

The sequence of your report should parallel the sequence of your investigation. You are taking the reader on a tour through the crime scene in the same sequence as when you went through it. The principal crime report prepared by the officer originally assigned to the case may be laid out to show how the crime is likely to have taken place with a hypothetical sequence, but your report should reflect the sequence of your investigation. Later, when you are putting your notes together or prepare your report, you will also prepare a summary statement to explain everything you did at the scene, such as collection of so many items of evidence, casting tool marks, sketching the scene, taking 14 Polaroid photos, videotaping the scene, and taking 87 photographs.

Next, your list of evidence should be laid out so that the other people have a complete list of evidence at their fingertips. For example, your evidence list should start like this:

1. Latent fingerprints found in living room, #5, 9, 14.

2. Man's white shirt and light blue pants found on floor in master bedroom saturated with what appears to be dried blood, #27, 28 (sizes and brands, if indicated).

3. Plaster casts of two shoe prints found in the mud below and outside the front window on the northwest side of the house, the point of entry; both prints appear to have been made by shoes of the same size #2, 3.

4. And so forth, listing all evidence.

The numbers should correspond with photograph numbers and also be located in your sketch. Describe each item so that it will not be confused with other evidence of a similar nature.

Chain of Custody

After you have listed all the items of evidence, present in your report an account of the journey and destination of each item. To save space and to assure accuracy, you may wish to include the numbers you have designated to each item in your summary. For example: "Items 37 through 42 and 64 through 110 were taken to the evidence lab for analysis and handed to criminalist Mr. P. Sorvino. All other items numbered as follows . . . were placed in the evidence room accepted and logged by B. Pearlman, supervisor of Evidence Custody." Some items may be sent directly to laboratories out of state, such as the FBI and Cell-Mark. Report who sent the packages and by what means, such as Federal Express, and when you receive the return receipt or verification of receipt, report the name of the persons who signed for the objects at those labs.

Corpus Delicti

The primary officer assigned to investigate the crime is responsible for explaining all of the elements of the *corpus delicti* that can be proven by testimony and evidence to justify the crime report. Your crime scene investigation report should demonstrate that all the evidence essential to the *corpus delicti* has been collected in accordance with the existing statutes, case law, and the Constitution. A perpetrator who breaks into a building and is caught before he or she can steal anything is still guilty of burglary is some states, but because there is no evidence of the perpetrator actually stealing or committing a felony, the prosecutor may decline to prosecute for anything other than misdemeanor vandalism or trespassing. The basis for rejection is that without evidence of more than mere entry, a jury would probably not find the defendant guilty of the more serious felony. Sometimes the more serious crime has been committed, but sloppy or incomplete investigations fail to produce the evidence necessary to sustain the charges. Be careful that you do not fall into the "sloppy" or "incomplete" categories.

Reporting Your Photographs

When you took photographs, you numbered or lettered them sequentially, or used some other method to separate them from items of evidence. List the photos in sequence and describe what each one is expected to depict. Your report should also include a statement that your sketch, if you made one, includes a symbol and number (or letter) representing where the camera was placed and in what direction it was aimed. You should briefly describe the type of camera that you used, but because you do not intend to represent yourself as an expert, do not go into detail about film and lens and other matters that you are not expected to know. All you have to do is testify that you took the pictures and that they represent the scene you saw in person. If you are a photo expert, be prepared to spend a lot of your time under cross-examination in an effort to discredit you by insinuating what you might have done in the darkroom to make the photos show what you wanted to show. Even if you are an expert, we suggest that you don't supply information unless the prosecutor asks for it.

FACCCT

The California Commission on Peace Officer Standards and Training uses the acronym FACCCT when teaching report writing to police academy students. This easy to remember system helps ensure that all relevant information is included in the report. It stands for the following:

Factual: Each report must be an objective accounting of the relevant facts.

Accurate: There must be no inconsistencies or discrepancies between what took place and what is documented in the officer's report.

Clear: There should be no doubt or confusion on the part of the reader as to what the officer is reporting.

Concise: Reports should be brief and yet contain all the relevant information the users will need to do their jobs.

Complete: The reader should be able to identify the what, when, where, who, how and why regarding the event or incident based on the information provided.

Timely: Evidence can be lost, suspects or witnesses may disappear, and the support and good will of the community can be lost if action toward resolving a case is delayed.

Bear in mind that when you submit your report, it becomes memorialized for decades to come and is going to be reviewed by literally dozens of people, including the people who evaluate your work, investigators, prosecuting attorneys, defense attorneys, judges, news reporters, involved parties, and a myriad of other people. Your whole department is going to be judged on the work that you do and the reports that you write.

Sketches

If you or another officer draw one or more sketches, include that information in your report. You will probably be the one to draw the rough sketch, and a draftsperson or architect from the public works or city engineer's office may later prepare a detailed drawing. In your report, be sure to describe how the sketch ties in with the photographs and other items of evidence. Make certain that all the numbers and letters match so that when you refer to evidence number 34 it is not confused with a photograph number 34.

Statements of Others

As we said earlier in this chapter, your *primary* role is to investigate the crime scene and to usually leave questioning witnesses and victims to the primary officer on the case. However, while you are doing your work, if you overhear conversations between witnesses or suspects, or if the victim talks with you about the crime, be sure to prepare a supplemental report for the follow-up investigators that covers all the information you gleaned from the conversations. Do not take it for granted that another officer will get the same information. To include information such as this in your crime scene report would dilute the value of the CSI report.

PHOTOGRAPHING THE SCENE

Keep an accurate log of all photographs you take and keep a separate numbering system for each camera you use, such as 35mm, SLR, Polaroid, digital, fingerprint, and any others. Whenever you take a photograph, place a symbol in your sketch at the location from which you took each picture and the compass direction you aimed the camera. In your photo log, describe what it is that the photo is expected to depict (Figure 11.1 and Figure 11.2). When you eventually have the photos developed and arranged in sequence, it is possible that some of them will come out unclearly, not in focus, or are in some other way unacceptable to present in court as evidence. Do not discard those. Include them along with the others. When asked by the follow-up investigators, or the prosecutor, or even the defense attorneys during discovery proceedings or at the trial, you will have the bad photos to show and it will be obvious why you did not use them. If you discard the bad shots, someone may say that you just destroyed those photos that did not help your case. A rule of evidence is that evidence suppressed is presumed to have been suppressed for a reason, the reason being that perhaps it helps the other side, in this case, the defense. Let the other side see for itself that what you did was simply take a bad picture.

Figure 11.1   Numbered placards are used to identify pieces of evidence within the crime scene.

Figure 11.2   Mid-range photographs are important to identify an item of evidence.

People tend to be visual learners. The ability to look at an image and comprehend the severity of an injury or the complexity of a scene can be greatly enhanced through the use of photographs. Picture this. You have been called to the scene of a suicide at a residence. Upon arriving, you grab your camera, notepad, and latex gloves, and an officer directs you to the master bedroom of the subject's residence.

The first photograph you take is an overall view from the doorway looking south into the bedroom. The room is 13' X 13' with white walls and light gray carpet. Along the east wall is a dresser made of light maple wood and a mirror attached to the top. There are miscellaneous items such as a change sorter, a few pictures in frames, and a pair of glasses. To the right, or south, of the dresser is a large closet with mirrored doors. Continuing around the room along the south wall is a window covered with white miniblinds and a muslin material drape tied back to the left side held above by a metal rod with spiral shaped decorative ends. To the right of the window is a nightstand, which is also made of a light maple wood with two drawers. On top of the nightstand is a white clock radio, a hardback copy of the book, "The Testament" and a contemporary-looking table lamp with a chrome base, wooden stand, and white shade. Adjacent to the nightstand is a queen size mission-style bed made of light maple wood. The bed is made and has an off-white comforter on top. There are two full size pillows leaning up against the headboard and three square, red, white and blue accent pillows in front of that. Above the bed is a large photograph of a baby in a pumpkin in a light-colored wood frame with a white mat.

The victim is in a seated position on the floor with his back against the bed facing the mirror. His legs are extended out in front of him. His left hand is draped down his left side while his right hand is in his lap with what appears to be a Smith & Wesson stainless steel revolver with wooden grips. The victim's head slumps forward and there appears to be blood coming from his mouth. Upon close examination, the victim's right index finger is still on the trigger of the weapon. The victim is dressed in blue denim shorts, a dark blue t-shirt and white "Nike Air" high top shoes.

Now close your eyes and imagine what this scene looks like from the description given above. Once you have a good mental image of what this scene looks like, take a look at the real photograph taken from this crime scene (Figure 11.3). Does your mental image accurately depict what you see in the photograph? Is there anything else that you see that was not described before?

We have all heard the expression that a picture is worth a thousand words. This is a prime example of why photographs and video are so important to the crime scene investigator. Often times, words alone cannot adequately convey the seriousness or totality of a crime scene, evidence or victims' injuries. Photographs are also easy to understand, especially when dealing with people or who are illiterate, disabled, or not old enough to read. But by showing a juror, for example, a photograph, they instantly understand what it is that you are talking about. Thus, no other medium can capture a moment in time as well as the photograph.

Figure 11.3 The photo described in the report.

PHOTOGRAPHY

<u>Getting Back to the Basics</u>

Understanding how valuable a photograph can be in a case requires that the crime scene investigator properly capture that image as it appeared at the time the photograph was taken. Oftentimes while on the stand in court, the police officer or crime scene investigator will be asked if a picture truly and accurately depicts the scene as it appeared when he or she took the photograph. The utmost care must be taken so that the image is in focus, properly exposed and composed so that the item being photographed does not distort the facts.

While many of today's cameras work nearly flawlessly in the "automatic" mode for general photography needs, the crime scene investigator must understand the basics so that he or she is able to preserve the evidence under a variety of abnormal conditions. Examples of such conditions might include close-up photography, night-time or low light photography, aerial photography, and photography in inclement conditions, such as rain or snow,

Figure 11.4   SLR camera.

just to name a few. Many books have been written solely on the topic of forensic photography. This chapter will discuss some of the basics of photography while focusing attention on situations you may encounter in the field.

The Camera

For the most part, many departments rely on the 35mm single lens reflex, or SLR, camera (Figure 11.4). These cameras allow for manual or automatic control over settings such as exposure and focus. They also allow the user to interchange lenses to best suit their needs. For the purposes of this text, we will be referring to features commonly found on this type of camera. These features are also found on other cameras like a medium format or digital camera.

The Lens

The ability to interchange lenses or use a zoom lens is a powerful tool. Lenses are generally labeled by their focal length in millimeters. This refers to the lens's magnification and angle of view. The focal length of a lens is measured from the center of the first element in the lens to the point at which the image is focused.

Fixed focal lenses are lenses that are set to one focal length. The most common is the 50mm, which gives the viewer a true-to-life view of what the scene actually looks like with the human eye. Generally a 40-55mm lens is considered a standard or normal lens. Wide-angle lenses are generally anything less that 40mm. This type of lens is invaluable when you want to show a large area. For crime scene photography, this is best suited for overall photos in tight spaces such as a bedroom or bathroom. But be aware that wide angle lenses can distort the relative distance between objects. Telephoto lenses are typically any lens with a focal length of more than 70mm. These are ideal for focusing attention on a distant object. However, be forewarned that when using a telephoto lens, camera shake or blurring can occur when slow shutter speeds are used.

Zoom lenses are ideal for most uses since they allow a photographer to go from a wide-angle lens to a telephoto lens with just a twist of the barrel. Imagine being in the doorway of our crime scene described in the beginning of this chapter. With a 28–105mm lens, you could shoot a wide angle or overall shot with the lens set at the 28mm and then shoot a close-up shot of the gun by turning the lens to the 105mm setting, all from the same position.

There are two or three controls found on almost any lens. First and foremost is the focusing ring. Your ability to take a sharp, focused photograph is critical in preserving evidence. When you focus on an object in the foreground, the background will become blurred or out of focus, or vice versa. The area that is in focus is referred to as the depth of field. The depth of field is controlled by two factors. First is the type of lens being used. A wide-angle lens will have a greater depth of field than a telephoto lens. Second, the aperture has a direct correlation with the amount of depth of field your image will have. The general rule of thumb is that the smaller the aperture, the greater the depth of field. When focusing on an object, the depth of field is generally carried about one third in front of the object and two thirds behind it. This can be an important rule to remember while focusing on a long skid mark or blood trail.

Inside the lens is an adjustable opening called the aperture. This is the next control typically found on the lens. Some modern cameras have the aperture controls on the camera body instead of on the lens. The aperture works like the iris in your eye by opening and closing to allow more or less light to pass through. The position or size of the aperture is measured in units known as f-stops. The larger the f-stop number, the smaller the opening in the aperture. While this may sound backwards, think of the f-stop as a fraction. Then you will agree that 1/4 is larger than 1/16, thus f4 is a larger aperture opening than f16. While lenses vary, a typical range of f-stops will be 2.8, 4, 5.6, 8, 11, 16, 22, and 32. These are referred to as full stops. Each full f-stop lets either twice as much light or half as much light through the lens depending on which way you go. Keep in mind that when you are focusing through the lens, the aperture is typically wide open, thus giving you the least depth of field. The camera does this to allow the most light

Figure 11.5   f5.6 gives a shallow depth of field.

Figure 11.6   Depth of field is improved at f22.

through the lens to help you view the image for composition and focusing. However, when you take your photograph, the aperture may close down, giving you a greater depth of field than what you saw through the lens. Some cameras come equipped with a "depth of field preview" button. When you press this button, the aperture will close down to the f-stop you set, thus showing you what the depth of field will be in the final image (Figure 11.5 and Figure 11.6).

The Shutter

The shutter controls the amount of time that the camera allows light to pass through the lens and strike the film. Shutter speeds can vary from as fast as 1/8000th of a second to minutes or hours. The shutter speed and aperture work together to properly expose the film with just the right amount of light for any given film speed. Shutter speed is also critical for stopping motion in moving subjects.

A good rule of thumb for taking a sharp photo is to make sure that your shutter speed is not too slow. If it is, camera shake will occur, causing blurred images. To remedy this, you can either mount the camera to a tripod or use a faster shutter speed. To determine if your shutter speed is fast enough to avoid camera shake, take the focal length your lens is set at and turn it into a fraction. For example, if you are using a 50mm lens, the shutter equivalent should be 1/50 or faster. Since there is no 1/50th shutter speed, round up to 1/60th. Regardless of what your shutter speed is, it is crucial that you use two hands and hold the camera securely while slowly depressing the shutter release when taking a photograph.

For crime scene photography, the ability to "drag" the shutter, or use long exposures like 15 seconds gives you the ability to make nighttime crime scenes look like daylight or more true to what your eye sees. Figure 11.7 and Figure 11.8 are examples of photographs taken in a carport. The photo in Figure 11.7 is taken using the camera's electronic flash, and the photo in Figure 11.8 is taken without a flash, but instead, the camera is mounted to a tripod and exposed for approximately 15 seconds at f5.6. While both images are properly exposed, the one taken using only the flash shows detail out to about 15 feet. The photo taken using a longer exposure and a tripod gives the viewer a more realistic view of what the scene looked like the night of

Figure 11.7 Photo taken with electronic flash.

Figure 11.8 Photo taken without a flash but with 15 second exposure.

the crime. While it may take longer to set up a tripod and shoot photos this way, you can see the value of knowing how to properly expose an image to more accurately document the crime scene.

Exposure

Exposure refers to giving the film enough light for the correct amount of time to properly record the image. This is controlled by three factors. As we have already discussed, the aperture and shutter control how much light strikes the film and for how long. The third factor is the film speed. This is measured by an ISO or ASA number, which is labeled on the film packaging. With respect to this, the higher the ISO rating, the more sensitive the film is to light. For photographs taken outdoors in bright sun, ISO 100 is the best choice. For low light conditions or when you want to stop action with a fast shutter speed, choose ISO 800 or faster. ISO 400 speed film is a good all-around speed film for both outdoor and flash photography.

Most cameras have a built-in light meter that automatically sets the exposure. This type of light meter is called a reflective meter because it measures light that reflects off of the subject and passes through the lens. The camera then tries to set the scene to a standard of 18 percent gray. In most cases this is appropriate, but given an arson scene where everything is black, the automatic setting will overexpose the scene.

When shooting outdoors on a bright sunny day, keep this rule in mind. It is called the f16 rule. The rule is that under sunny conditions if you set the cameras aperture at f16 and the shutter speed to a setting that closely resembles the film speed, you will get a proper exposure. For example, if you're shooting 100 ISO film on a bright sunny day, a proper exposure would be f16 at $1/125^{th}$ of a second. For ISO 400, a proper setting would be f16 at $1/500^{th}$ of a second. This is a good rule to know in the event that your camera is fooled by what the meter in the camera is reading.

Aside from the automatic or program mode setting on the camera, there are three other settings commonly found on cameras today. One is the aperture priority mode. This setting allows the photographer to set the desired aperture while the cameras light meter will then select the proper shutter speed. This feature is helpful when trying to expand your depth of field by selecting a specific aperture. The other setting is the shutter priority mode. This allows the photographer to set the appropriate shutter speed while the camera sets the corresponding aperture based on the light meter's reading. Last but certainly not least is the fully manual mode. This setting allows the photographer to set the aperture and shutter speeds independent of each other. The camera's light meter will oftentimes still try and suggest what it thinks is the proper exposure though. However, when photographing evidence in the lab, the camera's light meter is unaware of other studio flashes you have synched to the camera. In such a situation, the photographer will need to rely on a handheld meter to measure the proper exposure.

Film

While we have already discussed what the ISO or ASA numbers mean in relation to their sensitivity to light, there are other factors that must be taken into consideration when selecting film for crime scene investigation. Slower films may have drawbacks in low light situations, but they generally yield a higher quality image. This is because slower films are able to capture better color saturation and tonal range, and they have a tighter grain pattern to them which results in a sharper more true to life image. Faster films sacrifice color and show more grain in order to capture less light.

Most crime scene photography is shot with color negative film. This type of film is usually developed with a standard C-41 process and gives a photographic negative, or opposite, of the true colors. When the negative is then printed onto photographic paper, the result is a color positive print like the original subject. If contrast and detail is critical, black and white negative film should be used. Black and white photography results in images with a much higher contrast range, which results in greater detail. Almost all fingerprint, footprint, firearm and tire mark evidence is photographed in black and white. The black and white images show critical details and individual characteristics far better than color film.

But let us not forget about the cameras that use pixels instead of grain to record images electronically. We are talking about digital imaging. And while some "die hards" still contend that conventional film is the only way to go, digital imaging is catching up, and, in some respects, has surpassed, sliver-based films. The debate between these two mediums alone could span a chapter or a book for that matter, but for the purposes of this text, we will highlight a few of its advantages.

- Digital photography is safer to the environment, since there are no chemicals used to develop the images. There may be chemicals and inks used to print them, though.

- Digital imaging is almost instantaneous. The need for instant film has been almost completely eliminated. This is a huge cost savings, considering instant film costs over one dollar per image.

- The digital format lets you email an image of a fingerprint from the crime scene back to the lab for a search in the automated fingerprint identification system.

- Digital images can be quickly imported to image editing software for enhancement or dissemination to others via email.

- High mega-pixel image cameras yield photographic prints equal in quality to conventional film.

There are a few downsides to digital imaging that must also be addressed. The most common argument against digital imaging is that the images can be manipulated on a computer. While this statement is true, the same can be said for conventional film. For it is just as easy to scan a piece of film and alter it. Any image can then be printed out or recorded back to conventional film without detection. This is where chain of custody and the use of a digital imaging management system and protocol comes into effect. If your department wants to use digital imaging at crime scenes, then there must be safeguards in place to assure that an unaltered or archived image taken at the scene is kept on record and not allowed to be enhanced, altered, or manipulated. Copies of these images may be enhanced depending on the circumstances. This is a very controversial subject in the field today. But digital imaging has been accepted by the courts.

What to Photograph

Obviously, each crime scene is different and will require a modified approach, depending on time of day, weather conditions, available light, equipment on hand, type of crime, and how much time you have to conduct the investigation. The crime may be indoors or outdoors or both. It may be a traffic collision, an arson, a robbery, a burglary, a criminal homicide, or any of a number of crimes against persons or property. Following are a few general rules for photographing most crime scenes.

1. Take orientation shots of the location where the event occurred. When you watch a television show or movie, you first see a view of the outside of the building before you see the scene inside the apartment, or the outside of the precinct station before the scene shifts to the detective division office on the second floor. In CSI photos, these "orientation shots" show the viewer the general location of the crime, starting with the street signs at the intersection, then the view from the corner down the street to focus on the house or building where the crime took place. Next,

photograph the front of the building, the entrance, the point of entry, if different than the customary method of entry, the hallway leading to the room or rooms where the actual crime occurred, and a view of each room from the door looking in.

2. Introduce the viewer to each room or area where the crime took place. Take the first picture from the doorway, then take pictures from each compass point, moving in a clockwise course. In your sketch, show the location of the camera, sequence of photographs, and direction the camera was pointed for each photo. While you are rotating around the room and taking general overview shots and significant objects are in the picture, such as a victim's body or a broken window, move in on the object and take another picture before you move on to the next location. If you are using a camcorder for your orientation tour, zoom in and back out as you focus on crucial objects to show the viewer approximately where the object is located in relationship to the rest of the room.

3. Take close-up shots of each item of evidence in place as you find it and before touching or attempting to remove it (Figure 11.9). If you are working with a partner, one of you should take the photos while the other leads the search and identifies each object as it is found and photographed. You should decide beforehand how you are going to divide the workload, including making the photo log. If you search a second time, reverse roles that one of you may find something that the other one may have overlooked.

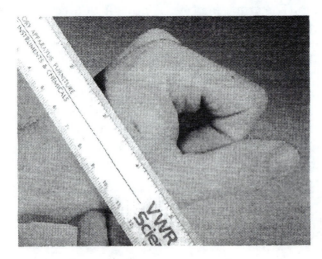

Figure 11.9 Close-up photographs should always be taken with a scale.

4. After you have completed photographing everything that you intended to, go back and retrace your steps. Take additional photos of items that you consider extremely important, perhaps from a different angle or with a different f-stop, shutter speed, and lighting. Your objective is to get clear, high-contrast photos that show each item of evidence in detail. You are not aiming for portraits, but you want to depict the scene and the objects in it exactly as they appear to the naked eye while you are taking the photos. This second time around, if you have the time, you may see objects differently than you did the first time, perhaps because of ambient lighting or a serial number on an object that you did not see from a different angle (Figure 11.10). Be sure to catalog these photos to correspond with the photos of the same scene or object the first time around. For example, photo 67 and 68 may be of the same piece of evidence as photos 34 and 35, but from a new perspective. All four of those photos may enhance your presentation of the case better than just the first two photos by themselves.

5. After you have finished your crime scene investigation and packaged all the evidence for transportation back to the office, take a few additional shots of the other investigators and bystanders, perhaps using just a snapshot camera, to help you later remember the faces you saw while you were working at the scene. You may need to go back and get elimination fingerprints and shoe prints of some of those people, so that their prints may be separated from those of the perpetrator,

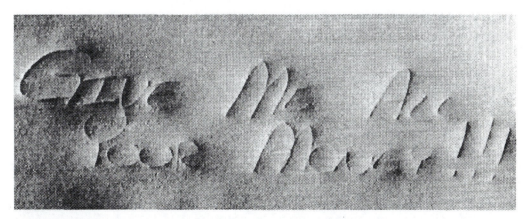

Figure 11.10   Oblique lighting across this blank piece of paper reveals what was written on the paper above it in a notepad.

who might have returned to the scene to check up and see how the investigation was going. Sometimes a review of photos from several crime scenes may show one or two faces that seem to be at every burglary you investigate. It could be mere coincidence, or you might have a picture of the perpetrator.

Basic Guidelines for Taking Photographs

Whenever you take close-up photos of evidence items, such as weapons, tools, prints, or other traces, place a ruler or evidence tag with a ruler printed along the edge of the tag. In the darkroom you or the person who develops the photos can adjust the image projected onto the print paper with another ruler in the darkroom so that the ruler in the photo and the ruler you place on the projected image are superimposed so that you will be able to develop the picture to show the actual size of the piece of evidence. This is known as a 1:1 (one-to-one) photo. This may be very critical, especially if you want to demonstrate that a tool was exactly three-quarters of an inch wide at the tip and the mark probably made by that tool is approximately three-quarters of an inch wide, allowing for the elasticity of the wood in which the impression was made.

When photographing charred or burned objects, remember to adjust the camera and the lighting to compensate for the absorption of light by the dark surface. Also, to get a profile shot of the surface of burned wood, shoe prints, or fingerprints, try taking a shot or two with the overhead lighting subdued, and use an oblique light that will make ridges and depressions in the material to look more like hills and valleys, illustrating the detail of the surface more graphically.

PRESENTATION OF PHOTOGRAPHS IN COURT

Bring with you all the photographs you took at the scene and also bring the negatives. You should be able to account for every single numbered shot that you took, although you may show only some of those photos. You must have them, however, for discovery purposes and to refute any claim that you did not bring photographs that were favorable to the defense. You and the prosecutor will go over which photos you should present and in what sequence. This will be very simple for you if you kept an accurate photo log. Sometimes the court will not allow certain gruesome or graphic photos of the victim because it tends to incite or inflame the jury, causing jury members to render a verdict based on a skewed emotional attitude rather than on the facts presented to them.

When you present the photographs while on the witness stand, your testimony should be about who took the pictures, when, and where, to lay the foundation. Then you will be asked if they fairly represent what you saw at the crime scene while taking the pictures. You may be asked to present the negatives to prove that you did not do anything in the development process to change the images. One reason why you do not want to represent yourself as an expert (unless the prosecutor insists that you do) is that experts can play tricks in the darkroom, such as removing a face from the picture, or superimposing the face of someone who was nowhere around when the photos were shot. A sharp defense attorney may sow the seed of doubt in the mind of at least one juror that someone falsified the evidence in some way. Testify honestly and thoroughly and let the attorneys fight it out.

Photography Success Story

A shootout erupted at a wedding reception. Many in the wedding party are gang members and took chase, shooting an innocent bystander whom they mistook for a shooter simply because he was running away and hid behind a car.

Later, during the investigation, photos were discovered of a member of the wedding party posing with a gun in his waistband with the wood grip clearly exposed. The photos had been taken just hours before the shooting at the reception. The gun was subsequently recovered during a warrant search, and ballistics matched the gun to the bullet recovered from the victim. Close examination of the gun showed unique individual characteristics visible in the wood grip. The photo also showed a great amount of detail because the photo was taken by an expert photographer.

The gun was then photographed under lighting conditions similar to those when the photos of the gang member carrying the weapon in his waistband. The two images were then merged using Adobe Photoshop a computerized imaging program. By overlaying the photo taken of the gun in the lab over the photo taken at the wedding, the individual characteristics were matched up. The wood grain pattern in the grip also matched, showing that the recovered gun was the same gun the gang member posed with just hours before at the reception. The use of photography and digital imaging aided greatly in putting the murder weapon in the possession of the suspect.

SKETCHING THE SCENE

Along with the photograph and the report, the sketch is the third in your trilogy of tools to take the observer back to the crime scene to see it as it presented itself to you. The sketch you will produce most frequently will be your *rough sketch*, which is the easiest to make. You may make this sketch in the field with a pen, graph paper (or regular unlined paper), and a ruler. You may have more sophisticated drawing instruments with you, but you will probably use them to prepare a more detailed sketch later in the office, after you have left the crime scene and deposited all of your evidence appropriately and while you are preparing your report.

Types of Sketches

1. *Locality sketch.* This is an overall view of the scene and its environs, including neighboring buildings, roads leading to the scene, and the location of the crime or collision in relationship to the surrounding landmarks. What you are doing here is drawing a map similar to one that you find on a college campus or in a large building that pinpoints the place where you are standing and is labeled, "You are here." In your sketch, use a star or arrow to pinpoint the exact location of the crime scene.

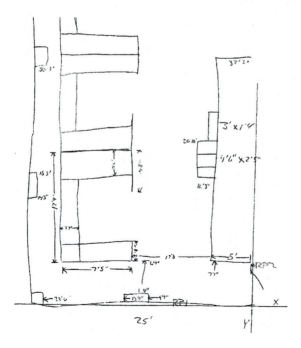

Figure 11.11 A rough sketch taken at a crime scene with the necessary measurements included.

2. *Grounds sketch.* Make a grounds sketch when your objective is to show the collision or crime scene in context with its general surroundings. A grounds sketch would show where the collision occurred, including the skid marks, the location where the vehicles were located when the drivers first knew the collision was going to take place (the "point of awareness"), the skid marks, the point of impact, and the final resting place of the vehicles. This sketch should also show the traffic controls, the streets, the nearest intersection, view obstructions, and lighting devices, all critical to the investigation. If the crime was committed outdoors, the grounds sketch would show the street or road, and other identifiable landmarks for reference, such as a tennis court, barn, or house, location of lights (if any), entrances to the area, driveways, pathways, or parking lots in the immediate vicinity of where the crime occurred.

3. *Building sketch.* This is similar to the grounds sketch, except that it is an interior view. For example, if a robbery occurred in a convenience market, you should sketch the entire building, indicating the location of the convenience market relative to the other business in the same building. The sketch should include the entire unit showing the main sales room where the crime took place and a general floor plan of the entire unit, including doors and windows.

4. *Location sketch.* The location sketch shows the total crime scene, as marked off with warning tapes or barricades, excluding the surrounding neighborhood as in the locality sketch. If an entire house is involved in a crime, such as a burglary where the perpetrators ransacked the entire house, this sketch will be the same as a building sketch, supplemented by one or more detailed sketches where the evidence is located.

5. *Detailed sketch.* This is a close-up view of the immediate scene by itself, such as the room or rooms where the actual crime took place. For this sketch, you are "zooming in" so that you can show the locations where evidence has been found and provide a blueprint for the reconstruction of the crime scene. When you draw a detailed sketch of one room at a time, you should consider drawing in the "cross-projection" mode. To do the cross-projection, draw the walls folded down as you would fold down the sides of box, giving the viewer a multidimensional

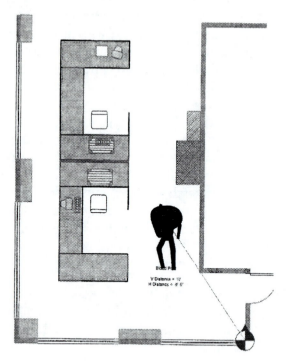

Figure 11.12 Final diagram using a computer-based crime scene diagram program.

view of the room by sketching evidence found on the floor and also critical evidence in the walls, such as bullet holes, doors and windows, pry marks, or broken glass. You are looking down from the ceiling, which makes it possible to present the sketch in three dimensions.

6. *Finished drawing.* This is done in the office, usually for courtroom presentation in more serious crimes. Usually a trained draftsperson prepares this with drafting equipment and computer, using your field sketch as the reference for the more finished product (Figure 11.12). In cases where drawings of this type are prepared, it is not unusual for the prosecutor also to have scale models of the scene prepared for presentation.

Basic Rules for Sketching

Whether you estimate dimensions in your sketch or measure them, in all cases you must indicate which way you do it. It is not wise to mix measurements by estimating some and actually measuring others. Measurements must be precise when measured, and the legend should state that they are exact. If you estimate measurements, be sure to put that in the legend as "all measurements are estimated." Even though you know for sure that your shoes are precisely eleven and a half inches long and you pace off 23 steps, you must state that all measurements are estimated and you would list the 23 paces as "approximately 22 feet."

Although a rough sketch will not be drawn to scale, it should be in proportion, so that there is less chance of distorted perception of the relative objects in the sketch. When you use a scale, try 1/2 inch = 1 foot for detailed sketches, or 1/4 inch = 1 foot for a large scene. Try 1/8 inch = 1 foot for location sketches or 1/2 inch = 10 feet for larger areas. Whatever scale you use, try to keep the sketch on one sheet of paper to accompany your reports. Later you may choose to prepare a finished drawing on posterboard for courtroom presentation, but large items are too cumbersome to place in file cabinets or to duplicate. You should also keep the sketch reasonably sized so that you may make transparencies for court presentation instead of using the larger boards.

1. *NORTH arrow.* In every sketch, you must include a NORTH arrow, or a symbol showing all four compass points, but the NORTH arrow is mandatory. It is best also to draw the sketch so that NORTH is at the top of the page. One of this book's authors got lost in Paris once because the map provided by the hotel had west at the top instead north, and there was no compass anywhere on the map. As you know, just because the house is situated on North Alpine does not mean that the street goes north to south. Use a compass and indicate true north in your sketch. Although many photographers do not follow the procedure, we suggest that you consider making a plywood or cardboard NORTH arrow to place in each scene you photograph.

2. *Title block or legend.* Either print it directly on your sketch or use a standardized card that you can attach securely to each sketch on which you print a least all of the following information: case number, date and time of the crime or collision, date and time the sketch is prepared, who prepared the sketch, including the person who took measurements (if measurements were taken). State the location of the event, including the street address (if any) and the exact location where it took place (tennis court, living room, intersection, other). Indicate whether the sketch is to scale or estimated and what the scale is. Use a numbering and lettering system for evidence and photo spots, and list all those items in the legend space.

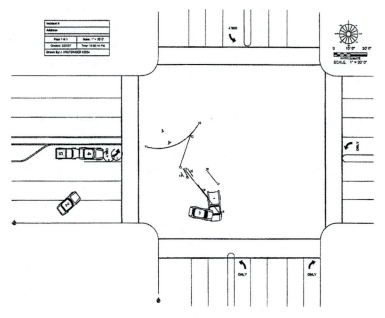

Figure 11.13   Traffic collision scene.

3. *Collision scene.* Show the exact point of impact and the skid marks of the vehicle(s). Measure the width of the streets and sketch them in proportion to other objects in the sketch (Figure 11.13). Locate and identify the lights, signals, and traffic signs, such as "Speed Limit," or "Stop," or "Yield." Name the streets and highways, locate and label vision obstructions that you observe, and list the type and condition of the road surface, such as "asphalt, wet from recent rain."

4. *Crime scene.* If the crime was committed in an open area, such as a public park or a front yard, show the locations where the parameter warning tapes or barricades were put up, familiar landmarks, and permanent objects at the location, such as trees and buildings. Be sure to sketch everything that appears to be related to the case.

   If the crime was committed inside a building, show the points of entry and exit, doors, windows, and large items of furniture and their relationship to each other and to the different items of evidence. Sketches of crimes against persons should show the location where the assault took place, as a discarded weapon might be nearby. Sketches of crimes against

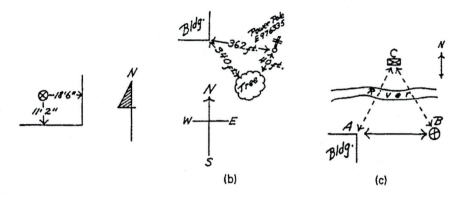

(b)   (c)

Figure 11.14 Measuring methods: (a) coordinates (b) polar coordinates (c) triangulation.

property should show locations of pry marks and other trace evidence. Be sure to draw your sketch so that the information coincides with the information in your report and the numbers and letters assigned to the evidence and photos.

5. *Locating methods.* There are five methods for sketching the locations of various items of evidence used for crime and collision scene sketches. They are (a) straight line, (b) diagonal baseline, (c) coordinate, (d) polar coordinate, and (e) triangulation. The straight line method speaks for itself, measuring from one object to another and recording the distance. See Figure 11.4. For the diagonal baseline method, measure from an imaginary line that stretches diagonally from one corner of the room to the opposite corner and the distance from that line to the object, such as a tool or weapon.

For the coordinate method, draw a line and measure the distance from one wall to the item of evidence, and a line from the object to the wall at a right angle from the first wall, such as the east wall, then the south wall. For the polar coordinate method, measure the distance from your object, such as a weapon, to a permanent fixture, such as a dishwasher (or a tree if outdoors), and another measurement from the evidence item to another large object that is not likely to be moved. For the triangulation method, draw a line from your evidence item to each of two permanent objects that are some distance apart. When you draw the lines to each stationary object from the third item you want to locate, it is possible to place the evidence in your sketch where the two lines from the permanent objects meet and cross each other.

SUMMARY

No matter how great a job you do searching for and collecting evidence, nobody will know what kind of a job you have done unless you prepare accurate and complete reports, take good photographs, and draw sketches that explain themselves. The visual presentation is as important as the report, as they each complement the other, and they serve as memory joggers and scene management tools. There may be times when you will overlook a very crucial piece of evidence while conducting the initial search. Then later when you are reviewing the photographs (and videotape if you were able to use a camcorder), you will see what you missed, and you may be able to retrieve it before it is destroyed or disappears.

A professional athlete is only as good as his or her last game, coupled with the statistics. Your statistics will be based on how well you use these three tools in recording your investigation of crime scenes: the *report*, the *photographs* and the *sketch*.

SUGGESTED OUTSIDE PROJECTS

1. Draw a sketch of an imaginary traffic collision scene involving two cars and a pickup truck with injuries involved. Draw a sketch of a burglary scene that appears to you to have been "rigged" by the "victim."

2. Take a 36-exposure roll of photos of various items that might be considered evidence. Arrange the lighting, the flash, and focus the camera so that the pictures come out clear and distinct.

3. Take at least a dozen photos with a digital camera and one dozen using traditional film. Compare the prints for clarity and quality, and make an oral presentation in class defending your choice of the better mode.

DISCUSSION QUESTIONS

1. What is the value of taking along a voice-actuated microcassette recorder while you are investigating a crime scene?

2. What is the advantage of videotaping the crime scene?

3. Do you believe first person or third person reporting is better?

4. What is the purpose of putting in your report what you do not find during your investigation?

5. For what reason should a crime report reflect the *corpus delicti* of a crime?

6. What is a "location shot"?

7. What is the purpose of changing f-stops on your camera?

8. Why would you use a Polaroid camera if you have a perfectly good 35mm SLR camera?

9. Which is best—film or digital?

10. Describe the sequence of photos you should take as you approach the crime scene.

11. What is the purpose of placing a ruler in close-up photos?

12. Do you think it is a good idea to put a north arrow in a sketch?

13. Should all sketches be drawn to scale? Why? or Why not?

14. Describe how you locate an object by triangulation.

15. Explain how you will present your photographs in court.

Chapter Twelve
The Crime Lab

INTRODUCTION

After you complete your job at the crime scene and take the evidence you have collected to the laboratory, the criminalists and other technicians go to work. One word you will seldom if ever hear from those unsung heroes is *can't*. A forensics laboratory, or crime lab, as we usually call it, is more like a research lab rather than a quality control lab, where minimum standards for certain products are maintained. What you will hear often is "Let's give it a try." New discoveries are made almost every day in crime labs around the world. For example, one of the most significant applications of DNA technology was done by an English doctor in a criminal case. In this chapter we will cover some of the miracles criminalists can work with those instruments. For more detailed information on the science of criminalistics, check the references at the end of the book for some excellent books by the experts.

THE MICROSCOPE

Without a doubt, this is probably the most valuable instrument in the lab. It was certainly one of the first, which gave scientists the magnification necessary to examine substances that are impossible to study with the naked eye. The magnification can be almost without bounds. For example, the scanning electron microscope (SEM) magnifies an object over 100,000 times, whereas the standard lab microscope is considerably less, but still quite effective for many analyses. With the standard microscope it is possible to identify substances such as marijuana seeds and particles, weave characteristics of cloth, patterns of different species of wood and grains, rocks, minerals, sand, and soil.

With the aid of the microscope, criminalists can determine the presence of sperm and bacteria in semen and blood and a person's blood type. They can identify materials, such as snagged clothing or traces of hair or blood, that adhere to a tool or weapon, or to a brush or shrub. They also can tell whether the substance is animal, vegetable, or mineral.

COMPARISON MICROSCOPE

The comparison microscope (or photomicrograph, Figure 12.1) is used to study the relative characteristics of bullets and the gun barrels they are believed to have been fired through. When the matching characteristics of the two are aligned, the expert will photograph the two magnified objects simultaneously so that the distinguishing characteristics that show the bullet probably traveled through that barrel. Handwriting exemplars can also be compared with the original writings, putting the images of the two side by side so that the expert can show their similarities to the investigators and eventually to the judge and/or jury at the trial.

BIOLOGICAL MISCROSCOPE

The biological microscope magnifies material in two stages. The image is first magnified, then a second lens magnifies it further for a closer examination. It is used by serologists for blood-typing and when searching for

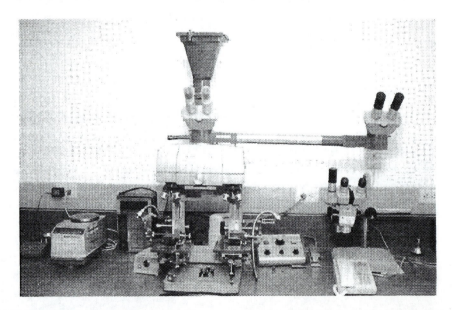

Figure 12.1   A comparison microscope with a 4 × 5 camera attached to the top.

spermatozoa in blood in rape and sexual abuse cases. The expert also uses this instrument to examine the medulla, cortex, and scale patterns of hairs. Another common use of the biological microscope is to test for various drugs, narcotics, and other controlled substances.

STEREOSCOPIC BINOCULAR MICROSCOPE

The stereoscopic binocular microscope is used for almost any type of microscopic examination. This instrument has a separate microscope for each eye, giving the criminalist a three-dimensional view of the material under the glass (Figure 12.2).

BALLISTICS EXPERT

The ballistics expert uses a comparison microscope to compare bullets that are found in shooting crimes with bullets that he or she test-fires in the laboratory to look for similarities in their rifling and other marks made while they passed through the gun barrel. The ballistics expert will also use the same kind of gun that was fired at a crime scene, load it with the same type of ammunition, and fire into a piece of meat with the fatty side out to

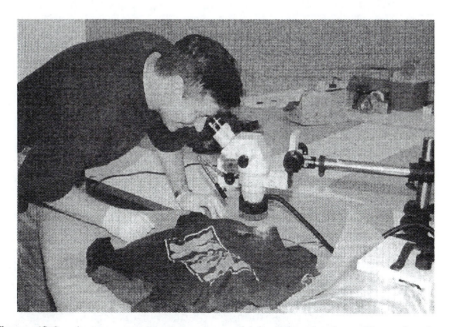

Figure 12.2 A stereoscopic microscope, which allows for three-dimensional viewing, is used here as small particles of lead are removed from around the hole in this homicide victim's clothing.

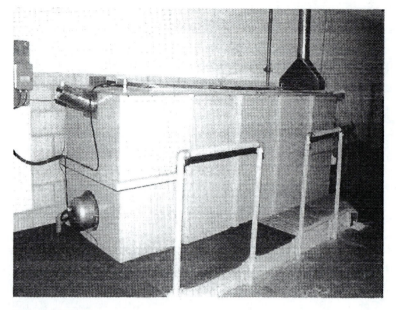

Figure 12.3a

approximate a human being shot. The expert shoots from different angles to determine the angle of the shooter to the victim and different distances to determine how far the shooter was from the victim. When the fired bullet leaves the barrel of the gun, small shavings of the bullet and other residue from the blast also fly out of the barrel. The shavings will make a pattern of particles called *tattooing*, which will be embedded on the clothing and skin of the victim. The pattern is smaller the closer the gun is to the victim at the time it is fired. The microscope is used to facilitate this test as well. See Figures 12.3a and 12.3b.

The ballistics expert also examines the hands and clothing of the suspected shooter for residue from the explosion and can compare what he or she finds with similar materials on the victim and on the gun.

GAS CHROMATOGRAPH

The gas chromatograph is used to identify the ingredients of liquid substances. The expert dilutes the liquid and injects it into the intake port of the instrument. With few exceptions, most compounds are different although they may contain the same ingredients. For example, there is enough difference between Texaco gasoline and Shell gasoline that samples of those brands can be compared with the suspect substance and identified as one

Figure 12.3b   Large water tanks like these are used to collect firearm-related evidence. Often five or six feet of water is enough to stop a bullet while maintaining the striations needed for comparison.

or the other gasoline product. An exception to this would be the independent gas station that buys surplus gasoline from whichever company it can get the best price, and its gas tanks may have a mixture of three or four different brands of gasoline.

The gas chromatograph scans over 400 different ions and weighs them, then prints out a graph with several different patterns of lines, each pattern representing a different compound. The contents of a kerosene can found at the home of a suspect may be compared with the flammable material that you found on the charred wood at the point where the arson fire was started. The two charts will compare positively, giving the criminalist a probable match.

SPECTROPHOTOMETER

A spectrographic analysis will be used to examine traces or fragments of materials found at the crime scene, and the analysis is recorded on photographic film. The substance in question is burned, which disturbs its characteristic atomic structure. Each substance burns with different colors unique to that substance. The colors are actually waves of energy expressed

Figure 12.4 The laboratory makes possible many processing techniques that cannot be done in the field.

in color. This light is projected through a prism onto the photographic plate. If black-and-white film is used, the light variations will be printed onto the photographic film as a series of parallel lines of varying density, from light gray to black. When color film is used, the bands show up as different colors of the spectrum. Each substance will cast a different arrangement of the lines, and the expert will be able to identify the materials being examined. See Figure 12.4.

NEUTRON ACTIVATION ANALYSIS

In neutron activation analysis, the specimen is bombarded with a stream of neutrons, and the instrument measures the wavelength and intensity of the radiation given off by the substances that have been made radioactive by the neutrons. At least 70 different elements can be identified and quantitatively determined by measurements of the interaction of their stable isotopes with the neutrons, known as radionuclides, as they decay. This result appears on the chart as lines that resemble peaks and valleys, which the criminalist studies. The criminalist interprets the various patterns as specific elements.

WET CHEMISTRY

When you are discussing all of the instrumentation in the laboratory, do not overlook the value of chemistry to forensic science. Many suspected substances can be isolated and identified by mixing them with specific chemical formulae, or *reagents*. With wet chemistry it is possible to identify thousands of substances, including drugs, narcotics, and blood. Through chemistry, the expert can determine whether the blood is animal or human, and from which type of animal the blood came. Blood types and DNA are determined with the aid of blood analysis. You may have been provided a collection of *reagents* in different vials so that you can conduct field tests for drugs, blood, and other liquids. When the suspected liquid is dropped into the reagent, the reagent changes colors, and you can tell what the suspected liquid is by what color and shade it changes to.

X-RAY

The X-ray is a better and safer way to look into a package without opening it, especially when the package contains a bomb or other dangerous material. Used extensively for airport security for several years, the X-ray can speed up the passenger screening process by looking into most containers without opening them. The container should be nonmetallic, and the metal objects inside show up in silhouette on the screen.

Valuable original paintings that have been painted over with another painting will show up in X-ray, as the newer painting will be more transparent than the older one. Jewelers and appraisers, as well as jewel theft officers, use X-ray to examine diamonds, pearls, and other gemstones to verify their authenticity and their value in addition to the usual method of using the ten power loop for examination and appraisal.

X-ray diffraction photography (the photo is called a radiograph, and in the medical lab the expert is known as a radiologist) will distinguish objects that are chemically identical but that differ in atomic arrangement. Auto grease stains, for example, can be distinguished from other grease compounds, such as kitchen grease. Barbiturates can be identified and compared with X-ray diffraction.

INFRARED LIGHT

Infrared light can be used to make some things appear that would otherwise be invisible or nearly invisible. Infrared heat sensors are used by the military and the police to look into darkened areas to search for living objects, particularly humans who are missing or lost or who might be trying

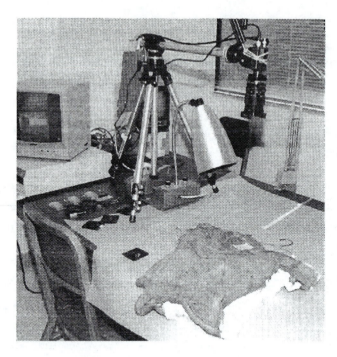

Figure 12.5 Infrared video is used to document gunshot residue on clothing—residue that is otherwise invisible to the naked eye.

to evade detection in the dark. Obliterated writings on surfaces that have been inked over may be made visible because the original writing shines through the overwriting under the infrared light. With the use of infrared light you may be able to read the letter inside an envelope without having to steam open the envelope or break the seal. If an erasure is not complete, you may find that you can bring out the erased writing with infrared light. See Figure 12.5.

A very popular type of pointer is the one that beams an infrared beam across the room. This is the same type of pointer that can be attached to a handgun, a rifle, or a shotgun and lighted to point to the spot where the bullets will strike the target (Figure 12.6). Infrared light is also used for night vision cameras and binoculars.

ULTRAVIOLET LIGHT

Some substances, such as semen, rouge, and lipstick, will fluoresce under ultraviolet light. Urine, milk, saliva, and erased writings will become visible under ultraviolet light. If you have a multicolored surface and cannot bring up latent prints because of the conflicting colors, use fluorescent fingerprint powder instead of the customary powder, and the prints will glow

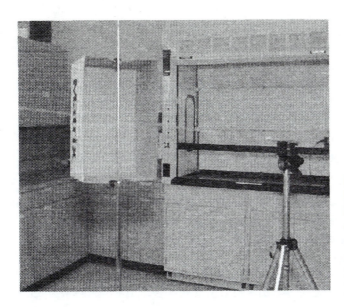

Figure 12.6 A laser beam is used to show bullet trajectory in this example. The laser is useful because its range is nearly endless and, more importantly, perfectly straight.

quite distinctly under the ultraviolet light. Many different inks and papers will fluoresce under the light, and undercover officers will make buys of contraband with money marked with inks and dyes that are invisible to the naked eye but which fluoresce under ultraviolet light. Many aerosol tear gas and pepper spray manufacturers mix in a dye that also fluoresces under the light.

EVIDENCE VACUUM

In the crime lab you will find one or more vacuum cleaners that have been sterilized and equipped with a special clean filter. The technicians vacuum clothing of suspected narcotics users and dealers for residue or powder from the pockets and surface, and they vacuum other places for narcotics or controlled substances. The sterile filter will insure that matter collected by the vacuum comes only from the place the technician vacuums.

SOUND SPECTROGRAPH

This device is more commonly known as the *voice print analyzer*. Voice patterns are transformed into visual patterns on a graph that moves through the instrument at a controlled speed, and patterns are drawn on the paper as it moves. By comparing the print patterns of two people who sound alike to you and me, the expert can tell you which one is the impersonator of the other. By analyzing the charts, some manufacturers claim, you can compare a tape of an individual's "normal" speech pattern with a tape of the same person being questioned about his or her involvement in some type of crime or other misbehavior. You can tell the person is stressed and probably untruthful. Such a device has yet to be used in a courtroom, where many people are known to have lied under oath.

AUTOMATED FINGERPRINT IDENTIFICATION SYSTEMS (AFIS)

Since fingerprints were first used for identification purposes and classification systems were developed for indexing and searching the files for comparison purposes, fingerprint technology has been the most consistently reliable method for positively identifying the owner of a set of prints. To this date, no two people have been found to have identical fingerprints. When you send latents to the laboratory and also submit all the elimination prints that you took of victims and witnesses at the scene, the technicians will try for a match (or elimination) with all the prints you submitted. Then the technician takes advantage of the automated fingerprint systems that connect your department with virtually every other department that is connected to the system (Figure 12.7). If there is a match, it will take only a few minutes compared with the months or years it would take an expert to search the files.

Figure 12.7 This Automated Fingerprint Identification System, or AFIS, workstation can search unknown fingerprints against a database of millions of known suspects.

DNA ANALYSIS

The genetic fingerprint of an individual is so unique that the experts are projecting that it is impossible for any two people, except identical twins, to have identical genetic codes. Blood, hair follicles, bones, tissue, body fluids, and almost any cell of a person's body will yield sufficient data so that the laboratory can identify the owner and match it to materials found at the scene. This discovery has made it possible for people in prison to be freed many years after their conviction because DNA tests showed that they were not the ones who committed the crimes, and other suspects have been located and their DNA matched. Some larger departments have teams of officers assigned to long-time unsolved murders, some cases still open for over 20 years, and they are solving some of those crimes with the aid of DNA analysis. DNA is also used to identify remains of people whose bodies have decayed so much that bone marrow samples are used to determine their DNA and their identity. In 1997, Nicholas II, Czar of Russia, and his family, killed by communist revolutionaries in 1918, were finally identified by their DNA and given a royal funeral in July 1998. Their DNA was determined by taking samples of their bone marrow and comparing it to that of Prince Philip, husband of Queen Elizabeth of England and a direct descendant of Nicholas II.

The application of DNA science to crime investigation has been one of the great discoveries of the twentieth century, and it promises to be a tremendous ally during the 21st century. Eyewitnesses make mistakes, but fingerprints and DNA do not.

FORENSIC TOXICOLOGY

The toxicologist studies the fluids and organs of the bodies of living or deceased persons and attempts to identify toxic substances that cause illness or death. This expert has an extensive knowledge of drugs and poisons and is called upon frequently to apply his or her skills to criminal homicide and other drug-related crimes.

FORENSIC ANTHROPOLOGY

The forensic anthropologist is called upon to examine bodies in various states of decomposition or in their whole condition. Through a study of the bones and whatever remains of the body, the anthropologist determines whether it is animal or human. These scientists have been known to estimate the approximate age, sex, race, height, weight, period of time since the person died, and nature of skeletal injuries sustained by the victim. Sometimes the anthropologist can reconstruct a face over the skull that will give investigators a fair idea what the victim looked like before death. The anthropologist can tell if bones belong to the same person and can take samples of bone marrow to send to a DNA laboratory for possible identification of the deceased.

COMPOSITE DRAWINGS, COMPUTER IMAGING

Eyewitnesses are often asked to work with a sketch artist or an expert who attempts to recreate an image of the suspect. Not every department has access to an artist, but many departments have a composite specialist who may use a computer or a collection of transparencies. From the description provided by the witness, the specialist selects face shape and size, then adds a hairline and hairstyle, eyes and ears, and so forth until the piece-by-piece construction of the suspect's face resembles the description provided by the witness. One of the earlier composite kits in the 1950s consisted of a box full of line drawings on transparent sheets of plastic. There were transparencies of eyes, noses, ears, chins, heads, hair, and other parts of the face that were used to put the composite together. Many improvements have been made since then, including utilization of the computer to prepare the image (Figure 12.8). A real treasure is to have an artist who can take the composite, then add scars or tattoos and fill in the composite to make a finished product that resembles a more realistic likeness of the suspect.

Figure 12.8   A PC-based digital imaging workstation.

POLYGRAPH, THE LIE DETECTOR

This "many graph" instrument measures and records body functions, which are drawn onto a chart that moves through the instrument at a measured rate. The lie detector is the person who operates the instrument, and the examiner's competency determines the reliability of the polygraph. Although the polygraph has been around for many years (one of your authors was qualified as an examiner in 1960), the results of a polygraph are not admissible in court except by stipulation of the judge and both attorneys, and its principal function is as an investigative tool.

The polygraph measures and records pulse, blood pressure, respiration, certain body movements, and galvanic skin response, or the changes in a small electric current sent through the body by way of electrodes attached to one finger in each hand. As the examiner asks questions that must be answered with on a "yes" or "no," the pens are recording on the chart the various body functions. As each question is asked and answered with an affirmative or negative response, the GSR (galvanic skin response), and squirming or similar body movements (all instruments do not have sensors under the subject's legs to record body movements). After a series of questions that the subject knows of in advance, the examiner will repeat the test once or twice and then analyze the chart. If certain changes on the chart appear to coincide with the answers given, the examiner may interpret the physical changes as emotional reactions to the question and answer. The interpreter then determines whether or not these changes indicate deception. The principle of the polygraph is based on the belief that most people have a conscience and they cannot lie to themselves. When they do lie, they have inner turmoil, which shows on the charts as changes in the body functions. The tests are conducted in a clinical atmosphere, and the only two people in the room during the test are the examiner and the subject.

PRINT AND TRACE EXPERTS

In the larger forensics laboratories, there are experts who specialize in such subjects as footwear identification and comparison, tire impressions, blood spatters, and mechanical matching of broken pieces of evidence. Most departments do not have the luxury of such a breakdown in specialties, and it is not uncommon for each criminalist in the lab to be a triple threat, doubling up on his or her competencies as an expert. A hair and fiber analyst may also work with soils and rocks, for example, whereas all are usually experts with wet chemistry and the use of the microscope.

SUMMARY

The crime laboratory is very much like an experimental lab. Even though the experts they may be carrying a heavy load already, most of the experts in the lab do the best they can to help the investigators solve the crime. Before you are assigned to investigate crime scenes as a specialty, you should visit several of the crime labs in your area and see how the criminalists work so that you may hone your CSI skills and you will have a better understanding what the lab can and cannot do.

SUGGESTED OUTSIDE PROJECTS

1. Visit the largest forensics lab in your area and take along with you the list of instruments and services described in this chapter. Compare our list with what you find on your visit. What does the lab have that we did not mention? How do they use the instruments? Write to the authors of this book with your findings so that we may update our next edition.

2. Take a polygraph exam. Some local examiner probably will be glad to use you as a subject to demonstrate how it works. Write a paper on how the polygraph works and whether or not you believe the results of a test should be admissible in court.

DISCUSSION QUESTIONS

1. List five types of evidence that are examined in the lab with the standard microscope.

2. Explain how two bullets are compared in a ballistics test.

3. For what kind of a case would the lab use the gas chromatograph?

4. What instrument would you use to find out if a valuable painting by one of the masters, such as Van Gogh, had been painted over to smuggle it out of the country?

5. What are some uses of infrared light?

6. For what types of cases would the lab use ultraviolet light?

7. What is the probability of two people having the same DNA, or genetic code?

8. According to the text, how accurate is the polygraph? What does your instructor say about the accuracy of the polygraph?

9. Can an anthropologist determine the sex of the deceased by examining his or her skeleton?

10. What is a comparison microscope, and how does it work?

Chapter Thirteen
Going to Court

INTRODUCTION

Your job is not done until you have performed another very important function in the crime scene investigation. That function is testifying in court and presenting the evidence that you discovered and processed. You are the first link in the chain of custody, and your role is to make your presentation and testimony factually and without embellishment. As you know, the criminal trial is an adversarial proceeding where prosecution and defense attorneys fight a pitched battle to get the results that they are paid for to represent their clients to the best of their ability. Your role in this battle is not the same as that of the attorneys. Your role is to present your evidence and testimony professionally and impartially so that the judge and jury will have your contribution to the case to determine truth, legality, and guilt or innocence. Too many officers who testify in court assume an adversarial stance the minute they get on the stand, purring like well-oiled machinery and presenting their testimony in a friendly and businesslike manner while being questioned by the prosecutor. Then, when the defense attorney gets up to cross-examine the officer, you actually see the change in that officer's attitude. The officer will assume a defensive position physically, such as holding the hands together or folding the arms, and actually change facial expressions as though the defense attorney were the devil himself. Hostility and reluctant cooperation replace the friendly and businesslike manner, which is readily apparent to all who observe the transition.

Actually, in some cases you might receive a subpoena from the defense attorney to be a witness for the "other side," as you see it. Keep in mind that your role is not to take sides with either prosecution or defense. You represent truth and fact, and your presentation should be a forthright and businesslike presentation of the facts with *truth* being your own ally. You may sometimes be required to give testimony that is favorable to the defense (heaven forbid, you think), but remember the rule of evidence that "evidence suppressed is presumed to be favorable to the defense." It is not your responsibility to find the defendant guilty or to administer the punishment. Your job is simply to tell the truth.

THE SUBPOENA

When you receive a subpoena, check out all the information about the case to see if it is one that you had anything to do with. Sometimes the attorneys do not prepare the subpoenas; they leave it up to a clerk in the office, who issues subpoenas for every person named in the report even if they are not familiar with the case. You may have been driving by a crime scene being investigated by a colleague and advised that your assistance was not needed, but your name was put in the report because you offered your services and then left the scene. Another example would be such a statement as, "We questioned the suspect in Sergeant Quimby's office," and you are Quimby. You were not even in the office that day and the officers used your office because you were on vacation. But you still get a subpoena. Notify the office of the attorney that issued the subpoena and have the office excuse you. Do not ignore the subpoena, as you could be arrested for contempt for not showing up in court.

If the case is one that you investigated, review all of your notes, the reports, and check to see what has been done with all the evidence. Although some attorneys are too busy to talk with you until the actual day of the trial, we suggest that you contact the attorney who subpoenas you, tell him or her that you are prepared, and set up a time for a pretrial consultation.

PETRIAL CONFERENCE

Meet with the attorney and discuss all of the evidence and testimony that you are going to bring to the trial. When you talk over the case, don't leave anything out. There should be no last-minute surprises when you are on the stand, such as revealing information that you did not give to the attorney. One good rule for attorneys is that they should never ask a question without knowing the answer. This conference is primary for the attorney to find out what kind of a witness you are going to be and to plan strategy so that you will be called upon for your contribution at a logistically and strategically good time during the trial.

EXPERT OR EXPERIENCED?

Because of your education, training, and experience in police investigative matters, you know more about what you do than the average person on the street, or the average police officer for that matter, and you would probably be considered an expert. As an expert, you are qualified by the court to go beyond presentation of your perceptions to also render opinions in categories of your expertise. This extra privilege to be qualified as an expert may sound good, and indeed it may be good for your presentation. Yet this is a two-sided "monster" in some cases. For example, as an expert crime scene investigator, you may be asked by a defense attorney about the qualifications and performance of the other officers at the scene. If one of those officers really "screwed up" and you know that he or she did a rotten job, as a lay witness you present your testimony and evidence and leave. You will not be asked about your opinions of the competency of your colleagues. But, as an expert, you may have to point out how your colleague messed up the investigation so badly that you were afraid that the whole case would be lost. Whether the prosecutor will have you take *voir dire* and have the court recognize you as an expert is up to the prosecutor. Discuss that matter before you are sworn in and get on the stand.

If you are presented as an expert, be sure to do your homework and be prepared to answer all kinds of questions about your area of expertise, whether related to the current case or not. Good attorneys would not be worth their salt if they did not try to discredit you on the stand. Your authors have testified as lay police witnesses and as experts, and they have found that each case is different and that the attorneys should plan the strategy of how they are going to use you as a witness.

WAITING TO TESTIFY

When you arrive in court, be sure to let the attorney who called you know that you are present and available. If the attorney is not going to get to you for a while, you may ask to be put *on call*, so that you can go back home or to your job and wait to be called with about a half hour's notice, or more, depending on how far you will be from the courthouse. The attorney may or may not consult with you at that time about your testimony and the evidence you are going to present. You may be required by the court to wait outside the courtroom while others testify. This is usually a move by a defense attorney who does not want two partners in a case to hear each other's testimony so that they can synchronize their testimony. You are outside while your partner is testifying, then you are called to the stand while he or she is meeting you in the aisle on the way out, giving you no time to compare notes. Don't worry about your testimony not being exactly the same. If you are telling the truth from your own perspective, there is no doubt that there are going to be inconsistencies, because you each interpret your observation through your own cognitive system.

While waiting outside the courtroom for your turn to testify, it is better not to strike up conversations with other people who are waiting outside for similar purposes. You never know who you are talking to, and it could prove embarrassing if you were to reveal information that the other person should not know. The best advice is to keep your counsel while waiting to testify.

TESTIFYING AS A WITNESS

Now is your time to shine! Everyone has stage fright before and during his or her appearance as a witness. You may be shaking and sweating, and for that you should be thankful. It shows that the adrenal glands are working, and the adrenaline pumping through your body will prepare you for this unusual event. Public speakers, teachers, athletes, and performers all experience this "rush" and most learn to use it to their advantage, as it sharpens your senses and your capabilities.

Whether you should wear a uniform in court depends on what you usually wear while on duty in your regular assignment. If you work in street clothes, then you will not be required to go out and buy a new uniform because the old one does not fit anymore. If you wear a uniform on duty, wear a clean and neatly-pressed one to testify. The judge may have specific requirements about sidearms and may require that you hand any weapon you might be wearing to the bailiff when you enter, and the bailiff will return it to you when you depart.

If you are required to wait in the spectator area behind the bar, be careful not to draw attention to yourself by waving to other officers or making obscene gestures to the defendant. Until you are called before the bar to the witness stand to testify, your demeanor should be that of a disinterested bystander. You have no personal axe to grind, and you are there as a witness, not an adversary.

When you are called to the witness stand, you will be required to take the oath or affirm that your testimony will be truthful. Please take that oath seriously and speak only the truth during your testimony. In the author's opinion, for an officer to lie from the witness stand in court is as bad as a minister blaspheming God from the pulpit. Answer all questions as they are put to you. If you do not hear or do not understand a question, say so. Give your answer then keep quiet. The attorneys will ask for an expansion of your reply or ask you to explain an answer if they choose to. It is their show. Sometimes an overzealous witness will start offering answers to questions that have not yet been asked or which will never be asked because the attorneys have reasons for running the examination as they are. There is a time and place for certain information to be given or evidence to be presented, and that should be left up to the attorneys.

EXAMINATION AND CROSS-EXAMINATION

During the direct examination by the attorney who called you as a witness, usually the prosecutor, the attorney will ask you questions that can be answered with a "yes" a "no" or a narrative response, such as, "Now that you testified that you were at that location on the night of August 14 at 9 p.m., tell the jury what you saw." The attorney is not allowed to ask leading or argumentative questions during direct examination in most cases. An exception to this is if the witness is noncooperative. In those cases, the attorney will then ask the judge to approve questioning of the witness as a "hostile witness." The general rule for testifying is to answer the questions and present your evidence as the attorneys ask you to do, and don't volunteer any additional information.

After the prosecutor is finished questioning you, the defense attorney will cross-examine you. The purpose of cross-examination is to challenge the truthfulness and accuracy of a witness. Be prepared to answer leading questions such as, "Officer Virtue, isn't it true that you actually arrived at the scene at 9:30, and not 8:30 as you testified during direct examination?" The general rule for answering questions during cross-examination is the same as for direct examination: Answer fully and honestly without trying to explain an answer unless asked to do so, and do not volunteer answers to questions that are not asked. The defense attorney may try to make you angry or confused and perhaps say things without thinking. Be careful, because some attorneys love to badger police witnesses, and, I suspect, there are some judges who love to see the badgering going on. A judge is less likely to interfere when an attorney is giving a police officer witness a bad time than if the witness were a child or a woman or another lay witness.

USE OF NOTES

Consult with the attorney before you refer to any notes that you have brought with you. Show the attorney what you are going to use to refresh your memory when necessary, but don't "spring" notes on him or her from your pocket without any advance notice. Also, before you testify from those notes or any other document, the opposing attorney must have the opportunity to examine them. Use your notes and reports whenever you need them to assure accuracy in your testimony. If your notes regarding that particular case are in a book that includes notes about other cases or other information concerning your work or private life, those portions may be blocked off by paper clips or staples. Contrary to popular belief, attorneys have no right and no business to go through the parts of your notebook that are not directly related to the case in hand or that you are using to refresh your memory.

TESTIMONY IN OTHER MATTERS

You may be called upon to testify during preliminary hearings, pretrial motion hearings, coroners' inquests, or administrative hearings, such as for workers' compensation or a school board. The rules are generally the same as far as responding to a subpoena and testifying during the proceedings. The prosecutor will point out to you the minor differences, such as hearsay is not admissible in a trial, but an experienced officer may testify to hearsay during certain preliminary proceedings. Some proceedings are more formal than others, but your demeanor should always be that of the professional police witness whose sole duty it is to present the facts in a concise and factual manner.

SUMMARY

You will be required to present your evidence and testimony in court as the final step in your crime scene investigation process. The general rule to follow is to be on time, be professional, and be truthful. Always remember that you are a witness and not an adversary. Your testimony and evidence should speak for themselves as to your honestly and efficiency, and any impassioned plea to the emotions of one side or the other will not enhance your image as a professional crime scene investigator. Be prompt, be honest, and be seated. Then, when you have finished testifying, ask the judge if you may be excused and leave. Don't hang around after you have testified to make sure the "scumbag gets his due." Read about it in the newspaper the next day or call the prosecutor in a day or two and ask about the outcome of the case. Not only must you be impersonal and professional in your persona, but you must be those things in the eyes of others.

SUGGESTED OUTSIDE PROJECTS

1. Spend at least 15 hours at a trial or visit three short trials for a total of 15 hours. Pay particular attention to the professionals who testify, such as police officers and expert witnesses. Write a critique on their performances and their behavior in the courtroom before and after testifying.

2. In this chapter we did not cover appearance before the grand jury. Visit your local prosecutor and ask how a witness would be handled for an appearance before that tribunal. What about examination and cross-examination, or is there any cross-examination if attorneys are not allowed to be present during witness testimony?

DISCUSSION QUESTIONS

1. When you receive a subpoena, describe what you must do before you go to court.

2. How does a witness qualify as an expert witness?

3. How does the testimony of an expert witness differ from that of a lay witness?

4. Why are witnesses sometimes required to wait outside the courtroom until it is time for them to testify?

5. Why ask the judge to excuse you after you testify as a witness?

6. How would you go about getting to use your notes during your testimony?

7. What do the authors mean when they say that a trial is an adversary hearing?

8. If you receive a subpoena and find that you had nothing to do with the case, what do you do?

9. What types of questions may be asked during a direct examination?

10. What types of questions can be asked during cross-examination?

Appendix
Career Profiles

Susan Clark

Agency: Monterey County Sheriff's Department

Job Title: Forensic Evidence Technician

Description: I am on an on-call basis for responding to homicide scenes. Once I am called out to a scene, it is my responsibility to work with the investigation team to process the scene. We photograph, videotape, and sketch to document the scene. We document blood stain patterns and collect samples and control samples. We also search for any evidence and collect it to be worked on at the lab in a more controlled environment. My daily duties include processing items of evidence for latent prints, digital photography, latent print tracings and entering into the state ALPS system and latent print comparisons to inked fingerprint cards.

Years of Experience: 13

Education: Associates Degree in Evidence Technology

How did you enter the field? I was going to school to be a Radiologic Technologist and was doing my internship in my last semester when I saw the movie "Manhunter." I was intrigued by the scenes that included the lab technicians working on the evidence. I did some research locally and found a school in my area and switched my major. After spending my two years in school which included an internship at the San Diego Police Department Latent Print Unit, I was able to get a job with the Monterey County Sheriff's Department as a Trainee. I have spent my entire career here and have enjoyed it.

Most satisfying aspects of the job: I have been in this field for 13 years now and am never bored. Each day, each new case brings something new to the table. There is always new technology to learn in this field. I enjoy working and learning each day. I am happy that I found a career that keeps that "spark" of interest for me.

Least: Working on cases that involve children. It is very hard to deal with that aspect of the job. I would also have to say the "smells" of some of the cases.

Advice to those entering the field: There are so many avenues in the forensic field that you can take; find one that you enjoy and learn from it. Always keep an open mind that unexpected "twists" in cases will occur. Most of all like what you do. I can honestly say that I love my job.

Rocky L. Edwards

Agency: Santa Ana Police Department

Job Title: Forensic Firearm and Toolmark Examiner

Description: I am responsible for the examination of firearms, ammunition, and ammunition components, including the microscopic examination of questioned bullets, cartridge cases, tool marks, obliterated serial numbers, fractures, and physical matches. I determine the distance from which a firearm was fired by gunshot residue and shotgun pattern analysis. I produce written reports of my findings and present them in court. I also instruct other crime lab personnel in the collection, preservation, and examination of firearm and toolmark evidence.

Years of Experience: 13

Education: B.S. degree from the University of State of New York
A.A. degree from El Paso Community College

How did you enter the field? I was a special agent with the United States Army Criminal Investigation Division. I was accepted as a student in the Army's Crime Laboratory located at Fort Gillem, GA where I spent two years training in this area of forensics.

Most satisfying aspects of the job: Educating people about the science of forensic firearms and testifying in court. I enjoy working cases brought to me by detectives and assisting on cases that otherwise might not have been solved.

Least: The lack of personnel and high-stress environment that is often required on high-profile cases.

Advice to those entering the field: Major in the natural sciences in college including biology, chemistry, or physics. Volunteer at a crime laboratory and get to know people by working with them. Seek sponsorship by the examiners of the firearm unit so that you can go to the Firearms Examiner Training School sponsored by the Bureau of Alcohol, Tobacco, and Firearms.

John Falk

Agency: Laguna Beach P.D.

Job Title: Police Officer II, FTO, Field CSI

Description: I am a field patrol officer and field training officer. I have the collateral duty of being a field crime scene investigator. I respond by request of other patrol officers, dispatch, or the watch commander as needed for most types of calls. Major crimes in my city require the assistance of the Orange County crime lab, which I have trained with and would assist if they were called in.

Years of Experience: 16 as an officer, about 3 years officially as a CSI. I have, however, conducted basic CSI my entire career.

Education: A.A. degree in Fire Service Technology, Advanced POST, 80-hour field evidence technician course, numerous adjunct CSI courses such as a 24-hour advanced fingerprint course, and an 80-hour field-training program with the OCSO forensics unit.

How did you enter the field? I felt it was an area lacking at my agency, and I developed our own field CSI unit modeled after other agencies in the area. As such, I wanted be a part of the CSI unit, as I have always been interested in the field.

Most satisfying aspects of the job: Knowing that with a little patience and knowledge, you can identify a suspect who would have otherwise gotten away with the crime. Getting to participate in the most interesting cases as a rule.

Least: It can be a very dirty, and at times tedious, job. Spending one to two hours examining a crime scene and coming up empty handed can be frustrating.

Advice to those entering the field: Investigate the programs in your area. Some agencies use only sworn officers, some use only civilian employees. It may require you do your time in a different job function until an opening comes up.

Greg Ferguson

Agency: Monterey County Sheriff's Department

Job Title: Forensic Evidence Technician

Description: Documenting the scenes of crimes to include photography, videotape, sketching, collecting and processing evidence and vehicles, evaluating and comparing fingerprints, attending autopsies, computer processing and digital imaging, presumptive drug testing, testifying to all of the above in court.

Years of Experience: 6 1/2

Education: A.S. Evidence Technology, A.S. Legal Systems/Court Management
    A.S. Corrections

How did you enter the field? While in the Navy, I began taking classes at the local junior college. The administration of justice field was interesting to me, evidence technology in particular. While taking classes, I began an internship at a local police department crime laboratory. After working in the crime laboratory for a year and a half, I began working at this job.

Most satisfying aspects of the job: There is something new every day. We respond to immediate requests both in and out of the lab. The challenges of solving crimes with old and new technologies. And to quote Ralph Waldo Emerson, "If one life has breathed easier because you have lived, then your life has been a success."

Least: Crimes against children, politics, and bureaucracy.

Advice to those entering the field: Be methodical, deliberate, and systematic. Be prepared to encounter *anything* on any given day. You can never have too much training or education.

Heather Heider

Agency: Santa Ana Police Department

Job Title: Forensic Specialist II

Description: My duties include documenting crime scenes using photography, written reports, and computerized drafting. I possess expertise in the recognition, collection, and preservation of evidence, chemical processing of items for biological, trace, or fingerprint evidence, and comparing fingerprints to known subjects.

Years of Experience: 6

Education: B.S. degree in Physics

How did you enter the field? While working for the Chino Police Department, I received training in how to handle all non-emergency calls, including burglary, vandalism, missing persons, traffic collisions, and stolen vehicle reports. I also assisted at major crime scenes including fatal accidents, homicides, and rapes. This experience combined with my academic study prepared me to enter the field of forensics.

Most satisfying aspects of the job: The knowledge that the work you do directly impacts lives by perhaps taking a violent offender off the streets or providing a victim or their family a tiny bit of solace, is extremely satisfying. It's also great to be right in the middle of things like the flashing red and blue lights, sirens, and helicopters that are always fun!

Least: This line of work can be emotionally draining. Every day, and several times a day, you are a witness to the worst part of a person's life.

Advice to those entering the field: Do not take your job lightly. Enjoy it, but realize that this field, more than many others, changes lives on a daily basis. Keep an open mind and never make assumptions. Go home and kiss your family.

Victor Lurz

Agency: Monterey County Sheriff's Department

Job Title: Supervising Forensic Evidence Technician

Description: Processing evidence submitted by deputies for latent finger-prints using powders and chemicals; comparing latent prints to inked fin-gerprints and testifying in court to the results; responding to crime scenes to photograph, video, sketch, and collect items of evidentiary value. Main-taining custody of the evidence and properly packaging and preserving ev-idence for long-term storage. Presumptive drug testing, physical comparisons of shoe and tire impressions/prints. Preparing budgets; maintaining schedules and assigning work for personnel in the unit; preparing evaluations; and helping to ensure that an even workload is maintained.

Years of Experience: 20

Education: A.S. degree in Evidence Technology at Grossmont College
     Many DOJ, FBI, and private training sessions in all aspects of evidence technology

How did you enter the field? My eyesight was too poor to pass the vision requirement to be a sworn officer, so I started taking classes at Grossmont College towards my degree in Evidence Technology. While attending school, I had an opportunity to intern 20 hours per week at the San Diego Police Department Crime Lab. After 6 months there, I applied for a trainee Evidence Technician job at the Monterey County Sheriff's Department. I've worked here for the past 18 years.

Most satisfying aspects of the job: Being a part of a much larger system that provides appropriate punishment for those in society who choose to il-legally take advantage of others.

Least: Being exposed on a daily basis to citizens who fall into the "less de-sirable" category, thereby being reminded that the world is not a perfect place. There is always someone who is waiting for an opportunity to pros-per at your expense. Without keeping life in the proper perspective, it can lead to a very negative outlook of the world and the people in your life.

Advice to those entering the field: Work hard and pay your dues, espe-cially when first entering the field. Don't be intimidated by a task that seems difficult. Be prepared to work long hours from time to time, under less than desirable conditions. Before you make the commitment to work in the field, do some volunteer work or internships with a lab to get an idea of what the job is about. Make sure that the job is something that you will always enjoy; don't believe all the glamorous images that you see on T.V. It is a great job, and a very rewarding way to make a living.

Magda Perez

Agency: Santa Ana Police Department

Job Title: Forensic Specialist

Description: As a crime scene investigator, my primary function is to identify, photograph, diagram, collect, and preserve evidence from crime scenes. I may also be responsible to chemically process evidence found at crime scenes for possible biological, trace, and/or fingerprint evidence. I also photograph and obtain fingerprints and/or evidence from victims and suspects. Another function is to lift, preserve, and compare fingerprints taken from crime scenes and to assist with the development of photographs and their preparation for courtroom exhibits. I prepare written reports, testify in court, and perform other related duties.

Years of Experience: 11

Education: B.S. degree from the University of La Verne

How did you enter the field? I was a college intern in the Santa Ana Police Department Crime Lab while in college. As a result, it was during this time that I changed my focus and became interested in CSI. I was introduced, intrigued, and challenged with the work done in the crime lab.

Most satisfying aspects of the job: Oftentimes, this is a thankless job, but the day comes when a victim remembers you and explains how the positive impact the 30 minutes I spent with them had on their life. And then there are those times when you become the victim's voice by the evidence you find and you are able to give the family some sense of justice by your work. Finally, I enjoy working out in the streets and the excitement of hearing the call come out over the radio and then helping to put the puzzle together.

Least: The lack of opportunities. Many agencies do not have much of a career ladder and have small CSI units. Unfortunately, when you go into forensics you will not have the flexibility to transfer in and out of assignments, and there are fewer promotional opportunities for non-sworn personnel.

Advice to those entering the field: Research the field and finish your education before accepting a full-time position. For those wanting to enter the crime lab, it is best to obtain a degree in biology, criminalistics, chemistry, or biochemistry. For those seeking a position in the field, any BA or BS degree will generally suffice, but a BS degree (especially in those listed above) is preferable.

Faye Springer

Agency: Sacramento County District Attorney Office, Forensic Services Laboratory

Job Title: Criminalist IV

Description: I scientifically analyze and interpret physical evidence from a criminal investigation in the areas of trace materials, firearms, and basic serology. I also do crime scene and blood spatter reconstruction.

Years of Experience: 32

Education: B.S. degree in Biochemistry

How did you enter the field? I applied to Santa Clara County Criminalistics Laboratory after seeing a job announcement that was mailed to me from the University of California job placement center.

Most satisfying aspects of the job: I think the most satisfying aspect of my profession is being part of the criminal justice system, where my work is used to protect the public interest.

Least: The work can be tedious and at times unappreciated by attorneys.

Advice to those entering the field: Criminalistics is a rewarding field. It does require one to be meticulous in laboratory techniques and note taking. After completing an examination, a report is written and oral testimony is given in a court of law. Therefore, a strong scientific background, along with good writing and oral skills, is essential to being a good criminalist.

For Further Study

Bodziak, William J. *Footwear Impression Evidence*. Boca Raton, Florida: CRC Press Inc., 1995.

CA Criminalist Institute. "Latent Print Comparisons." Classroom text/handouts, n.d. California Department of Justice, Sacramento.

Cassidy, Michael. *Footwear Indentification*. Ottowa, Canada: RCMP GRC, 1987.

Hilderbrand, Dwane S. "Footwear, The Missed Evidence." Classroom text/handouts, n.d. California Department of Justice, Sacramento.

Redsicker, David R. *The Practical Methodology of Forensic Photography*. New York, New York: Elsevier Science Publishing, 1991.

Smith, Ron. "Demystifying Palm Prints." Classroom text/handouts, n.d. California Department of Justice, Sacramento.

Staff, FBI, Carl Collins. "FSI Advanced Latent Fingerprint School." Classroom text/handouts, n.d. FBI, Washington, DC.

Index